US NATIONAL SECURITY
AND FOREIGN DIRECT INVESTMENT

INSTITUTE FOR INTERNATIONAL ECONOMICS

US NATIONAL SECURITY
AND FOREIGN DIRECT INVESTMENT

EDWARD M. GRAHAM AND DAVID M. MARCHICK

Washington, DC
May 2006

Edward M. Graham, senior fellow since 1990, has been an adjunct professor at Columbia University since 2002. He was associate professor in the Fuqua School of Business at Duke University (1988–90), associate professor at the University of North Carolina (1983–88), principal administrator of the Planning and Evaluation Unit at the OECD (1981–82), international economist in the Office of International Investment Affairs at the US Treasury (1979–80), and assistant professor at the Massachusetts Institute of Technology (1974–78). He is the author, coauthor, or coeditor of numerous studies, including *Does Foreign Direct Investment Promote Development?* (2005), *Fighting the Wrong Enemy: Antiglobal Activists and Multinational Enterprises* (2000), *Global Corporations and National Governments* (1996), and *Foreign Direct Investment in the United States* (3d ed. 1995).

David M. Marchick is a partner with Covington & Burling, where he advises US and foreign companies on foreign investment and international trade issues. He is widely recognized as an expert on the Exon-Florio Amendment. He served in the State Department during the Clinton administration (1993–99) as deputy assistant secretary of state for transportation affairs, deputy assistant secretary for trade policy, and principal deputy assistant secretary of commerce for trade development. He also held trade policy positions at the White House and the Office of the US Trade Representative and is a senior adviser to Kissinger McLarty Associates.

**INSTITUTE FOR
INTERNATIONAL ECONOMICS**
1750 Massachusetts Avenue, NW
Washington, DC 20036-1903
(202) 328-9000   FAX: (202) 659-3225
www.iie.com

C. Fred Bergsten, *Director*
Valerie Norville, *Director of Publications and Web Development*
Edward Tureen, *Director of Marketing*

Typesetting by BMWW
Printing by United Book Press, Inc.
Cover photo: Getty Images

Printed in the United States of America
08 07 06   5 4 3 2 1

Library of Congress Cataloging-in-Publication Data

Graham, Edward M. (Edward Montgomery), 1944–
   National security and foreign direct investment / Edward M. Graham and David Marchick.
     p. cm.
   Includes bibliographical references and index.
   ISBN 0-88132-391-8 (alk. paper)
     978-0-88132-391-7
   1. Investments, Foreign—United States—Political aspects.   2. National security—United States.   I. Marchick, David.   II. Title.

HG4910.G745 2006
332.67'30973—dc22
                2006009285

To my wife, Kathryn,
and to all the nurses, physician assistants,
technicians, and physicians on the seventh floor
of Georgetown University Hospital
who ensured that this book would be finished
and that more could follow.

— EMG

To my wonderful wife, Pamela Kurland,
and my father, Richard Marchick,
who has inspired me since I was a child.

— DMM

Contents

Figures

Boxes

Preface

A perennial issue in US policy has been whether foreign ownership and control of productive assets in the United States poses a risk to national security. This issue first arose in 1914, the year World War I began in Europe. New laws were passed, most notably the Trading with the Enemy Act, giving the US government the right to effectively nationalize foreign-controlled assets in times of national emergency. The immediate issue was extensive control of US industry by German interests, especially in chemicals, the high-tech sector of the day. During the early 1920s, Congress passed a number of laws to shield other US sectors from foreign control, notably broadcasting, telecommunications, aviation, and petroleum, where again the main issue was national security. The same issue arose following the outbreak of World War II.

US economic predominance led to a fading of concern with foreign ownership during the 1950s and 1960s, but concerns reemerged following the first oil crisis of 1973–74 and then again during the second oil crisis of 1979. The specific issue at that time was rising investment in the United States from the members of the Organization of Petroleum Exporting Countries (OPEC). Because of these concerns, the interagency Committee on Foreign Investment in the United States (CFIUS) was created by executive order in 1975, and the International Emergency Economic Powers Act (IEEPA) was passed in 1977. I personally served as the second chairman of the CFIUS during 1977–81 and led the administration team that worked out the IEEPA legislation with Congress.

Concern with OPEC control of the US economy faded somewhat after it became clear that most foreign direct investment (FDI) in the United States came from Europe and Canada rather than from OPEC nations. But rising FDI from Japan and other nations during the mid-1980s sparked another round of concern. A number of measures to regulate or curtail this investment were proposed, and a major outcome was passage of the Exon-Florio Amendment to the Omnibus Trade and Competitiveness Act of 1988, which enabled the president to block any foreign acquisition of a US firm that impaired, or even threatened to impair, US national security. This book is largely about the Exon-Florio Amendment, how it has been used, and how it might be modified in light of recent concerns.

In 1988 the Institute for International Economics published a major study of foreign investment in the United States by Edward M. Graham and Paul Krugman entitled *Foreign Direct Investment in the United States*. A second edition was released in 1992 and a third in 1994. This analysis showed that, in terms of its economic effects, FDI was overwhelmingly positive for the United States and that virtually none of the negative effects then being suggested could actually be observed. We believe that this analysis contributed significantly to the debate on FDI at the time and, in particular, that the strong findings of positive economic effects helped to counter a number of proposals for regulation of such investment that would have proven counterproductive.

Since 2005 a new round of concern with the national security implications of FDI in the United States has taken hold. This round has largely focused on investment from China, beginning with the takeover of the personal computer operations of IBM by Chinese firm Lenovo and reaching a crescendo with the (subsequently withdrawn) bid by the China National Offshore Oil Corporation (CNOOC) to buy US oil firm Unocal. The furor within Congress died down after CNOOC withdrew its offer but then again reached fever pitch when the United Arab Emirates–based Dubai Customs and Free Zone Corporation (Dubai Ports World) bought the port operations of the UK-based Peninsular and Oriental Steam Navigation Company (P&O), which would have given Dubai Ports World control of operations at six US ports. Although this transaction easily passed a CFIUS review, many members of Congress deemed the transaction unacceptable. The upshot has been that Dubai Ports World agreed to sell its interest in the six US ports, and a number of bills (at last count about 20) have been introduced into Congress that would modify Exon-Florio, the CFIUS process, or broader foreign investment laws.

This book is directed to this latest surge of concern over FDI in the United States and its national security implications. It is coauthored by Edward M. Graham, a senior fellow at the Institute and coauthor of our previous study, and David Marchick, a partner in the law firm Covington & Burling, who served as deputy assistant secretary of state for transportation affairs and for trade policy and worked on CFIUS issues. It examines FDI in the United States and the Exon-Florio law in the current policy context of post–9/11, a worldwide "war on terrorism," and new concerns over the economic and political rise of China.

The book examines these issues in historical context and updates the economic analysis contained in the earlier study by Graham and Krugman. It includes a detailed legislative history of Exon-Florio, an analysis of how it has been implemented, a chapter addressing the special concerns being expressed over investment from China, a detailed examination of a number of Exon-Florio cases that have become politicized, and the authors' recommendations on how to, and how not to, "reform" Exon-Florio and the CFIUS process.

The Institute for International Economics is a private, nonprofit institution for the study and discussion of international economic policy. Its purpose is to analyze important issues in that area and to develop and communicate practical new approaches for dealing with them. The Institute is completely nonpartisan.

The Institute is funded by a highly diversified group of philanthropic foundations, private corporations, and interested individuals. Major institutional grants are now being received from the William M. Keck, Jr. Foundation and the Starr Foundation. About 33 percent of the Institute's resources in our latest fiscal year were provided by contributors outside the United States, including about 16 percent from Japan.

The Institute's Board of Directors bears overall responsibilities for the Institute and gives general guidance and approval to its research program, including the identification of topics that are likely to become important over the medium run (one to three years) and that should be addressed by the Institute. The director, working closely with the staff and outside Advisory Committee, is responsible for the development of particular projects and makes the final decision to publish an individual study.

The Institute hopes that its studies and other activities will contribute to building a stronger foundation for international economic policy around the world. We invite readers of these publications to let us know how they think we can best accomplish this objective.

C. Fred Bergsten
Director
April 2006

Executive Summary

Foreign acquisitions of American companies and assets have long been a controversial and hotly debated subject in the United States. Americans take pride in the words "made in America" and, to a lesser extent, "owned by Americans." A March 2006 poll by The Pew Research Center for the People and the Press found that 53 percent of Americans believed that foreign ownership of US companies was "bad for America."[1] Similarly, 58 percent agreed that Congress acted "appropriately" when it blocked the acquisition of six US port terminal operations by Dubai Ports World, a company owned by the government of the United Arab Emirates, in the spring of 2006. The subject attracted intense interest far beyond Washington and New York elites: 41 percent of Americans said that they tracked the Dubai Ports World transaction "closely," only 2 percentage points lower than interest in the war in Iraq (43 percent). The same poll showed that the Dubai Ports World transaction ranked seventh among political stories that generated the most news interest in the last two decades, just below the 1996 federal government shutdown and the 1993 controversy over whether to allow gays in the military.

It is partly encouraging that 53 percent of Americans believed that foreign ownership of US companies was "bad for America": In 1989 that figure stood at 70 percent. The 1989 poll was taken at a time of great uncertainty about the competitiveness of the US economy, at the height of US concerns about mergers and acquisitions from Japan, and shortly after Congress passed the Exon-Florio Amendment to the Defense Production Act in the Omnibus Trade and Competitiveness Act of 1988. The Exon-

---

1. The Pew Research Center for the People and the Press, *Survey Reports*, March 15, 2006, available at www.people-press.org.

Florio Amendment gave the president broad powers to block a foreign acquisition or takeover of a US company if that transaction threatened to impair US national security. That amendment and the national security implications of foreign direct investment (FDI) in the United States are the subjects of this book.

Chapter 1 traces the history of the impact of FDI on the US economy and the US reaction to FDI, particularly during World War I and II and in the late 1980s, when Exon-Florio was enacted. FDI played a significant role in the development of the US economy in the late 19th and early 20th centuries, particularly in the chemical, radio broadcasting, telecommunications, and transport machinery sectors. FDI in the United States—most of which was new, or "greenfield" investment, as opposed to an acquisition—grew to $7.1 billion by 1914. As the United States moved toward entering the war, national security concerns arose about FDI, particularly investment from Germany. These concerns led to the passage of the Trading with the Enemy Act (TWEA) in 1917, which authorized the president to seize assets owned by foreign persons. President Woodrow Wilson invoked the TWEA in 1917 and 1918, seizing virtually all US assets owned by German companies, as well as assets owned by US citizens of German origin. The US government subsequently transferred or sold these assets, including patents for chemical products, to US companies, such as DuPont and General Electric. After World War I, Congress, encouraged by the US Navy, passed sector-specific prohibitions on FDI in radio broadcasting, telecommunications, air transport, shipping, and oil. Except for FDI in telecommunications, which was liberalized in 1996, these laws remain on the books.

President Franklin Delano Roosevelt invoked the TWEA again in 1941, though this time there were very few German assets to seize since German investment in the United States after World War I was very little. The low level of postwar German investment stemmed not only from the poor health of the German economy but also from foreign investors' lack of confidence in US willingness to allow them to keep their holdings. Postwar FDI in the United States grew modestly, to $2.5 billion in 1946, and investments flowed primarily from the United Kingdom and Canada. The stock of US investment abroad stood at $7.2 billion in the same year.

By contrast, FDI in the United States grew quickly between 1956 and 1977, particularly as European economies rebounded. It grew even faster in the late 1970s and 1980s, reflecting a worldwide trend. Between 1977 and 1984, FDI in the United States grew almost thrice as fast as US investment abroad. From 1985 to 2004, the stock of FDI in the United States increased more than eightfold, from about $185 billion in 1985 to almost $1.7 trillion at the end of 2005.

The specific security concerns over FDI in the United States have changed since World War I. At that time the main concern was that foreign companies would dominate new, strategically important technologies. This dominance was reflected in the fact that most FDI in the United States was of a "greenfield" nature). But since then, US firms have come to be at the cutting edge of such technologies. FDI thus has shifted away from greenfield investments and toward mergers and acquisitions, so that the modern concern is more acquisition by foreign firms of US-developed technologies than foreign-firm dominance of these technologies. Even so, in all its forms, FDI has become critical to the vibrancy and vitality of the US economy. Moreover, with rising levels of FDI in the United States have come rising concerns over its national security implications.

In chapter 2, we analyze the legislative history that led to the adoption and implemention of the Exon-Florio Amendment. As originally introduced, the amendment would have allowed the president to block investments that affected not only US national security but also essential commerce and economic welfare. The latter two provisions became the focus of intense debate and brought a threat of veto by President Ronald Reagan. President Reagan and Congress eventually agreed to narrow the bill to allow the president to block a transaction only on "credible evidence" that the foreign acquirer might take action that "threatens to impair the national security" and only if no other provision of law allowed the president to protect national interests. Congress did not define the words "national security," and the Committee on Foreign Investment in the United States (CFIUS), the 12-agency body that reviews foreign investments, interprets this term as broadly as possible.

On multiple occasions, Congress has attempted to amend, broaden, and deepen Exon-Florio. As we go to print, the Senate Banking Committee, led by Senators Richard Shelby (R-AL) and Paul Sarbanes (D-MD), passed a bill by a 20-0 vote that would require greater scrutiny of certain acquisitions, lengthen reviews, and create much more congressional involvement in and oversight of the CFIUS process. More than 20 similar bills have been introduced in both the House and the Senate. These efforts mirror many earlier attempts to amend Exon-Florio, although at the time of this writing, it appears almost inevitable that Congress will pass legislation to amend Exon-Florio.

That Congress never defined "national security" has had important consequences, particularly after the terrorist attacks of September 11, 2001. Since then, and along with the addition of the Department of Homeland Security to CFIUS, CFIUS has more heavily scrutinized foreign investments, imposed tougher requirements before approval, and enhanced enforcement of security agreements negotiated through the Exon-Florio process. Chapter 2 discusses the security agreements CFIUS used to mitigate national security concerns in the telecommunications and defense sectors. These agreements have become increasingly intrusive and restrictive, particularly in the telecommunications sector, and have evolved according to CFIUS's expanding view of national security. Today, CFIUS's focus on protecting "critical infrastructure" is a high priority.

Chapter 3 examines the effects of FDI on the US economy—in particular, on US workers, research and development (R&D), long-run US economic growth, and positive or negative externalities or "spillovers." The United States depends heavily on continued inflows of FDI, because US savings, net of the drain of public-sector deficits on these savings, are insufficient to finance domestic investment. In 2005 the current account deficit was slightly more than $800 billion and growing, implying that the United States needed to import in excess of $2 billion each day to close the gap between domestic investment and saving.

In 2003 US affiliates of foreign investors employed 5.3 million workers in the United States. On average, particularly within major manufacturing subsectors with significant numbers of foreign-controlled firms, US affiliates of foreign firms pay higher annual wages and salaries than US firms. Similarly, foreign-controlled firms employ at least 100,000 workers in the United States in eight manufacturing subsectors; in seven out of the eight, foreign firms pay more than the overall US average wage and salary within those subsectors. There may be some selection bias in the data, but while the extent of the wage differential can be debated, it is clear that FDI creates desirable US jobs at higher-than-average wages.

Our analysis also shows that while US parents of US-based multinational firms invest slightly more in R&D as a percentage of overall contribution to US GDP than do US affiliates of foreign-owned firms, the difference is rather small. It is rather surprising that foreign investors' R&D spending as a percentage of value added approximates R&D spending by the parents of US-based multinationals, given that most firms tend to concentrate their R&D activities close to their worldwide headquarters, typically located in a company's home country. In some subsectors, including computer manufacturing and communications equipment, affiliates of foreign firms spend a greater portion of value added on R&D than US parents do. While it is hard to pinpoint the precise impact of FDI on economic growth, it is closely correlated with the amount of international trade, and studies have clearly shown that increased international trade aids economic growth. Microstudies also indicate that, in some sectors at least, FDI has generated positive spillovers: For example, in the auto industry, rising productivity and improved product quality both have almost surely been stimulated by the greater competition in the United States created by the local operations of foreign-owned automobile producers.

Chapter 4 discusses the national security implications of FDI from China, which became an important issue in 2005 with the sale of IBM's personal computing division to Lenovo and the failed attempt by the China National Offshore Oil Corporation to acquire Unocal. In less than 30 years, China has transformed itself from one of the most isolated and autarkic economies in the world to the second-largest recipient of FDI, but outward investment flows from China remain small. China's central government, which controls significant parts of the Chinese economy, began encouraging Chinese enterprises to invest abroad only less than five years ago. Chinese outward investment is growing, reaching $44.8 billion in 2004, but it pales compared with the total stock of FDI in China, which was $562 billion in the same year.

From a broad, strategic perspective, Chinese acquisitions present CFIUS with different issues and concerns than do acquisitions by companies of other major trading partners. Of the United States' 10 largest trading partners, China is the only one not considered a strategic or political ally. Similarly, more than any other major trading or investment partner, the Chinese government owns or controls most Chinese companies with the resources and size to invest abroad. A recent study[2] estimates that only about 20 of approximately 1,300 publicly listed companies in China in 2004 were genuinely private; the rest were all ultimately controlled by the state. A Chinese company seeking CFIUS approval will likely have a heavy burden of convincing the committee that it is not government-controlled, and under the Byrd Amendment to Exon-Florio, CFIUS can more closely scrutinize companies owned or controlled by foreign governments.

Other factors can also lead to extra scrutiny by CFIUS of Chinese investments in the United States. The possibility of sensitive, export-controlled technology being transferred to other countries is a factor in virtually all CFIUS reviews, regardless of the home country of the acquirer. It is a particular concern for acquisitions by Chinese companies largely because of a series of high-profile breaches of US export control laws and regulations by Chinese companies in the late 1990s and early 2000s. China's espionage activities have also become a concern and a higher priority at US counterintelligence agencies, including the Departments of Justice, Defense, and Homeland Security, as well as the Federal Bureau of Investigation. So long as the Pentagon views China suspiciously, CFIUS will likely assess Chinese acquisitions of US companies in part by their impact on China's military strength.

Notwithstanding concerns associated with Chinese investment in the United States, we believe that the Exon-Florio Amendment gives the president and CFIUS ample authority and power to scrutinize investments and mitigate national security concerns—and if such concerns cannot be mitigated, the president has ample authority to block individual transactions.

The United States should continue to support China's integration into the global economy, and Chinese outward foreign investment should be viewed as a natural and positive step in China's economic development. For close to two decades, through Republican and Democratic administrations, the United States has encouraged China to lower tariffs, eliminate nontariff barriers to trade, privatize state-owned enterprises, allow inward investment, and participate in—and play by the rules of—the global econ-

2. See testimony of Pieter Bottelier before the US-China Economic and Security Commission, April 16, 2004.

omy. A US policy that encourages American companies to invest in China, but frowns upon Chinese investment in the United States, is neither sustainable nor sound from an economic perspective. Rather, the United States should simultaneously encourage China to allow FDI and make clear that Chinese investment in the United States is not only welcome but also encouraged. Notwithstanding the serious and legitimate policy concerns related to espionage, technology transfer, and state control of many Chinese corporations, CFIUS should focus on the marginal increase in risk to US national security, if any, that a particular transaction creates. It should not try to use individual transactions to resolve the broad set of problems in the US-China economic relationship. At the same time, the president should not hesitate to block a foreign investment, from China or any other country, that genuinely threatens to impair US national security.

Chapter 5 shows how the CFIUS process has become increasingly politicized. The very nature of an Exon-Florio review involves two highly sensitive political issues: foreign ownership over US assets and national security. Each of these issues independently can grab attention, and when they combine, they can produce a combustible political mix. Companies have sought to influence or politicize the CFIUS process to raise costs for potential foreign acquirers, reopen the bidding process, or advance other commercial interests unrelated to national security. In 1990, 119 members of Congress wrote to the president asking for an investigation of the proposed hostile acquisition by the UK firm British Tire and Rubber (BTR) of the Norton Company, based in Massachusetts. Encouraged by Norton, these members of Congress suddenly changed their tune when a French company, Compagnie de Saint Gobain, bid $15 more per share than did BTR. It is hard to see how a British acquisition of a US company raised national security concerns while a French acquisition did not. Similar examples have occurred over the last 18 years, including the uproar over Dubai Ports World's proposed acquisition of the Peninsular and Oriental Steam Navigation Company (P&O), the UK company that operated terminals at six US ports.

The catalyst for the political controversy surrounding Dubai Ports World appears to have been a small stevedoring firm based in Miami, Eller & Co. Eller had a long-standing commercial dispute with P&O and sought to block the deal to increase its leverage in its negotiations with P&O. It first tried to intervene with CFIUS, which, appropriately, decided not to factor a commercial dispute into its national security analysis. Eller then stoked the flames on Capitol Hill. A spokesperson for Senator Charles Schumer (D-NY), the leading opponent of the transaction, stated that "Eller was really the canary in the mineshaft for many people on the Hill" regarding the Dubai Ports World/P&O deal.[3]

---

3. Neil King Jr., and Gregg Hitt, "Small Florida Firm Sowed Seed of Port Dispute," *Wall Street Journal*, February 28, 2006, A3.

We conclude in chapter 5 that politicizing the CFIUS process costs the United States. It increases uncertainty for foreign investors, employees, and customers of the parties to a transaction. If the politicization of the process continues unabated, foreign investors could shy away from acquiring US companies, chilling the investment market and lowering values of US companies. A politicized review could create higher risk for foreign investors than for domestic investors because of the uncertainty associated with it. As a result, in highly politicized transactions, foreign investors could be forced to pay more for an asset than would domestic investors. Alternatively, if a domestic company seeks to be acquired by another company, and the only interested parties are foreign, the domestic company might see the value of its assets diminished because of the CFIUS process. A failed foreign transaction would also hurt the United States if the foreign investor would have brought improved technologies and new capital that enhanced productivity and job creation. All of this translates into higher costs for the US economy and, in some cases, diminished benefits.

To avoid the costs of politicization, CFIUS should make it clear that it frowns on competitors or their representatives interfering in the national security review process for commercial rather than national security reasons. Such a statement would only be hortatory, as distinguishing between commercial and national security considerations depends on the desires of the leaders of each CFIUS agency to do so. However, Congress did not set up CFIUS to block politically difficult or unpopular transactions; it intended for the president to block only those transactions that create national security risks to the United States.

Reforming the CFIUS process has become one of the top priorities for the 109th Congress in 2006. While we believe that CFIUS can be improved through changes to regulations and not the statute, pressure for changes in law seem to be so substantial that Congress is likely to pass legislation. Chapter 6 offers a number of ideas for improving Exon-Florio, as well as those that should be rejected. Improvements to the process should include

- **adding protection of critical infrastructure as a factor for CFIUS consideration**. The Department of Homeland Security has identified 12 sectors that it considers to be critical infrastructure. Together, these sectors account for 24.4 percent of US nonfarm civilian workers, a huge swath of the US economy. But if protection of critical infrastructure is going to be a high priority for the federal government, which it should be, then CFIUS, and particularly the Department of Homeland Security, should clarify exactly how it would protect critical infrastructure.

- **establishing security standards for employment of nonnationals in sensitive positions**. Traditional screening mechanisms may not be available to conduct background checks on non-American citizens or non-US employees working abroad. US security agencies can have foreign nationals employed in sensitive positions screened by their own governments or by independent screening agencies operating under the laws of a particular individual's home country. Doing so would require CFIUS to recognize the validity, through mutual recognition agreements, of background checks undertaken by friendly foreign governments.

- **enhancing disclosure of information to Congress.** CFIUS should enhance the quality and quantity of information provided to Congress on the operation of the Exon-Florio Amendment. Greater information disclosure should include aggregate rather than detailed, transaction-specific data. Congress should not demand, nor should CFIUS provide, any confidential business data that parties to a particular transaction give to CFIUS.

- **clarifying the standard by which CFIUS determines whether there is "foreign" control.** The standard by which CFIUS determines foreign control is one of the most restrictive in the US government. CFIUS agencies should clarify the critical elements of the test and consider raising the 10 percent threshold of ownership above which control is presumed.

- **developing international standards for national security review processes.** A number of countries have moved to either impose tighter national security–based restrictions on FDI or define such restrictions in broader economic and strategic terms, or both. To minimize the chilling effect on FDI of these new or expanded foreign investment review measures, members of the Organization for Economic Cooperation and Development (OECD), joined by China, India, and Russia, should develop principles that govern laws for national security–related screening processes for foreign investment.

The executive branch and Congress should also reject a number of ideas that will chill investment without enhancing national security. These include

- **establishing a mandatory filing requirement.** Creating a mandatory filing requirement is both unnecessary and inconsistent with the philosophy underlying Exon-Florio and broader US international economic priorities. Mandatory filings would completely overwhelm the CFIUS process, force CFIUS to focus on transactions that do not raise national security issues, and divert attention from cases that do raise national security concerns.

- **moving the CFIUS chair.** Designating Treasury as the CFIUS chair was consistent with the legislative intent of Exon-Florio to maintain an open investment environment while protecting national security. No other US government agency is better equipped to chair the process than Treasury is. At the same time, Treasury should defer to security agencies with expertise on particular transactions and should strengthen its own security expertise.

■ **introducing an economic security test**. The Exon-Florio Amendment is perhaps most frequently criticized for not allowing CFIUS and the president to consider economic as opposed to national security issues. Adopting an "economic security" or "economic effects" test would undermine the United States' long-standing policy of welcoming foreign investment, be extremely difficult to implement, and further politicize the CFIUS process.

Without FDI, US manufacturing, employment, competitiveness, and innovation will all be at risk. Unless the United States remains open to foreign investment, it will alienate its allies and could find itself increasingly isolated in an increasingly interdependent world. There are those who would restrict foreign investment in the name of strengthening the economy and national security. If they have their way, the United States will lose an important source of economic vitality, resulting in the opposite of what they set out to achieve. Maintaining an open environment for FDI is in itself deeply in the national security interest of the United States.

Acknowledgments

This book has been a labor of love for both authors. It was written in about a year, at a time when the story changed almost faster than we could keep up, in large part due to events like the controversy over Dubai Ports World's proposed acquisition of six ports in the United States.

We first thank C. Fred Bergsten, the director of the Institute for International Economics. Fred was intimately involved in the Committee on Foreign Investment in the United States (CFIUS) during his time as assistant secretary of the Treasury and has been a keen observer and commentator on the process ever since. We are grateful for his support of our efforts, his insightful input, and the institutional support from the Institute to produce the book in a timely fashion. We also thank Ted Truman, a senior fellow at the Institute and also a former assistant secretary of Treasury for international affairs, where he served as the policy level chair of CFIUS. Ted provided us with important and critical feedback on an early draft of the book, comments that helped shape later drafts.

Our work also benefited from, and in many ways reflects the collective learning of, the extraordinary team of lawyers and policy experts who form the core CFIUS team at Covington & Burling. This team includes Stuart Eizenstat, Alan Larson, Mark Plotkin, David Fagan, Jonathan Gimblett, Meena Sharma, and Patricia Johnson. In particular, David, Jonathan, and Meena spent countless hours making important contributions to and collaborating on this project. Without Meena's phenomenal research skills and attention to detail, publication of this book would not have been possible. A number of Covington summer associates also provided important research and memos from which we have drawn. They include Sarah Bannister, Clara Brillembourg, Jeremy Marwell, Dakota Rudesil, and Charlie Trumbull. Finally, David's assistant, Renee Walker, and his colleague at

Covington, Dena Parnis, incorporated the edits into the manuscript and successfully interpreted the authors' terrible handwriting.

We also benefited from typically astute observations and commentary from four highly regarded professionals in the field: Jesse Chang, a prominent lawyer in Beijing; Arnold Kantor, a CFIUS and China expert with the Scowcroft Group; Ted Moran, who holds the Marcus Wallenberg Chair at the School of Foreign Service at Georgetown University; and John Reynolds, a CFIUS expert at the law firm of Wiley, Rein and Fielding. We are grateful for their time and input.

The publications team at the Institute was also terrific. Valerie Norville, Madona Devasahayam, and Marla Banov supervised the editorial and production process with skill and grace and pushed us to respond to editorial suggestions and changes in a timely fashion. Brian Slattery served as a great copyeditor, tightening, refining, and improving our writing. Giwon Jeong was of great assistance with data, particularly the often confusing and contradictory official Chinese data.

Finally, David would like to thank his wife, Pam Kurland, for her support and indulgence while we worked on this project, and his wonderful kids, Hannah and Zachary.

David Marchick is a partner at the law firm Covington & Burling and advises US and foreign companies on Exon-Florio issues. As would be expected, Covington & Burling's clients have a range of views on international investment and Exon-Florio issues. This book represents the two authors' views and not the views of Covington & Burling or its clients. Any information on particular companies mentioned in this book was derived from public sources.

■　■　■

Three and a half years ago, I was handed a medical diagnosis that suggested that I might never produce another book in my life. But this book was produced in spite of this diagnosis and indeed might not be my final book. For this I owe a bundle to a truly fine team of healthcare providers at Georgetown University Hospital (GUH), where Dr. John Marshall heads my team. He and his close colleague Dr. Jimmy Huang are among those to whom this book is dedicated. But my dedication is also to all team members who serve or have served in the trenches. They include most especially the nurses, physician assistants, technicians, and physicians on the seventh floor of GUH Main, and they are Amy, April, Catherine, Jennifer, Joy, Kash, Latisha, Marjorie, Mary, Mercedes, Nina, Pari, Quiana, Rita, Rory, Sonia, Suzie, Terry, and Zam-zam. Finally, I also dedicate this book to the homecare team, which consists solely of my wife, Kathryn. My thanks and love to all.

—EMG

1

Introduction

For close to 100 years, foreign direct investment (FDI) has been a vital and beneficial part of the US economy. The US economy depends on FDI for its vibrancy and vitality today more than ever, yet FDI has often created bitter and emotional debates about its implications for US national security. During World War I, FDI from Germany raised national security concerns, and goaded by the Navy, Congress passed sector-specific prohibitions on FDI as well as the Trading with the Enemy Act (TWEA), which gave the president broad powers to block or expropriate foreign investment. In 1985 FDI in the United States, which had been building up since the 1970s, began to draw public attention. Shortly thereafter, there was a surge of foreign acquisitions of US companies and assets, particularly by Japanese companies. In response, in 1988 Congress gave the president a powerful new tool to address the national security implications of FDI: the Exon-Florio Amendment, which authorized the president to block a foreign acquisition of a US entity if the acquisition threatened US national security. The amendment has been at the center of debate about FDI and its effect on national security ever since.

The post-1985 surge of FDI in the United States stimulated concerns in Congress that the resulting loss of domestic control to foreign investors might harm US economic and security interests. These concerns waned during the early 1990s, as the rate of growth of FDI into the United States slowed, and perhaps more important, the economic growth of Japan, a significant and symbolic investor nation, came to a virtual halt. This ended widespread fear that Japan would soon overtake the United States as the world's preeminent economic power. Simultaneously, the US economy entered a sustained period of faster economic growth than had been seen since the 1950s. This boom bolstered US confidence and reduced anxiety and uncertainty about foreign control of US assets.

1

But as Yogi Berra, the famous catcher and manager for the New York Yankees, once said, it is "déjà vu all over again." Today the debate in the 1980s over Japan is being repeated with respect to China as a rising economic and military power. The proposed takeover of Unocal, a US publicly traded energy company, by the state-owned China National Offshore Oil Corporation (CNOOC) during the summer of 2005 is just one impetus for the fears generated by the prospect of more Chinese FDI entering the United States. This fear persists even though Chinese direct investment in the United States has been to date quite limited, and even though it is doubtful that most Chinese investment is detrimental to US interests. In early 2006 the political eruption in Congress over the proposed acquisition of the Peninsular and Oriental Steam Navigation Company (P&O) by Dubai Ports World, a company owned and controlled by the government of the United Arab Emirates, made the CNOOC controversy look like small potatoes. In the chapters that follow, we examine these fears and concerns in some detail.

FDI occurs when a foreign investor exerts direct control over domestic assets. Technically speaking, it is the book value of the equity held by the foreign investor that is attached to the asset. In most cases, the asset is a US firm, and the equity consists of two components: ordinary (common) stock and retained earnings. If both foreign and domestic investors own the common stock, then only the portion held by foreign persons is considered to be FDI, and only if a threshold percentage is attained that is deemed to give the foreign investor control of the business. In the United States, for most purposes, this threshold stands at 10 percent.[1] As already suggested, foreign investment can take place in one of two ways. First, foreign investors can establish new firms in the United States, which they control, or they can enlarge their holdings in firms that they already control. Second, foreign investors can acquire controlling interests in previously established domestic firms, or spin-offs of such firms. Both forms of FDI have raised and continue to raise national security issues in particular transactions.

FDI in the Early 20th Century

FDI has played a significant role in the development of the US economy since at least the 1870s. In the late 19th century, the vast majority of foreign investment in the United States originated in Europe. In some cases, this investment changed from foreign to domestic when major shareholders became US citizens. Carnegie Steel (later, US Steel), which for some

---

1. In this instance, FDI would also include a share of retained earnings in proportion to the foreign investor's share of the common stock. If the foreign investor held 50 percent of the stock, 50 percent of retained earnings would be considered FDI along with that stock, at book value.

time was the largest US industrial corporation, changed from being a foreign investment to a domestic holding when the Scottish-born Andrew Carnegie became a US citizen.

Apart from steel, in the late 19th and early 20th centuries, FDI contributed to the development of a number of emerging and important US industrial sectors, including chemicals, radio broadcasting, telecommunications, and transport machinery. Several foreign firms started plants to produce automobiles in the United States in the early 1900s. The FDI that helped foster the development of these sectors in the United States also gave rise to US government national security concerns, particularly in the early 20th century.[2] Although records of FDI flows during those years are sketchy, data indicate that in the early 1900s, there was substantial inward and outward FDI. FDI in the United States—again, most of which was from Europe—totaled $1.3 billion in nominal terms in 1914. US direct investment abroad was twice this amount, or $2.6 billion.[3] Comparing the number of affiliates established in Europe by US firms with affiliates established in the United States by European firms also suggests that the US direct investment presence in Europe exceeded that of Europe in the United States (Graham 1974, table 2.1). In addition, there was a significant stock of portfolio investment in the United States:[4] In 1914, the stock of all foreign investment in the country was $7.1 billion, equal in value to about 20 percent of annual GDP.[5] One reason this large amount of foreign investment, particularly in relation to GDP, raised few concerns was that systematic data were rather scant at the time. Data on foreign investment in the United States during that period are mostly scholarly "educated guesses." In 1915, when the US government began to investigate the amount of foreign investment in the United States, its size and extent startled policymakers. The quantitative data generated by this investigation triggered concern about how much of the US economy was under foreign control; these data were one reason a number of measures to restrict or regulate this investment were soon to be enacted.

US national security concerns regarding foreign investment in the early 20th century were triggered by the onset of World War I. It is safe to say

---

2. For very detailed histories of FDI in the United States, see Wilkins (1989) and Wilkins (2004). Much of the history recounted in this chapter is derived from the latter source, supplemented by other sources.

3. See Hymer (1960, table 1.1); original data from US Department of Commerce, Bureau of Economic Analysis (BEA). For a history of US business activity abroad, see Wilkins (1970).

4. While government and international agencies differ in the precise definition of portfolio versus direct investment, they agree in general that portfolio investment occurs when an equity investor exerts no managerial control over the investment, whereas a direct investor exerts such control.

5. See note 1, table 1.1, and accompanying text in Wilkins (2004).

that these concerns were more pronounced at the time of World War I and its aftermath than at any other time in US history, including the 1980s, when Americans became preoccupied with Japanese investment in the United States. German companies had made significant direct investments in the United States early in the 20th century, but it was only after hostilities broke out in late 1914 that questions were raised about the level of German involvement in the US economy. US concerns regarding foreign investment reached new heights after 1915, simultaneously with the growing antagonism between the United States and Germany that culminated in the United States entering the war. Public and official attention to German investment intensified following a 1915 incident in which a German diplomat accidentally left a briefcase on New York's elevated transit (Wilkins 2004, 31). Materials found in the briefcase indicated that some German-controlled operations in the United States were aimed at, or at least useful for, enhancing German war capabilities, reducing Allied capabilities, or spying on the United States. This revelation confirmed the suspicions of certain members of Congress that at least some German investment in the United States was meant to achieve sinister ends, even for cases in which the apparent purpose of the investment was purely for commercial gain.

The war years (1915–16) saw significant disinvestment from the United States, but some new FDI still entered the country, mostly from the United Kingdom, but also from Germany. Certain of these foreign investments helped create domestic production of dyestuffs, potash, and refined tin, much of which was imported from the United Kingdom and Germany before the war. By 1915 the conflict had extended into the North Atlantic, and shipments of these materials to the United States were disrupted. Thus the capacity to produce dyestuffs and other chemical products, including pharmaceuticals, in both British- and German-controlled plants in the United States was expanded during this time. This benefited the United States when it later entered the war: Because of foreign investment, the United States had the capacity to make these products that it might have lacked otherwise. The operations, including German-controlled ones, also benefited from inward technology transfer that would aid the American war effort a few years later.

The experience of World War I establishes an important point regarding direct investment. Such investment, even when it comes from antagonistic nations, does not automatically harm the defense or security interests of the nation that receives it. To the contrary, the investment can actually serve the interests of the receiving nation.

As World War I progressed, the United States sided increasingly with the nations allied against Germany. Finally, in the spring of 1917, the United States entered the war on the side of the Allied nations. With the United States at war, concerns about the security risks posed by German-controlled firms in the United States led to the passage of the TWEA in 1917.[6] The TWEA authorized the president, in times of war or declared national emergency, to take a number of measures affecting transactions between US subsidiaries of foreign companies and their parent organizations. Section 5(b) of the TWEA empowered the president to

> investigate, regulate, direct and compel, nullify, void, prevent or prohibit, any acquisition, holding, withholding, use, transfer, withdrawal, transportation, importation or exportation of, or dealing in, or exercising any right, power, or privilege with respect to, or transactions involving, any property in which any foreign country or any national thereof has any interest.[7]

This section and other TWEA provisions gave the president very broad but rather ambiguous powers to take action against foreign-controlled subsidiaries operating in the United States. Until the passage of Exon-Florio in 1988, the TWEA and International Emergency Economic Powers Act (IEEPA) remained the main laws by which the US government could regulate direct investments in the United States by foreign companies for national security reasons.

In 1917–18 President Woodrow Wilson invoked the TWEA to sequester and take title to US assets held by all German companies, as well as some non-German assets that were determined to be effectively under German control.[8] These assets were then administered by the US Government Office of the Custodian of Alien Properties. In practice, President Wilson's action meant that US subsidiaries of German firms were nationalized under legal provisions that would allow for their return to their original owners following cessation of hostilities. However, following the Treaty of Versailles in 1919, which brought the war formally to an end, most of these assets transferred to US ownership instead.

The main beneficiary of this transfer was the chemical industry,[9] which, at the time, was viewed by the US government as perhaps the most im-

---

6. *Trading with the Enemy Act*, Public Law 65-91, *US Statutes at Large* 40 (1917): 411, codified at *US Code* 50 (2000), App. § 1 et seq. In 1976, the TWEA was supplanted by the International Emergency Economic Powers Act (IEEPA). The changes effected by the IEEPA are discussed later in this chapter.

7. *Trading with the Enemy Act*, App. § 5(b)(1)(B).

8. Beginning in 1915, some German interests had attempted to acquire strategically important US firms via Denmark. Also, some German investments in the United States were jointly held with British investors. When these were seized in 1917, it affected British as well as German investments, even though the United States was allied with the United Kingdom.

9. In what follows, the reader should be aware that the technologies associated with dyestuffs, ammonia, and aniline film production were very close to those used to make high explosives. Moreover, German high explosives first used in war in 1914 were of much greater potency than explosives used in earlier conflicts.

portant industry to national security. As a result, forced transfers of chemical assets from German to US companies were especially prevalent. Except for dyestuff operations, US businesses held by the large German chemical company Bayer were sold to the US firm Sterling Products. The assets included the right to the Bayer name in the United States, which is why Sterling sells aspirin under the Bayer trademark to this day.

The massive postwar transfer of assets from German to US ownership was not limited to tangible property; it also included important intellectual property assets. In 1919 the alien properties custodian sold some 4,500 patents previously held by German chemical firms—excluding those of Bayer, which were already sold to Sterling Products—to the Chemical Foundation, a nonprofit US corporation established specifically to receive those patents. The Chemical Foundation then licensed the patents to US firms. This transfer resulted in important benefits for a number of US firms, including perhaps the biggest winner, E. I. du Pont de Nemours, which later acquired a number of other firms that had also purchased rights to intellectual property from the alien properties custodian.[10]

While certain US firms benefited economically from the transfer of physical and intellectual property, the US government's main justification for appropriation was that US ownership of these assets was needed for national security reasons.[11] German high explosives, unmatched in lethality, had wreaked havoc on Allied forces in the early months of the war, and for a time, the Allies could not reciprocate. To have the key technologies needed to produce such explosives within US-owned firms, and to do so efficiently, was seen as an American national priority. Even after the German defeat in 1918, the fear remained that German companies, which had dominated the chemicals sector prior to the war, would quickly regain their former strength because of their comparative technological advantage.

In 1920 a number of US chemical firms, including those that were former US affiliates of foreign firms, merged to form the Allied Chemical Company. For a time, Allied Chemical was the largest US chemical firm. After expropriating technology previously under German ownership, in 1921, Congress and the Warren Harding administration moved to protect the US chemical industry by adopting steep tariff increases. The Fordney-McCumber tariff of 1922 raised tariffs further for organic chemicals.

Although DuPont, Allied Chemical, and other US-owned chemical firms benefited from acquiring German patents, they soon found that there were missing links in the technology they had acquired. Thus as early as 1919, beginning with exchanges of technology for production of nitrates of ammonia between DuPont and the German firm Badische Anilin und

---

10. For an account of how DuPont benefited from transfer of intellectual property following World War I, see Zilg (1974, chapter 9) and Wilkins (2004, note 1, chapter 2).

11. *Federal Register* 7, no. 55 (March 18, 1942): 2165.

Soda Fabrik (BASF),[12] major US chemical firms that had acquired US operations of German firms began to establish ties with many of the same German firms from which the properties and technologies had originally been expropriated. The US firms used these alliances to buy additional technology. Although German firms were initially reluctant to sell the very technologies that had enabled them to dominate the market, in the circumstances following the war, they were in no position to refuse outright, and the management of German firms soon realized that significant profits could be earned from technology sales. Thus licensing technology to US firms became a major business activity for German companies as the 1920s progressed.

Within a few years, German companies began to reenter the US market, often in partnership with the same US firms that had acquired the German firms' former US assets. Bayer reentered the United States in 1923, setting up an alliance with Winthrop Chemical Company, a subsidiary of Sterling Products. Bayer's primary role in this joint venture was to supply technology to Winthrop. But as noted earlier, most of Bayer's US assets, except its dyestuff operations, had earlier been sold to Sterling Products, a US-owned firm, and Winthrop Chemical Company thus controlled former Bayer operations. Bayer made a similar arrangement with the Grasselli Dyestuff Corporation, a subsidiary of the US-owned Grasselli Chemical Company, which was merged later into DuPont. The US government sold Bayer's US dyemaking operations to Grasselli Chemical Company in 1918, immediately after the armistice ending World War I. Grasselli Dyestuffs was the subsidiary established for these operations. Thus by 1923, in effect, Bayer had entered into alliances with all of its former US affiliates, now under control of two different US-owned firms. A second large German firm, Hoechst, had lost its US assets in 1918. Many of these assets were sold to the US-owned National Aniline and Chemical Company. But in 1925 Hoechst reentered the United States by creating the General Dyestuffs Corporation in the United States, which then worked as a partner in a number of undertakings with National Aniline and Film.

In 1926 much of the German chemical industry, including the three biggest firms, Bayer, Hoechst, and BASF, was consolidated into one firm, I. G. Farbenindustrie, or I. G. Farben. This prompted similar consolidations in the United Kingdom, creating the firm known as Imperial Chemical Industries (ICI) (Hardie and Pratt 1966). US firms thus had to compete with very large European groups that wielded significant market power. In an effort to further increase its own power, I. G. Farben attempted but failed to merge with Allied Chemical in 1926. A year later, I. G. Farben entered into an agreement with Standard Oil of New Jersey (SONJ, today Exxon), through which I. G. Farben gave SONJ access to its hydrogenation

---

12. The British firm Brunner, Mond and the Belgian firm Solvay were also involved in this exchange (Wilkins 1974, 125–26).

technology for increasing oil-refining yields. The agreement also specified that SONJ would not enter the chemical businesses that I. G. Farben dominated. In 1928, DuPont acquired Grasselli Chemical, but Grasselli Dyestuffs was spun off to I. G. Farben, which named its new subsidiary General Aniline Works (later General Aniline and Film, or GAF). In turn, GAF acquired a 50 percent interest in Winthrop Chemical. In 1929 I. G. Farben took further steps to enlarge its US presence by combining all of its US operations into I. G. Chemical Corporation, a holding company. This reemergence of German interests in the US chemical sector would have important national security implications during the 1930s, as discussed later in this chapter.[13]

Interestingly, and unlike in several other sectors discussed below, Congress did not pass legal restrictions on foreign investment in the chemical sector. Thus by the late 1930s, the chemical sector was the leading industrial sector for FDI in the United States, and with a major German presence. Doubtless, despite the industry's perceived importance to US national security, Congress did not impose restrictions in the chemical sector because unlike in 1914, German firms operating in the United States did so in alliance with US-owned firms, which welcomed those alliances and the technology enabled by them. Even so, German participation in the sector came under some scrutiny by the US military following the rise of Hitler in Germany, and the sector would again become a focus of US national security concerns when World War II broke out, as discussed later in this chapter.

In World War I, as mentioned above, the chemical sector was identified as strategically the most important sector to the US war effort. But the US government identified other sectors as critical to US military efforts as well, and German-owned US assets, as well as assets owned by investors seen as German allies, were seized and effectively nationalized. As a result, by the end of World War I, the stock of overall FDI in the United States had fallen by more than one-third from prewar levels, from $1.3 billion in 1914 to about $0.9 billion in 1919 (Hymer 1960, table 1.1).

Even after the war ended, and despite the reemergence of foreign investment in the chemical industry, overall FDI flows did not return to their prewar levels for some time. In 1930 the stock of foreign FDI in the United States was only $1.4 billion, only slightly more in nominal terms, and significantly lower in real terms, than it was in 1914. The expropriation of German assets was one important reason for the drop in the real value of FDI. Moreover, in the eyes of German and other foreign investors, the US government had simply failed to protect foreign investment according to the standards required by international law, or even US domestic law. The

---

13. The events in the chemical sector in the 1920s are complex, and the above paragraphs highlight only a few of the events most relevant to the topic of this book. Bäumler (1968) gives a more complete account.

US investment environment was thus seen as fraught with political risk. FDI stagnated because of other factors as well, including significant economic imbalances—in particular, a large current account deficit—in the United Kingdom following the war, which led Her Majesty's government to take measures to restrict capital outflow. Although the United Kingdom had been the largest source of FDI in the United States prior to the war, UK-based firms were hard-pressed after the war to resume investment abroad. In addition, even without the expropriations, significant amounts of German investment in the United States would have been unlikely after 1918, because post–World War I Germany was in economic ruin. France, another source of FDI in the United States, was in even worse shape than Germany was, having suffered substantial physical destruction during the war. Some of the largest French investments in the United States had been in the oil industry; these assets were mostly sold to US interests in 1919 and 1920. However, an important reason for low postwar FDI was that, in the years immediately following World War I, Congress passed a number of sector-specific restrictions on foreign investment in the United States. As a result, 1919–23 were anemic years for foreign investment in the United States (Wilkins 2004, chapter 3).

Unlike the United Kingdom and continental Europe, the United States economy was not disrupted by the physical destruction of World War I. In fact, the United States had been a net international debtor nation at the outset of the war, but emerged as an international creditor nation, a position it maintained until Reaganomics brought the nation back into net international debtor status in the late 1980s. Accordingly, during the 1920s, US firms expanded their international presence, including in Europe (Wilkins 1974). By 1930, the stock of US direct investment abroad had risen to about $8 billion, from $2.6 billion in 1914 (Hymer 1960, table 1.1). US direct investment abroad in 1930 was almost six times greater than FDI in the United States.

But as noted above, despite the relatively small amounts of FDI entering the United States immediately following World War I, foreign control of business activity in certain sectors remained a security concern, and this deterred foreign investment. Perhaps the best example of this can be seen in the interrelated sectors of radio broadcasting and telecommunications, which were heavily affected. Security concerns in the radio broadcasting sector began to surface right after conflict broke out in Europe, well before the United States entered the war. In late 1914, the US Navy became concerned that espionage activities were being conducted over foreign-owned radio stations located in the United States. This concern led to action when, following the sinking of the British ship *Lusitania* in 1915, the United States seized, through executive order, the broadcasting facilities of the German electronics firm Telefunken and placed their assets under Navy control. At the time, the Telefunken seizure was seen as a temporary measure; indeed, it took place before the TWEA had established a legal basis for such action.

When the TWEA later came into effect, the Telefunken assets were transferred to the Custodian of Alien Property established under the Act, and employees of German ancestry, including US citizens, were barred from working at the facilities it formerly owned.[14]

The Telefunken seizure turned out to be the tip of the iceberg in the broadcasting sector. In 1917, after the United States entered the war, President Wilson seized all foreign-owned radio stations under the Radio Act of 1912, which authorized government control of all radio facilities in time of war. The largest seizure involved the broadcasting assets of the firm American Marconi, which was one-third owned by and under the effective control of British interests.

Not satisfied by the seizure of Telefunken's and Marconi's broadcasting assets, the US Navy later pressured Congress to pass a law restricting all foreign ownership of radio broadcasting facilities in the United States. Indeed, a bill to do so—the so-called Bullard bill, named after its drafter, Captain W. H. G. Bullard—was drafted by the Navy and introduced into the House of Representatives.[15] However, by that time, such a law was not needed and none was passed, because all radio broadcasting facilities were under US naval control.

With the Allied victory in World War I, one might have thought that the rationale for such restrictions would expire. However, in 1919, with the strong encouragement of the Navy, US General Electric (GE) bought the radio patents formerly held by American Marconi. This transaction, executed under threat of action by Congress to force the sale if Marconi did not enter into it voluntarily, effectively put American Marconi out of business.[16] GE subsequently transferred these patents to a newly formed company, the Radio Corporation of America, or RCA. At the time of its formation, RCA was effectively under US Navy control. With the US government's blessing, RCA proceeded to establish a monopoly over domestic wireless operations. Thus by 1919 the US Navy finally obtained what it had wanted since 1914: domestic, albeit not Navy, control over all radio broadcasting activity in the United States.

These actions alone did not preclude all future foreign investment in US broadcasting. That was largely achieved when Congress passed the Radio Act of 1927,[17] which prohibited foreign control of radio broadcasting activity, including by US corporations under foreign control. Control was

---

14. Sidak (1997) is the primary source for this subsection on telecommunications.

15. HR 19350, 64th Congress, 2nd sess., §§ 7, 9 (1916).

16. In 1918 Representative Joshua Alexander drafted a bill to nationalize all radio transmitters and put them under US Navy control. The bill was never introduced because of the sale described above.

17. *Radio Act of 1927*, Public Law 69-632, *US Statutes at Large* 44 (1927): 1162, codified at *US Code* 47 (1927), § 87.

found if either a director of the company was an "alien," a person not holding US citizenship, or if one-fifth or more of the voting stock of the company was held by aliens or could be voted by aliens. With the Radio Act of 1927, foreign-controlled firms could not effectively challenge the RCA monopoly. Although it was directed at the radio industry, the Radio Act also effectively precluded foreign ownership of telecommunications operations in the United States because the telecommunications sector increasingly relied on radio and, later, microwave transmissions (also covered under the law) for transmission of traffic. Most of the restrictions on foreign ownership in the Radio Act were incorporated into the Communications Act of 1934 and remained in place for more than 60 years.[18]

Thus in the name of national security, British radio and telecommunications interests were subject to almost the same treatment as the German chemical industry. Their US assets, including patents, were effectively expropriated by American interests, largely through US government intervention. As mentioned above, unlike in the radio or telecommunications industry, Congress never acted to preclude foreign investment in the chemical industry.

Why would FDI restrictions enacted during the 1920s have been directed toward British interests, as was the case in radio broadcasting and other sectors? The United Kingdom and United States had been allies during World War I, but after the war ended, there was some sentiment within both the US and British militaries that US and British interests were bound in the future to collide. During the 1920s, each military drew up contingency plans for a war with the other.[19] How much this sentiment affected US direct investment policy is difficult to ascertain after so many years. However, it seems to us unlikely to be a coincidence that most restrictions on FDI in the United States during the 1920s affected sectors of particular interest to the US Navy, and were directed toward British interests.

Other sectors besides radio broadcasting and telecommunications were also affected by measures restricting direct investment into the United States in the aftermath of World War I, including transportation, energy (mainly oil), and banking. In each of these sectors, with the exception of banking, security concerns played a major role in bringing about the restrictions.

In marine transport, as in radio broadcasting, the US Navy was a leading advocate of restricting foreign investment. As the war demonstrated

---

18. *Radio Act of 1927*, §§ 310(a), (b).

19. On these plans, see Peter Carlson, "Raiding the Ice Box," *Washington Post*, December 20, 2005, C1. The US plan, entitled "Joint Army-Navy Basic War Plan Red," was completed in 1930. It is now declassified, and a photocopy can be obtained from the National Archives of the United States; see also "Did the United States Have a Plan to Invade Canada During the 1920s?" at www.straightdope.com.

the need for shipping capacity, the Navy wanted to ensure that the United States maintained a sizable shipping fleet under US control. In response to goading from the Navy, Congress passed Section 27 of the Merchant Marine Act of 1920, or the "Jones Act,"[20] which required coastal shipping between American ports to be handled by ships built in the United States, registered in the United States, and owned by US citizens. Under the act, a firm was considered to be owned by US citizens if 75 percent of its common stock was held by US citizens.

In 1926 Congress passed the Air Commerce Act, regulating the airline industry.[21] In some ways, the Air Commerce Act mirrored the Jones Act. Once again, the Navy took a lead role, arguing that the United States should have a fleet of aircraft under its domestic control that could be used in the event of war to transport both personnel and material.[22] Under the act, only US citizens could register aircraft in the United States, and foreign aircraft had to obtain permission to fly over US territory. Commercial flights between any two points in the United States were reserved for US-registered aircraft. Certain provisions of the Air Commerce Act were more lenient than equivalent shipping provisions under the Jones Act. A firm was deemed to be controlled by US citizens only if a majority of common stock was held by persons holding US citizenship, although the act allowed only 25 percent of the voting power to be held by foreign persons. However, the Air Commerce Act also specified that the president of a firm holding US-registered aircraft had to be a US citizen, as did two-thirds of the officers and members of boards of directors. Many of the Air Commerce Act's foreign ownership restrictions were later incorporated into the Federal Aviation Act of 1958, the law that restricts foreign investment in airlines today.[23]

In 1926 Congress also passed the Air Corps Act,[24] which regulated the production of aircraft. The Air Corps Act stipulated that the US Army Air Corps could buy aircraft only from companies in which all of the directors were US citizens, with all manufacturing facilities located in the United States, and of which at least 75 percent of common stock was owned by US citizens. A special provision, however, allowed the US government

---

20. *Merchant Marine Act of 1920*, Public Law 66-261, codified at *US Code Annotated* 46 (West 1975 and Supp. 2005), App. § 883.

21. *Air Commerce Act*, Public Law 69-254, *US Statutes at Large* 44 (1926): 568.

22. In 1926 there was no US Air Force and, indeed, it was unclear which branch of the military would operate military air transport. In advocating this legislation, the Navy might have thus been hoping that it would get this role.

23. *Aviation Act of 1958*, Public Law 85-726, *US Statutes at Large* 72 (1958): 731, codified as amended at *US Code Annotated* 49 (West 1997 & Supp. 2005), § 40102.

24. *Air Corps Act*, Public Law 69-446, *US Statutes at Large* 44 (1926): 780.

to buy aircraft from a "domestic firm" listed on a US stock exchange. This seemed to be designed to benefit operations controlled by the Dutch-controlled Fokker interests (Wilkins 2004, 292).

Thus by 1926 exactly what constituted a US firm varied substantially from sector to sector: As discussed above, 80 percent US ownership was required for radio broadcasting; only majority ownership for commercial air transport; 100 percent for marine shipping, but holding companies with no more than 25 percent foreign ownership were deemed to be controlled by US citizens; and 75 percent for aircraft manufacturing if the product was to be sold to the US military, subject to the aforementioned exception. Congress did not rule out minority foreign participation in these sectors altogether, because it recognized that American entrepreneurs could in some cases benefit from raising equity abroad. What Congress sought, rather than 100 percent US ownership of the relevant activities, was US control over them (Wilkins 2004, 294).

Security considerations also played a significant role in enacting restrictions on foreign investment in the energy sector, mostly related to oil and gas production. Once again, the US Navy was the prime mover behind the legislation. However, the specific concerns over oil and gas were quite distinct from those in other sectors. In 1919, the Navy worried that the United States might eventually run out of oil and gas, even though at that time, the United States was by far the largest producer of both, and also held the largest proven reserves in the world. The Navy was concerned about the need to keep US warships fueled around the globe, and was intensely aware that the United Kingdom had near-exclusive rights to explore and develop oil in the Middle East, where the existence of petroleum reserves was well known. Accordingly, the Navy encouraged US oil firms to invest overseas. There was also significant foreign investment in the US oil industry in 1919, particularly by the Royal Dutch/Shell group, based jointly in the United Kingdom and the Netherlands. Among other assets, Shell owned significant tracts of oil-producing land in California. The Navy, however, did not see foreign ownership of oil reserves in the United States as a security concern; rather, it worried about the lack of US presence in, for example, Iran, where Royal Dutch/Shell held exclusive rights.

In response to Navy and other pressures, in 1920, Congress passed the Mineral Lands Leasing Act,[25] limiting foreign participation in leasing US public land to extract or transport oil (e.g., through pipelines) to only those companies from countries that allowed US investment in their oil sectors. The intent of the law was not to prevent foreign investment in exploration within the United States, however, but rather to assist expansion

---

25. *Mineral Lands Leasing Act*, Public Law 66-146, *US Statutes at Large* 41 (1920): 437, codified at *US Code* 30 (2000), § 181 et seq.

overseas of the US oil industry. The concept of reciprocity, unique among US foreign investment laws of the era,[26] provided that if the government of the foreign investor allowed US access to petroleum under its jurisdiction or control, then investors from that country could participate in leasing US public land. Meanwhile, the overseas industry would improve the Navy's ability to refuel its ships abroad (Wilkins 2004, 101–102).

In contrast to the sectors discussed above, foreign ownership of banking in the United States had been restricted since the 19th century. Since 1864, federal law had required that directors of US national banks be US citizens. Under New York law, foreign banks could not establish branches or take deposits in New York, forcing foreign banks wishing to operate in the dominant US capital market to operate as nondepository institutions. In 1919, Congress passed the Edge Act[27] to stimulate US bank participation in international trade finance, but even "Edge Act banks" required US citizens to own a majority of the bank and comprise a majority of its directors.

As noted, FDI, particularly portfolio investment, in the United States was making something of a comeback in the late 1920s, a time of robust economic expansion. However, that expansion would soon come to an abrupt end with the onset of the Great Depression in the 1930s. Portfolio investment in the United States was heavily affected; the stock of this investment plummeted during the Depression years. In contrast, the stock of FDI in the United States increased during this period, albeit only slightly, from $1.4 billion in 1930 to $2.0 billion in 1939.[28] US direct investment abroad, however, declined over the course of the decade, from $8 billion in 1931 to $7 billion in 1939.[29] Even so, by that year, US direct investment abroad was about three and one-half times greater than FDI in the United States.

Some of the FDI that flowed to the United States during the 1930s did not develop from normal economic circumstances, but from the creation

---

26. While the statutory framework governing investment in the US airline industry does not include concepts of reciprocity, the US Department of Transportation (US DOT) has given much more flexibility to foreign investors from countries with which the United States has liberal air services agreements and which provide US investors with similar opportunities to invest. See US DOT (2005).

27. *Edge Act*, Public Law 66-106, *US Statutes at Large* 41 (1919): 378, codified at *US Code* 12 (2000), § 611 et seq.

28. See Hymer (1960, table 1.1). However, Wilkins (2004) questions the accuracy of the data, noting that there were some foreign entries into the United States in the early 1930s, apparently in response to the very high Smoot-Hawley tariffs of 1930, but also a significant number of exits, in response to the poor economic conditions that prevailed after the onset of the Great Depression.

29. Hymer (1960, table 1.1). Specific cases of disinvestments by US firms are detailed in Wilkins (1974).

of a number of large-scale international cartels (Edwards 1944, Hexner 1945) that covered a wide range of sectors, but were especially significant in the chemical, steel, oil and gas, electrical equipment, and precision instrument industries—all sectors then considered "strategic" from a security point of view.[30] Some cartelization had begun during the 1920s. Indeed, as noted earlier, the agreement between I. G. Farben and SONJ contained cartel-like provisions, by which I. G. Farben agreed to stay out of the oil business if SONJ stayed out of the chemicals business. Where the two sectors overlapped in the "petrochemical" sector, the agreement delineated exclusive marketing territories (Hexner 1945). The Depression motivated further and more extensive cartelization of world markets for numerous industrial products. Cartelization occurred because the worldwide depression substantially reduced global demand for industrial products, creating worldwide overcapacity in many sectors. This, in turn, led to price-cutting, as firms sought to maintain their market shares. In sectors characterized by large fixed costs, price cuts often drove prices below average cost, a situation that could prove ruinous for all firms in a particular sector. Under these circumstances, firms had a strong incentive to collude, holding prices constant and monitoring others' activities. During the Great Depression, conditions were ripe for collusion.

In most cases, the cartels aimed to coordinate output reduction among competitors and prevent prices from falling. Much of the FDI entering the United States in cartelized industries during the 1930s amounted to "listening posts" within territories assigned under cartel agreements to operations by other firms. The listening posts monitored activities of rival firms, ensuring that output reduction agreements were not broken. In the early 1930s, DuPont entered into a number of agreements with ICI, effectively dividing world markets. But even so, each firm often created or maintained small operations in territories reserved for the other.

Because of cartelization, not only did FDI into the United States not dry up entirely, but some FDI of a "listening post" variety even entered the United States from Germany.[31]

During and following World War II, a number of international cartels were prosecuted under US antitrust laws and were found to be illegal. The arrangements between ICI and DuPont came under scrutiny as possible violations of US antitrust laws; both firms later were party to large-scale litigation that affected the entire chemical industry. Despite prose-

---

30. Senate Subcommittee on Scientific and Technical Mobilization, Committee on Military Affairs, *Hearings on Cartel Practices and National Security Before the US Senate, Subcommittee on Scientific and Technical Mobilization, Committee on Military Affairs*, 78th Congress, 2nd sess., August 29 and September 7–8, 12–13, 1944.

31. Graham (1974). Entry into the United States by the German electrical firm Siemens might be classed as of this nature.

cution, evidence emerged as late as the 1950s indicating that some cartel activity still persisted, for example, in the electrical equipment industry.

As noted earlier, there was some US scrutiny of the chemical sector after Adolph Hitler's rise to power in Germany in 1933. Under the Nazi government in Germany, a close relationship developed between Farben and the rearming German state. Such a relationship had existed earlier between the state and the predecessor firms of I. G. Farben, but it had grown somewhat cold after World War I. As a military power, Germany was particularly vulnerable to being cut off from its supplies of vital raw materials. But I. G. Farben's vast expertise in the chemical industry during the 1930s proved capable of providing the reemerging German war machine with domestic alternatives to many raw materials that Germany had before been forced to import. Since World War I, I. G. Farben had developed processes for manufacturing synthetic rubber and making gasoline out of coal, a product found in abundance in Germany. Because of I. G. Farben's growing ties to the German war machine, its businesses in the United States after 1934 came under increased scrutiny, from both the US and German governments. As noted earlier, much of the focus of I. G. Farben's US operations involved the sale of technology. But following the Nazi government's rise in Germany, under German government pressure, I. G. Farben began to withhold technology sharing, and thus effectively reversed its earlier strategy: It sought to become a net acquirer of technology. Under its agreement with SONJ, I. G. Farben should have shared its synthetic rubber technology. But it did not, even though SONJ made its own studies into synthetic rubber available. By the late 1930s this withholding of technology created concern for US military leaders, although no formal action was taken.

In 1941 after hostilities resumed between the United States and Germany, President Roosevelt invoked the TWEA, allowing the US government to seize German and Japanese assets in the United States. However, because German investment in the United States between the two world wars had been quite modest, there were fewer German assets to be seized. The alien properties custodian, charged with investigating the extent of German-controlled holdings in the United States, concluded that these holdings were considerably less significant in 1942 than they were in 1917.[32] The most substantial assets seized were, once again, held by the

---

32. Wilkins (2004, 518–19). Wilkins also reproduces the results of a US Treasury census of firms in the United States under foreign control as of June 14, 1941. At that time, there were reported to be 2,816 such firms, 1,985 of which were under the control of European investors. But the total value of these firms was reported as a rather modest $2.316 billion, and the value of enterprises under European control at $1.569 billion. The total number of enterprises under German or Swiss control—the latter of importance because, in many cases, Swiss holding companies masked German holdings—was 416, with a total value of $242.9 million. The small average size of the firms under foreign control supports the hypothesis that many of these firms were essentially listening posts.

German chemical industry, especially the already suspect I. G. Farben. Beginning in December 1941, the US government seized I. G. Farben's assets, including those of its main US subsidiary, General Aniline Works. Assets of other Axis nation firms were also seized, including those of the Harvard Brewing Company (owned by a German family), American Bosch, American Potash and Chemical, General Dyestuff, Schering, Mitsubishi Trading Company, and four Italian bank agencies. Patents held by German, Italian, and Japanese interests, most of which were in the electrical, pharmaceutical, and chemical sectors, met the same fate.

During World War II, US antitrust law remained a key weapon in the US government's arsenal against foreign firms and their US investments. In fact, the antitrust "weapon" had been deployed before the United States actually entered the war. In 1939 the United States brought suit against Allied Chemical and Dye and 41 foreign firms, including I. G. Farben and ICI, alleging anticompetitive activity in nitrogen fixation. The case against the "nitrogen cartel" was settled by consent decree in 1941. In addition, the United States launched a series of cases in 1941 targeting various other I. G. Farben activities, including one challenging its alliance with SONJ. After the United States entered the war, the number of cases expanded. Not all cases were directed against German firms and the US companies with which they had business relations, but a great many were. In 1943 the antitrust division of the US Department of Justice (DOJ) claimed to have uncovered more than 160 agreements by I. G. Farben alone that it deemed illegal and detrimental to the interests of the United States (Wilkins 2004, 536).

The question remains whether the US war effort was negatively affected by German ownership of US firms, or by the alliances entered into by US firms and later deemed by the DOJ to be detrimental to US interests. It is very difficult to make an overall judgment on this issue, but in certain cases, it is clear that during both world wars, certain former German subsidiaries made positive contributions to the war effort, as did US subsidiaries of other foreign firms, including some whose home nations were under Axis occupation. Under their new American owners, American Bosch Corporation, GAF, and American Potash and Chemical Corporation all received Army-Navy "E" awards ("E" was for excellence) for substantial wartime contributions (Wilkins 2004, 541).

One issue that has received considerable attention is whether or not I. G. Farben, by virtue of its pre–World War II activities and arrangements with US firms, impeded US development of synthetic rubber. From the record, the consensus within the US government during the wartime years appears to be that it did (see, e.g., Edwards 1944). But Mira Wilkins, who has investigated the issue intensively, concludes that I. G. Farben's holding back of synthetic rubber technology, if anything, actually stimulated US development of synthetic rubber, so that rubber supplies proved adequate even after the Japanese occupied Malaysia and its large rubber plantations, greatly restraining the supply of natural rubber in 1942 (Wilkins 2004, 542–43). I. G. Farben's withholding of certain aspects of the relevant technology led to the development of independent US research and development (R&D) needed to offset the omissions. Had it been otherwise, on the eve of the war, the United States might not have had independent capability to develop this technology. Meanwhile, the possibility of technology exchange by I. G. Farben hurting any future German war effort had also concerned the German government during the 1930s.

European affiliates of US firms located in Germany, or in countries occupied by German forces, also contributed to the German war effort. In one memorable raid, Ford Motor Company's German works, at the time producing German military trucks, was bombed extensively by the US Army Air Corps, using bombers that themselves largely came from Ford's US plants (Wilkins 1974). Wilkins indicates that there is little evidence that breaking corporate ties between Ford US and Ford Germany reduced the capacity of the latter to produce for the German war effort. One lesson, therefore, from the impact on the war of US subsidiaries in Germany, and German subsidiaries in the United States, is that the physical presence of an investment is frequently much more important from a national security perspective than the national affiliation of capital.

It might have been expected that World War II would cause FDI flows to dry up entirely. However, between 1939 and 1946, FDI in the United States increased modestly, from $2.0 billion to $2.5 billion. US direct investment abroad similarly increased modestly, from $7.0 billion to $7.2 billion (Hymer 1960, table 1.1). Some of this growth reflected asset exchanges between companies in the United States and Canada, or the United States and the United Kingdom. Rather than expanding FDI, these exchanges had more to do with consolidating and rationalizing wartime production. However, excepting government seizures, there was little retrenchment of FDI out of the United States. Most firms from Allied nations holding assets in the United States, and those from the United Kingdom in particular, retained these assets, and often expanded capacity to meet wartime needs.

Postwar Trends in FDI

In the years following World War II, the economies of nations that had been or would become major sources of FDI to the United States were, to an even greater degree than they were after World War I, in bad shape, if not in ruins. These poor economic conditions were present not only in the three foes of the United States—Germany, Italy, and Japan—but also in the United Kingdom, the largest source of inward FDI in the United States.

Rebuilding these economies began in earnest during the 1950s, and proceeded into the 1960s. Some FDI entered the United States in the early 1950s, but at modest levels, such that the stock of FDI in the United States increased only from $2.5 billion to $4.0 billion between 1946 and 1956 (Hymer 1960, table 1.1). FDI flows then grew steadily in the 1960s and 1970s, to $51.5 billion in 1977 (data obtained from US BEA, www.bea.gov). Thus between 1956 and 1977, particularly as European economies rebounded, FDI in the United States grew quite quickly, at an annual compound rate of about 13.5 percent. This high rate of growth, of course, was built upon a very small base, and partly reflects both US inflation and the significant depreciation of the US dollar against European currencies during the 1970s. Therefore, despite some growth, relative to the size of the US economy, foreign investment remained quite small. In 1977 the ratio of the stock of FDI to the net worth of all US nonfinancial corporations was about 2.6 percent (Graham and Krugman 1994, table 1.2). Relative to the size of the US economy, the foreign investment presence in the United States was almost surely lower in 1977 than it was in 1914, though this is difficult to confirm, given the limited amount and questionable accuracy of 1914 data.

US direct investment abroad, by contrast, grew throughout the 30 years or so following World War II, at rates as fast as or even faster than the rate of growth for FDI in the United States. Moreover, this rate of growth was built on a base that was three and one-half times larger than that of the stock of FDI in the United States. Beginning in the mid-1950s especially, direct investment abroad accelerated rapidly, creating over the next 20 years a significant US commercial presence throughout much, but not all, of the world. The vast majority of this presence was established in developed countries—Canada, most of Western Europe, Australia, and New Zealand—but not Japan or the then Communist world.

In Europe in particular, the multinational spread of US enterprise triggered fears of US domination via its commercial presence,[33] which was indeed quite large. By 1969, the stock of US direct investment abroad was close to $68 billion, of which almost $22 billion was in Europe (Hymer 1960, table 1.1). During the late 1960s, a project at the Harvard Business School identified 187 US industrial corporations that held major operations in Europe, many of which were established after 1955 (Vaupel and Curhan 1969, Vernon 1971). With few exceptions, these firms were among the top 200 of *Fortune* magazine's list of the 500 largest US industrial firms (Vernon 1971). By today's standards, in which FDI stocks are measured in trillions of dollars, $68 billon in foreign investment might seem like a modest sum. But at the time, this represented a very substantial increase over historical levels of foreign investment.

During the 1970s a number of academic studies addressed what the official US policy should be with respect to inward and outward FDI (Vernon 1971, Dunning 1958, Buckley and Casson 1976). C. Fred Bergsten,

---

33. In 1967 a best-selling book in Europe, *Le Défi Américain* (The American Challenge), warned of complete US domination if Europeans did not build firms that could match the competitive prowess of the emerging US multinational firms. See Servan-Schreiber (1967).

Thomas Horst, and Theodore Moran (1978) argued that US direct investment abroad, as well as FDI in the United States, largely served US interests but that the benefits could be diminished by government policies, including tax policies, investment incentives, performance requirements, and other government measures. Not all of the studies concluded that the effects of investment were positive, and some authors (e.g., Barnet and Mueller 1974) concluded that the United States should discourage it. But this position did not carry the day. Accordingly, when Bergsten became assistant US treasury secretary in the Carter administration, he successfully pushed for a formal US statement of policy toward direct investment, issued by President Carter in 1977. The statement indicated that US policy should be neutral, without a bias for or against either FDI in the United States or US direct investment abroad. In 1983 the Reagan administration issued a statement strengthening this position, adding that direct investment in the United States was welcome, at least if it was responding to market forces.

Despite the Carter statement on foreign investment, there was some consternation about FDI in the United States during the late 1970s, in particular from the Organization of Petroleum Exporting Countries (OPEC). Major oil price increases in 1974 and 1977, instigated by OPEC countries, caused concerns that the large amount of petrodollars being accumulated by these nations might be used to buy key US assets. Hearings by Congressman Benjamin Rosenthal (D-NY) in 1979, however, revealed that most FDI in the United States originated in Europe, and little investment emanated from OPEC nations. Following these hearings, the furor largely died out.

As previously noted, however, in 1977 Congress amended the TWEA through the IEEPA.[34] The amendments slightly reduced the president's power to seize and take title to foreign-owned assets in the United States. The TWEA gave the president the power to seize and take title to foreign assets in the United States in either time of declared war or any "international emergency," but what constituted such an emergency was vague. The IEEPA stipulated that, for the TWEA's powers to be invoked, the president must declare an international emergency pursuant to procedures stipulated under the National Emergencies Act of 1976.[35] The IEEPA also stipulated that, while the president could seize foreign-owned assets in the United States in time of a declared national emergency, the president could not take title because ownership of the assets would remain in the hands of foreign investors, such that control over them presumably would return to investors when the emergency ended, in contrast to the experi-

---

34. *International Emergency Economic Powers Act*, Public Law 95-223, *US Statutes at Large* 91 (1977): 1625–26, codified at *US Code* 50 (2000), § 1701 et seq.

35. *National Emergencies Act of 1976*, Public Law 94-412, *US Statutes at Large* 90 (1976): 1255, codified at *US Code* 50 (2000), § 1601 et seq.

ence of German and some British investors following World War I. Apart from the IEEPA limiting the president's authority to take title for foreign-owned assets, most other elements of the TWEA were retained. During a declared emergency, the president could continue to act under the TWEA framework to seize and take control of foreign-owned assets.

Between 1977 and 1984, trends in FDI with respect to inward and outward flows reversed. During the 30 or so years prior to 1977, US direct investment abroad vastly exceeded FDI in the United States, but after 1977, the latter grew sufficiently faster than the former, and the stock of FDI in the United States began to catch up with the stock of US direct investment abroad. As already noted, in 1977 the stock of US direct investment abroad was $146 billion, whereas the stock of FDI in the United States was a third of that total, or $51.5 billion. By the end of 1984, the stock of US direct investment abroad had risen by about 50 percent, to $218 billion, whereas FDI in the United States had risen by 220 percent, to almost $165 billion. US direct investment abroad grew at an annual compound rate of 5.7 percent, a robust figure, but FDI in the United States grew at the significantly faster rate of 16.5 percent.[36] Along with other factors, including international trade in goods and services, growing FDI would contribute to the "globalization" of the world economy—a term barely heard prior to the 1990s—and to increased consternation over the effects of foreign investment in the United States.

The FDI Expansion of 1985–2003

In 1985 a worldwide explosion in FDI began, in large part due to the rapid overseas expansion of multinational firms. This expansionary phase has continued to the present, albeit with some relative lulls. FDI growth and the expansion of multinational firms have been two of the main factors behind the globalization of the world economy. Significant economic interdependence has been created among many of the world's nations, albeit by no means all of them, and though such links have long existed, the recent pace of growth of global integration has accelerated considerably.

The effect of FDI on globalization can be gleaned from table 1.1, which indicates global stocks of inward FDI as reported to the United Nations Conference on Trade and Development (UNCTAD) in 1985, 1990, 1995, 2000, and 2004. This stock stood at somewhat less than $1 trillion in 1985, but at the end of 2004, it had grown to almost $9 trillion. From 1985 to 2004, it grew at an annual compound rate of almost 12 percent, an impressive rate on a high base. This rate of growth is even more significant in that it was sustained over an almost 20-year period. Table 1.1 also shows FDI stocks in developed and developing nations. As the figures indicate,

---

36. The authors calculated the growth rates using BEA data.

Table 1.1 Worldwide reported inward FDI stock at end of year, 1985–2004 (billions of dollars)

Location of FDI stock	1985	1990	1995	2000	2004
China	6.1	20.7	134.9	346.0	462.1
United States	184.6	394.9	535.5	1,214.3	1,473.9
Developing nations	402.5	548.0	916.7	1,939.9	2,226.0
Developed nations	569.7	1399.5	2,035.8	4,011.7	6,469.8
Total (world)	972.2	1950.3	2,992.1	6,089.9	8,895.3

Sources: China Statistical Publishing, *China Statistical Yearbook 2001,* 17-13, and *China Statistical Yearbook 2005,* table 18.13; other data from United Nations Conference on Trade and Development (UNCTAD), *World Investment Report 2004,* annex table B.3.

most FDI stock resides in developed countries, defined by UNCTAD to be those of the European Union, plus Australia, Canada, Iceland, Israel, Japan, Malta, New Zealand, Norway, Switzerland, and the United States. The predominance of FDI in developed countries ought to give second thoughts to those who think that globalization is mostly about transferring business from high-wage to low-wage countries. Indeed, the percentage of global FDI stock in developed countries in 2004 (72 percent) was considerably higher than it was in 1985 (59 percent), a trend that continues today, despite the very large growth of FDI into China, discussed below.

From 1985 to 2004, the stock of FDI in the United States increased more than eightfold, from about $185 billion in 1985 to slightly under $1.5 trillion in 2004. This represents a massive increase, with an annual compound growth rate of more than 11 percent over 19 years. Even so, the growth rate of FDI in the United States was actually slightly slower during this period than the global rate of growth. Moreover, the growth rate of FDI into the United States actually fell somewhat after 1985: Between 1977 and 1984, it had been about 16 percent. Also, although the stock of FDI in the United States grew to almost equal the stock of US direct investment abroad in 2000, in the first years of the 21st century the growth of the latter greatly outpaced that of the former (figure 1.1). At the end of 2004, the stock of US direct investment abroad was more than $2 trillion, or about one-third more than the stock of FDI in the United States.

Table 1.1 also indicates inward FDI into two large economies, the United States and China. The data underscore an important fact: While there was a large buildup of FDI in the United States between 1985 and the present, it was part of a larger worldwide trend. This fact was largely missed in the debate over FDI during the late 1980s and early 1990s, which led, among other things, to the passage of the Exon-Florio Amendment. During this period, many critics of FDI saw the rise as a phenomenon unique to the

Figure 1.1 US outward and inward investment, 1976–2004

trillions of dollars

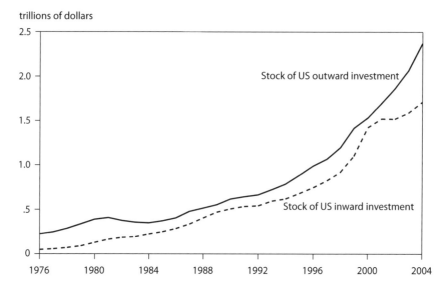

Source: BEA, International Investment Position, available at www.bea.gov.

United States, and an alarming one at that. In their eyes, the large flows of FDI into the United States hurt the United States. In chapter 3 we offer evidence that much of this criticism was misplaced, and that increased foreign participation in the United States enhances growth rates, investment in R&D, and innovation.

During the late 1980s and into the early 1990s, much of the debate over FDI in the United States focused on national security concerns. A number of sensationalist books were published, including *Selling Our Security* by *New York Times* correspondent Martin Tolchin and George Washington University professor Susan Tolchin[37] and *Rising Sun,* a novel by science fiction writer Michael Crichton (1992), which was later made into a movie starring Sean Connery, the original James Bond. These books, along with numerous others, suggested that FDI by Japanese firms, and especially FDI resulting from takeovers of US firms by Japanese firms, would diminish US technological capabilities, much of which would be shipped off to Japan. Lester Thurow (1992), then Dean of the Sloan School of Management, even posited a war in the near future between Japan and the United States, in which the United States would fare poorly due to this so-called "hollowing out" of US technology. Despite brisk book sales and hand-wringing about these issues at think tanks and academic institu-

---

37. See Tolchin and Tolchin (1992). This followed an earlier book by the same authors; see Tolchin and Tolchin (1988).

tions, the dire predictions simply never came to pass. Rather than decline relative to Japan in the 1990s, US technological capabilities rose, in large part because of the expansion of information technology–based industries in the United States.

Given that the growth rate of FDI into the United States actually fell during the late 1980s relative to a few years earlier, why did FDI become such a controversial issue? By the late 1980s, the extent of foreign ownership of US business activity had grown to the point that it was much more visible than it had been in previous years. It was less visible during the 1970s because, despite the fast growth of FDI into the United States, the percentage of US business activity under foreign control remained quite low. Also, many large foreign investors had come to be recognized by Americans, and even accepted as household names. Many Americans likely did not recognize such names as Shell, Lever Brothers, and Philips Norelco as those of foreign-owned firms. But during the late 1980s, a number of large foreign investors entered the United States for the first time, bringing with them names that were clearly foreign-sounding and not well known to the American public.[38] Thus not only did the United States witness an enormous expansion of activity under foreign control during the 1980s, before widespread recognition of the phenomenon of globalization, but also Americans became exposed to a multitude of new, unfamiliar corporate names. Moreover, Japanese economic growth considerably outpaced that of the United States, and Japan's strong economic performance stoked US anxieties that it might soon overtake the United States as the world's largest economy. These anxieties were soon to be allayed because during the 1990s the US economy would greatly outperform Japan's.

As table 1.1 indicates, as rapid as the pace of FDI in the United States has been since 1985, it was moderate compared with the growth rate of FDI in China. Between 1985 and 2003, the stock of FDI in China increased from $6.1 billion to over $500 billion, increasing at an annual compound rate of almost 19.1 percent. This turned China from one of the least globally connected economies into a global center for efficient manufacturing in less than 20 years. The rise of FDI in China has been mirrored by a high growth rate for the Chinese economy, which has hovered at close to 10 percent in recent years. FDI in China has been a major cause of the growth, albeit by no means the only factor (Graham and Wada 2001).

It is hard to overstate the magnitude of globalization, or the buzz that economic integration has created. Almost every day, it would seem, a new book appears on the topic of globalization, or related topics, such as the "offshoring" of production. A number of these books have been bestsellers (Bhagwati 2004, Friedman 2000, Friedman 2005, Stiglitz 2002, Wolf 2004). Table 1.2 summarizes additional data showing the extent and mag-

---

38. Many of these companies have now become household names; one thinks of Mitsubishi, Samsung, Siemens, and Sony. In 1989, these names were unknown to most Americans.

**Table 1.2   Impact of multinationals on world product and trade,
1990 and 2003**

	1990	2003
Gross product of foreign affiliates of multinational enterprises (billions of dollars)	1,454	3,706
Gross product of foreign affiliates of multinational enterprises (percent of world GDP)	6.4	10.2
World GDP at current prices (billions of dollars)	22,588	36,163
Exports of foreign affiliates of multinational enterprises (billions of dollars)	1,194	3,077
Exports of foreign affiliates of multinational enterprises (percent of total world exports)	28.0	33.3
World exports at current prices (billions of dollars)	4,260	9,228
World exports (percent of world GDP)	18.9	25.5

Sources: UNCTAD's *World Investment Report 2004,* table 1.3, and authors' calculations based on data from this table.

nitude of globalization. As discussed below, the gross product (value added) by foreign affiliates of multinational firms in 2003 accounted for more than 10 percent of total world GDP. The share of US GDP accounted for by domestic affiliates of foreign firms is about 4.5 percent, lower than it is in other highly industrialized countries. In 2003, the exports that these affiliates generated—again, not including exports by the parent firms—totaled about one-third of world exports, up from somewhat more than one-fourth of world exports in 1990. As the table shows, world exports themselves, another measure of globalization, accounted for about 25 percent of world GDP in 2003; this percentage stood under 20 percent in 1990.

It is against these measures that FDI in the United States, and other indications of the extent to which the US economy has become globalized, should be assessed. Table 1.3 indicates several such relevant measures for 2000 and 2003, the latter being the most recent year for which data are available.

A number of important points emerge from the data in table 1.3. Of the several measures of the extent of foreign ownership in the US economy, the most striking in size is the FDI stock ratio, which indicates the percentage of equity of all US nonfarm, nonfinancial corporations accounted for by inward FDI in the nonfinancial sector (FDI itself being a measure of equity). This measure is both high and growing: It was 15.7 percent in 2003, up from 15.1 percent in 2000 and 11.3 percent in 1992. These data reflect the fact that there have been substantial numbers of large foreign takeovers of US firms in the last 15 years, primarily by European firms.

Table 1.3   Extent of FDI in the United States, 2000 and 2003
(percent or billions of dollars)

Measure	2000	2003
a. FDI stock ratio (FDI stock, nonfinancial affiliates, as percent of net worth of all US nonfinancial corporations)	15.1	15.7
b. Share of foreign affiliate employment in total US employment	4.5	4.2
c. Share of foreign affiliate employment in US manufacturing employment	12.6	12.5
d. Share of foreign affiliates of US GDP	4.5	4.1
e. Share of foreign affiliates of US manufacturing GDP	17.4	19.1
Memorandum:		
f. FDI stock, nonfinancial affiliates, at year end	1,025.6	1,196.5
g. Total FDI stock, at year end	1,256.9	1,526.3
h. Net worth of all US nonfinancial corporations, historical cost basis	6,785.7	7,619.5
i. US GDP	9,817.0	11,734.4
j. US manufacturing GDP	1,238.5	1,190.2
k. Value added by all foreign-owned affiliates in the United States	447.3	486.3
l. Value added by foreign-owned affiliates in US manufacturing	215.7	227.7

Sources: Items a–e, authors' calculations based on data included as memo items; *Memorandum* items: (f) Bureau of Economic Analysis, Foreign Direct Investment in the United States, Balance of Payments and International Investment Position Data, available at www.bea.gov; (g) same as item f; (h) US Federal Reserve, Balance Sheets for the US Economy, available at www.federal reserve. gov; (i) Bureau of Economic Analysis, National Income and Product Accounts, available at www.bea.gov; (j) same as item i; (k) Bureau of Economic Analysis, Foreign Direct Investment in the United States, Value Added by US Affiliates of Foreign Investors, available at www.bea.gov; (l) same as item k.

Simultaneously, US firms have acquired an even larger number of foreign firms, including within Europe.

This growing level of merger and acquisition activity is mirrored in the share of manufacturing employment in the United States accounted for by foreign-owned corporations. As table 1.3 indicates, this share has been stable in recent years, at about 12.5 percent. The employment share is lower than the share of foreign firms in US manufacturing GDP—about 19 percent in 2003—because, as chapter 3 discusses in greater detail, foreign investment in the US manufacturing sector is more concentrated in subsectors that are relatively capital-intensive than in those that are relatively labor-intensive.

Table 1.4   Value added by majority-owned affiliates of foreign investors operating in the United States in major manufacturing subsectors and by entire domestic US subsector, 2003

Sector or subsector	Value added by majority-owned affiliates of foreign investors (billions of dollars)	Value added by entire domestic subsector (billions of dollars)	Value added by majority-owned affiliates (percent of value added by subsector)
All manufacturing	227.68	1,369.23	16.6
Food, beverages, and tobacco processing	16.26	170.62	9.5
Paper	4.24	46.44	9.1
Printing and related	4.62	44.55	10.4
Chemicals	49.95	174.36	28.6
Plastics and rubber	9.00	65.53	13.7
Nonmetallic minerals	14.73	46.16	31.9
Primary metals	4.50	38.67	11.6
Fabricated metals	7.83	109.10	7.2
Machinery	19.87	95.09	20.9
Computer and electronic products	22.85	125.64	18.2
Electrical equipment	5.51	48.58	11.3
Motor vehicles	31.78	129.92	24.5
Other transport equipment	3.41	64.98	5.2
All other	34.13	212.59	16.1

Source: Bureau of Economic Analysis, Foreign Direct Investment in the United States, Value Added by US Affiliates of Foreign Investors, available at www.bea.gov.

Despite the low double-digit percentage shares of foreign investment in the US nonfinancial corporate sector, and in the sector's manufacturing portion, the total share of foreign-controlled firms in the US economy, as measured by share of total GDP, was 4.1 percent in 2003—much lower than in the manufacturing or nonfinancial corporate sectors. This demonstrates that FDI in the United States tends to be made by large multinational companies and is heavily concentrated in manufacturing. The overall best measure of the total extent of foreign control over the US economy is the share of foreign-controlled firms in US GDP. Even today, notwithstanding growing FDI in the United States, foreign control of the economy is rather modest and significantly lower than the corresponding measure for the world as a whole.

In manufacturing, however, foreign investment is significant, as table 1.4 shows. It portrays foreign-owned firms' contribution in the manufacturing sector to US GDP, the value added by majority-owned affiliates of foreign investors in the United States by major manufacturing subsector, the value added by the entire domestic subsector, and the percentage of the latter contributed by the former. Note that 16.6 percent of value added in the entire manufacturing sector was generated by foreign-owned firms. However, there is a great deal of variance in the same percentage by subsector. In nonmetallic minerals, majority-owned affiliates of foreign investors contribute almost 32 percent of value added; most of this is glassmaking as opposed to mining. Foreign investors contribute almost 29 percent of value added in chemicals, which includes pharmaceuticals. But in other sectors—food, beverages, tobacco, paper, fabricated metals, and transport equipment other than motor vehicles—the share of value added for foreign-owned firms is under 10 percent.

The Impetus for This Book

Active debate continues over the role of foreign investment in the United States and its effect on US national security, despite the relatively low level of foreign investment in the United States, and notwithstanding strong empirical and anecdotal evidence that foreign investment benefits the US economy, even in industries considered sensitive to national security.

This chapter has emphasized that security-related concerns over FDI in the United States have quite a long history. However, this history has evolved over time, so that today's concerns are often quite different from those that arose, say, during World War I. For example, during the pre-World War I years, most FDI in the United States was "greenfield"—i.e., the foreign investor created US operations from scratch. Given this nature of FDI, the main concern then was that foreign-controlled operations might dominate US markets for strategic products and services so that critical technologies associated with these products and services would remain under foreign control. This was a relevant concern at a time when, in many sectors (e.g., chemicals in 1917), foreign firms indeed held technologies that were not available to their US-owned competitors. But in 1988, when security-related concerns over FDI again arose, US-owned firms were often (albeit not always) at the leading edge of the relevant technologies. Moreover, the majority of "new" FDI in the United States was then being generated by foreign takeovers of extant US firms (Graham and Krugman 1995). The national security concern thus was somewhat different than it had been in 1917. In particular, the concern became that, if foreign firms bought US-owned firms, then the foreign firms would come into possession of sensitive technologies not previously available to them, and this possession might create security risks for the United States. This concern led to the passage of Exon-Florio, which gives the president the power to block foreign takeovers of US firms for security reasons but not the power to intervene in foreign-controlled operations created by green field investment in the United States. Thus, one motivation for this book is to examine whether new circumstances in 2006 that have led to new security-related concerns over FDI in the United States require measures beyond those currently embodied in Exon-Florio or, alternatively, major changes in the existing law.

All of the issues covered in this study must be examined in the context of the current international economic position of the United States. The United States is now more dependent on foreign investment than ever, because US savings, net of the drain on these savings created by public-sector deficits, are insufficient to finance domestic investment. As a consequence, the United States must import savings from abroad, generating net capital inflows, or net foreign investment, into the United States. This deficit for 2005 was slightly less than $800 billion, implying that the United States needed to import in excess of $2 billion per day during 2005 to close the gap between domestic investment and domestic saving. Moreover, the deficit is expected to grow in coming years. Chapter 3 discusses this in greater detail, but generally the data suggest that the United States will require even more foreign investment, including acquisitions of US companies. In addition, and similar to the experience of the late 1980s, before the US current account deficit is closed significantly in the next three to five years, US assets could become much cheaper, and therefore more attractive, to foreign investors. As a result, there is likely to be a substantial increase in foreign investment in the United States, and an accompanying increase in the number and complexity of reviews by the Committee on Foreign Investment in the United States (CFIUS).

As this chapter demonstrates, the United States has tended to impose restrictions on FDI in times of conflict or insecurity. The TWEA and numerous sector-specific foreign ownership restrictions were adopted during and after World War I, and the United States seized the assets of foreign-owned firms operating in the United States during both world wars. Uncertainty about Japan and two high-profile transactions in the late 1980s—Sir James Goldsmith's attempt to buy Goodyear Tire and Rubber, and Fujitsu's attempt to acquire 80 percent of Fairchild—were the straws that broke the camel's back on investment issues, leading to the adoption of the Exon-Florio Amendment in the 1988 Omnibus Trade and Competitiveness Act. Three years later, in the wake of the controversial and ultimately failed attempt by the French government-owned firm Thomson to acquire LTV, a defense contractor, Congress passed the Byrd Amendment, requiring heightened scrutiny for acquisitions of US firms by foreign government-owned or government-controlled firms.

At the time of this writing, the CFIUS process was under fire on Capitol Hill. Focus on CFIUS intensified in the wake of the sale of IBM's personal computer division to Lenovo, a Chinese company, and reached a feverish pitch during congressional debate over the proposed CNOOC-Unocal transaction and Dubai Ports World–P&O acquisition. In addition, the Government Accountability Office (GAO), the congressional audit and oversight organization, released a highly critical report on CFIUS in late September 2005. That report, among other things, argued that

- the Treasury Department and certain other agencies take too narrow a view of the definition of national security;

- CFIUS, with Treasury as the lead, is reluctant to initiate investigations under Exon-Florio because of a perception that they would lead to a chill in inward investment;

- the 30-day timetable for reviewing foreign acquisitions of US companies does not afford national security agencies adequate time to fully assess the potential national security implications of a particular transaction; and

- CFIUS agencies disagree as to what criteria to use when deciding whether to pursue an investigation (second-phase review) under CFIUS, with the Department of Defense and "other officials" arguing for broader criteria that would allow for more investigations (US GAO 2005).

The GAO report was considered at two Senate Banking Committee hearings chaired by Senator Richard Shelby (R-AL) in October 2005.[39] Around that time, Senators Shelby and James Inhofe (R-OK) introduced two distinct amendments that would substantially toughen CFIUS reviews. The Inhofe Amendment would

- expand the definition of national security to include US national economic and energy security;

- give Congress the power to block any transaction investigated and approved by CFIUS, by joint resolution of the two houses;

- rename CFIUS as the Committee on Foreign Acquisitions Affecting National Security; and

- transfer chairmanship of the process from the US Treasury to the Department of Defense.[40]

---

39. One of the authors of this book testified at the second hearing. See testimony of David Marchick, *Hearings on the Implementation of the Exon-Florio Amendment and the Committee on Foreign Investment in the United States*, before the Senate Committee on Banking, Housing and Urban Affairs, October 20, 2005.

40. Inhofe Amendment, SA 1311 to S 1042, 109th Congress (2005).

The Shelby Amendment would

- extend the review period between notification of a transaction to CFIUS and a decision on whether to proceed to investigation to 60 days, up from 30;

- give Congress the power to request CFIUS investigations into acquisitions by foreign government–controlled entities that could affect US national security;

- require CFIUS deliberations to account for "the long-term projections of United States requirements for sources of energy and other critical resources and materials"; and

- allow Congress to block any transaction investigated and approved by CFIUS by joint resolution of the two houses.[41]

Senators Shelby and Inhofe are not alone. In the midst of the Dubai Ports World–P&O controversy, more than 20 bills were introduced by members of Congress to either block the Dubai Ports World acquisition, prohibit foreign ownership of key port operations, or amend Exon-Florio.[42] Given all of this debate and legislative activity, the authors and C. Fred Bergsten, director of the Institute for International Economics, thought a comprehensive discussion of the Exon-Florio Amendment, and the national security implications of foreign investment, particularly with respect to China, would be timely.

We have organized the book as follows. Chapter 2 discusses the Exon-Florio process for reviewing foreign takeovers of US firms for national security reasons in some detail, including the legislative history of the process, experience to date, and how Exon-Florio reviews have changed following the terrorist attacks of September 11, 2001. Chapter 3 examines the economic and political impact of FDI on the United States, recapping and updating the discussion in chapters 3 and 4 of Graham and Krugman (1994), which dealt with these subjects in considerable detail. Chapter 4 analyzes issues related to FDI in the United States posed by the rise of China as both an economic and geopolitical power, detailing the ways in which current issues regarding China are both similar to and different from those

---

41. Shelby Amendment, SA 1467 to S 1042, 109th Congress (2005).

42. *Foreign Investment Security Improvement Act of 2006*, S 2333, 109th Congress, 2nd sess. (2006); *Port Security Act of 2006*, S 2334, 109th Congress, 2nd sess. (2006); *Smart and Secure Foreign Investment Act*, S 2335, 109th Congress, 2nd sess. (2006); *Safe and Accountable Foreign Enterprises Proving Other Requirements to Secure (SAFE PORTS) Act*, HR 4814, 109th Congress, 2nd sess. (2006); *Port Operations Require Tough Security (PORTS)*, HR 4820, 109th Congress, 2nd sess. (2006); HR 4839, 109th Congress, 2nd sess. (2006).

raised 10 to 15 years ago regarding Japan. Chapter 5 discusses the increasing politicization of the Exon-Florio process, and includes several case studies in which domestic firms sought to use the Exon-Florio process for commercial gain. Finally, chapter 6 discusses policy issues and, in particular, whether and how the Exon-Florio process should be amended in light of current events.

2

The Exon-Florio Amendment

The United States has formally invited foreign investment since the late 1970s. In 1983 President Ronald Reagan publicly announced, for the first time by a US president, that the United States welcomed foreign investment, stating, "The United States believes that foreign investors should be able to make the same kinds of investment, under the same conditions, as nationals of the host country. Exceptions should be limited to areas of legitimate national security concern or related interests."[1] This national treatment policy, reinforced by the United States' attractiveness as the world's largest economy, has led to sustained increases in foreign direct investment (FDI) into the United States over the last 30 years, apart from a brief lull from 2000 to 2003. US affiliates of foreign multinational enterprises employed 5.2 million American workers in 2003, accounting for 4.2 percent of total private sector US employment. Capital expenditures by these same affiliates totaled $109 billion in 2004.

The path of the United States' open investment policy, however, has not been free from turbulence. As chapter 1 discussed, political pressures based on real or perceived threats to tighten the valves on FDI have arisen from time to time. While these pressures generally failed to carry the day, in 1988, they resulted in the establishment of an investment review law—the Exon-Florio Amendment—grounded in national security concerns.

In this chapter, we provide an overview of the Exon-Florio Amendment and its legislative history. We discuss how the Committee on Foreign Investment in the United States (CFIUS) has implemented Exon-Florio, including the national security issues that the committee has considered in

---

1. See Reagan (1983). President George Herbert Walker Bush also issued a statement on the subject; see George H. W. Bush, "White House Statement Announcing United States Foreign Direct Investment Policy," December 26, 1991.

applying the statute, and how the amendment has been applied more broadly since the attacks of September 11, 2001. Since, in practice, CFIUS has focused on mitigating the national security impact of a particular foreign acquisition, as opposed to blocking acquisitions altogether, we conclude this chapter with specific case studies in the telecommunications and defense sectors, and a discussion of the tools that CFIUS has used to reduce the perceived threats from foreign investments.

Overview of the Exon-Florio Amendment

In 1988 Congress enacted the Exon-Florio Amendment to Section 721 of the Defense Production Act of 1950.[2] Exon-Florio authorizes the president to investigate foreign acquisitions, mergers, and takeovers of, or investments in, US companies from a national security perspective. If necessary, the president may also prohibit a transaction that appears to threaten national security when other laws, except for the International Emergency Economic Powers Act (IEEPA),[3] are otherwise inadequate to mitigate the threat. In the words of the amendment, the president may block an acquisition if "there is credible evidence that leads the President to believe that the foreign interest exercising control might take action that threatens to impair the national security," and if other laws except for IEEPA "do not in the President's judgment provide adequate and appropriate authority for the President to protect the national security in the matter before the President."[4]

When Exon-Florio became law, the president delegated his initial review and decision-making authorities, as well as his investigative responsibilities, to CFIUS,[5] which had been established by executive order in 1975.[6] Thus an Exon-Florio review is often alternatively called a CFIUS review. CFIUS is chaired by the secretary of the Treasury and has 11 other members (box 2.1). The assistants to the president for national security affairs (the national security adviser) and economic policy (national economic adviser) are formally members of CFIUS, but they and their staff have tried not to participate actively in CFIUS deliberations in the initial 30-day review period of an investigation, in case they are called upon to

---

2. *Omnibus Trade and Competitiveness Act of 1988*, § 5021, Public Law 100-418, *US Statutes at Large* 102 (1988): 1107, codified at *US Code* 50 1988, App. § 2170. The original authorization was scheduled to expire in 1991 but was made permanent by Section 8 of *Defense Production Act Extension and Amendments of 1991*, Public Law 102-99, *US Statutes at Large* 105 (1991): 487.

3. *International Emergency Economic Powers Act*, §§ 1701–1706.

4. *Omnibus Trade and Competitiveness Act of 1988,* App. § 2170(e).

5. Executive Order no. 12,661 (1988).

6. Executive Order no. 11,858 (1975). As discussed below, CFIUS originally was established primarily to monitor and evaluate the impact of foreign investment in the United States.

Box 2.1   Members of CFIUS

Secretary of Treasury (Chair)
Secretary of State
Secretary of Defense
Secretary of Commerce
Secretary of Homeland Security
Attorney General
Director of the Office of Management and Budget
United States Trade Representative
Chairman of the Council of Economic Advisers
Director of the Office of Science and Technology Policy
Assistant to the President for National Security Affairs
Assistant to the President for Economic Policy

mediate disputes between CFIUS agencies, or to advise the president on a particular transaction. CFIUS is unique among executive branch interagency committees in that it purposefully includes agencies with distinct missions. Certain CFIUS agencies have law enforcement, defense, and homeland security as their mandate, while others are oriented toward promoting open trade and investment policies. This tension among member agencies is designed to elicit carefully considered judgments that account for a myriad of economic and security considerations.

By statute and regulation, CFIUS is authorized to review a transaction either upon a voluntary filing by either party to the transaction, or upon an agency notice filed by one of the committee's members.[7] The statutorily mandated timetable for the CFIUS review process is as follows (figure 2.1):

- initial 30-day review following receipt of notice;

- 45-day "investigation" period for transactions deemed to require additional review following the initial 30-day period (not all transactions are subject to this);[8]

- formal report to the president at the end of the 45-day investigation period;

- presidential decision within 15 days of receiving the formal report.[9]

---

7. Regulations Implementing Exon-Florio, *Code of Federal Regulations,* title 31, sec. 800, App. A (1988).

8. The term investigation is a misnomer; practically speaking, it is only an extended review.

9. Regulations Implementing Exon-Florio, *Code of Federal Regulations,* title 31, sec. 800, App. A (1988).

Figure 2.1   CFIUS process

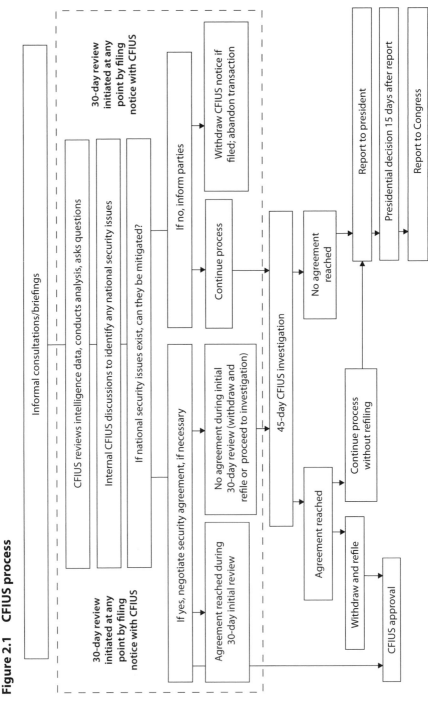

The statute also mandates investigations in certain instances. In 1993 the Byrd Amendment to the National Defense Authorization Act amended Exon-Florio to mandate an investigation "in any instance in which an entity controlled by or acting on behalf of a foreign government seeks to engage in any merger, acquisition, or takeover of a US entity that could affect the national security of the United States."[10] This language does not mean, however, that an investigation is required every time a company owned or controlled by a foreign government acquires a US company. CFIUS also considers whether the acquisition could affect national security. The presence of foreign government ownership is, however, a key consideration for CFIUS agencies when weighing national security risks, and typically leads to greater scrutiny.

The Byrd Amendment became the focus of intense debate in the controversy surrounding the Dubai Ports World (DP World) acquisition of P&O. Lawmakers were incredulous that CFIUS did not extend its review into the 45-day investigation period, given that DP World is owned by the government of the United Arab Emirates. Senators Carl Levin (D-MI), Hillary Clinton (D-NY), and Robert Byrd (D-WV), the last of which authored the Byrd Amendment in 1993, argued that the Bush administration was flouting the law by not pursuing an investigation of the transaction. They argued further that an investigation was mandatory under the Byrd Amendment and lambasted the administration's view that, because of the security agreement negotiated with DP World, the transaction "could not" affect US national security.[11] In response, Deputy Treasury Secretary Robert Kimmit argued that the Byrd Amendment provides CFIUS with discretion on whether to pursue an investigation.[12] This same issue of interpreting the Byrd Amendment was vigorously contested in briefs by New Jersey Governor Jon Corzine and the US Department of Justice (DOJ) in the case Corzine brought to block the DP World acquisition.[13]

The framework of the statute and implementing regulations provides broad discretion to CFIUS in a number of important ways. First, CFIUS authority is not time-limited, nor is there a statute of limitations. Exon-Florio simply authorizes CFIUS, through the president's designation, to initiate its investigation of a foreign merger, either upon a voluntary filing or, if the parties do not file voluntarily, at the instigation of a CFIUS member at any time. This can happen even after a transaction has closed.

---

10. *National Defense Authorization Act for Fiscal Year 1993*, Public Law 102-484, *US Statutes at Large* 106 (1993): 2315, 2463, § 837(a).

11. See Elana Schor, "Bush Administration Defends Ports Deal on Capitol Hill," *The Hill*, February 23, 2006.

12. See Christopher Rubager, "Rove Opens Door to Delaying Port Deal as Senators Slam CFIUS Review," *BNA International Trade Daily*, February 24, 2006.

13. Defendants' Response to Order to Show Cause at 18-21, *Corzine v. Snow et al.*, No. 06-833 (D.N.J.). Complaint at 10, *Corzine v. Snow et al.*, No. 06-833 (D.N.J.).

Second, while the sole purpose of the CFIUS process is to determine whether a particular transaction could threaten US national security, the statute does not define the term "national security." Rather, it identifies a number of criteria for the president to consider in evaluating the potential threat. These criteria include

- domestic production needed for projected national defense requirements;

- the capability and capacity of domestic industries to meet national defense requirements, including the availability of human resources, products, technology, materials, and other supplies and services;

- the control of domestic industries and commercial activity by foreign citizens as it affects US capability and capacity to meet national security requirements;

- the potential effects of the transaction on the sales of military goods, equipment, or technology to a country that supports terrorism or proliferates missile technology or chemical and biological weapons; and

- the potential effects of the transaction on US technological leadership in areas affecting US national security.[14]

CFIUS's considerations, however, are not limited to these criteria. The legislative history of Exon-Florio makes clear that "national security" is "to be read in a broad and flexible manner."[15] For this reason, and notwithstanding having received a number of comments and recommendations on what might be an appropriate definition of national security,[16] CFIUS intentionally decided to leave the term undefined in the US Treasury regulations implementing Exon-Florio. According to the preamble to these regulations, "The Committee rejected [all of the recommended definitions] because they could improperly curtail the President's broad authority to protect the national security."[17] Thus, CFIUS, at its discretion, has undertaken Exon-Florio reviews of transactions involving various industrial sectors beyond the defense industrial base, including technology, telecommunications, energy and natural resources, manufacturing, and transportation.

---

14. Exon-Florio Amendment, App., § 2170(f).

15. Statement of Senator Exon, *Congressional Record* 134 (April 25, 1988): S4833.

16. Regulations Implementing Exon-Florio, *Code of Federal Regulations*, title 31, sec. 800, App. A (1988), noting that definitional guidance was "a major theme of the public comments" and that "[c]ommenters had a wide range of recommendations on this point."

17. Regulations Implementing Exon-Florio, *Code of Federal Regulations*, title 31, sec. 800, App. A (1988).

Third, there is considerable breadth in the term "foreign control," as defined in the statute and clarified in the regulations. The statute authorizes the president to act on transactions that could result in foreign control of entities engaged in interstate commerce in the United States. The regulations interpret control to mean

> the power, direct or indirect, whether or not exercised, and whether or not exercised or exercisable through the ownership of a majority or a dominant minority of the total outstanding voting securities of an issuer, or by proxy voting, contractual arrangements or other means, to determine, direct or decide matters affecting an entity.[18]

In theory, the breadth of this definition enables CFIUS to review transactions that, as a practical matter, give the foreign acquirer very little actual control. The regulations create a rebuttable presumption of foreign control if a foreign person acquires 10 percent of a US company's equity.[19] They also do not distinguish between direct control, or ownership of shares in a US company by foreign citizens, governments, or other entities, and indirect control, or foreign acquisition of another foreign corporation, which then controls a US company.[20] Thus, CFIUS has in the past, and could in the future, determine that a foreign person controls a US entity regardless of the foreign person's actual ownership percentage. If the foreign owner's rights include seats on the board of directors, veto rights over certain corporate actions, or the right to appoint or reject certain key personnel, foreign control could be deemed to exist even if the percentage of equity ownership is de minimis.

Fourth, CFIUS has never defined what constitutes "credible evidence," the standard in the statute for the first prong of the two-part test for whether the president should block an acquisition.[21] In practice, CFIUS views the credible evidence standard as a fairly low threshold: It accepts evidence as credible so long as it is "worthy of belief."[22] CFIUS's reluctance to define "credible evidence" is not surprising. The regulations were

---

18. Regulations Implementing Exon-Florio, *Code of Federal Regulations*, title 31, sec. 800.204 (1988).

19. The rebuttable presumption of control if a foreign person acquires more than 10 percent of equity in a US entity arises in practice from the regulations exempting from the requirements of Exon-Florio a purchase of equity that results in "ten percent or less of the outstanding voting securities of the US person." *Code of Federal Regulations*, title 31, sec. 800. 302(d)(1) (1988).

20. Regulations Implementing Exon-Florio, *Code of Federal Regulations*, title 31, sec. 800.213 (1988), defines "foreign person" as a foreign national or any entity "over which control is exercised or exercisable by a foreign interest."

21. Specifically, the first prong is whether there is "credible evidence that leads the President to believe that the foreign interest exercising control might take action that threatens to impair the national security." See *Omnibus Trade and Competitiveness Act*, App. § 2170(e).

22. Interview with CFIUS official.

designed to give the president maximum discretion to make national security determinations under Exon-Florio. Even if CFIUS agencies were inclined to clarify what constitutes "credible evidence," it would be a challenge to do so. US courts have had difficulty providing useful guidance on the terms. The US Supreme Court has never defined "credible evidence," and state supreme courts that have attempted it have failed to do so precisely. The Missouri Supreme Court concluded that "credible evidence" exists where a "term is sufficiently plain and meaningful and does not require definition."[23] The New York Supreme Court defined credible evidence as "evidence that proceeds from a credible source and reasonably tends to support the proposition for which it is offered."[24] These definitions are circular, and do not substantively clarify the term.

In sum, CFIUS has given itself exceptional flexibility to decide whether a particular transaction so concerns national security that it requires an investigation or, when an investigation has been undertaken, whether the president should be advised to block the transaction.

Enactment of the Exon-Florio Amendment

Since September 11, 2001, a number of transactions, or potential transactions, subject to Exon-Florio review have engendered heated policy debates over their impact on both economic and national security, the threats posed by investments from particular countries (e.g., China), and the loss of US leadership in purportedly sensitive industries. In reality, the legislative history of Exon-Florio demonstrates that such political pressures are not new. Many of the economic and broader policy arguments proffered today for limiting foreign investment in the United States spurred the legislation initially proposed by Senator James Exon (D-NE).

The original Exon amendment was introduced in 1988, when the Reagan administration's open investment policy, a weak dollar following the 1985 Plaza Accord, mounting US indebtedness, and attractive stock prices were working together to create an impression that American firms were "increasingly vulnerable to takeover" (Alvarez 1989, 56).[25] Predictably, the perceived weakening of the American economy compared with foreign competitors created a domestic political backlash. As noted in chapter 1, the increase in FDI at this time mirrored similar increases in worldwide investment. With a wealth of capital at their disposal, Japanese companies were becoming active in acquiring, or attempting to acquire, US com-

---

23. *State v. Thresher*, 350 S.W. 2d 1, 9 (Mo. 1961).

24. *Cusick v. Kerik*, 305 A.D. 2d 247, 248 (N.Y. 2003), citing *Meyer v. Board of Trustees*, 90 N.Y. 2d 139, 147 (1997).

25. For additional background information on Exon-Florio, see Menard (2002) and Shearer (1993).

panies, sparking widespread concern in the United States about Japan's supposed challenge to US economic leadership.

Two specific transactions created a stir in Congress: Sir James Goldsmith, the famous British corporate raider, attempted to take over Goodyear Tire and Rubber, and the Japanese company Fujitsu attempted to acquire an 80 percent interest in Fairchild, a large semiconductor manufacturer located in California (Alvarez 1989). The proposed takeovers sparked intense debate on Capitol Hill and in the US business community. Opponents of the Fairchild takeover argued that the merger would harm US competitiveness, grant Japan access to vital US technology, and make the United States dependent on Japan for production of semiconductors (Alvarez 1989, 58). Some industry observers compared the takeover to "selling Mount Vernon to the Redcoats" (Alvarez 1989, 57).

While the Reagan administration worried that blocking the sale would chill foreign investment and hinder efforts to open the Japanese market, it nonetheless acquiesced to pressure from Capitol Hill, and had CFIUS initiate a review into any security risks that the Fairchild merger might pose. At that time, CFIUS was authorized to review any investment that "might have major implications for United States national interests."[26] But as a purely advisory body to the president, it was not empowered to pass regulations or take substantive action short of recommending that the president invoke the IEEPA. Accordingly, the Reagan administration, through the DOJ, said that it would scrutinize the transaction under the Hart-Scott-Rodino Act.[27] Even though the administration was unlikely to block the merger, Fujitsu eventually abandoned the transaction, announcing that "rising political controversy in the United States" made the deal undesirable (Alvarez 1989, 62).

Despite Fujitsu's abandonment of its attempt to acquire Fairchild, the Reagan administration's perceived lack of concern with respect to the transaction concerned a number of business leaders and policymakers. Senator Exon took the lead in criticizing the administration's inaction, introducing a bill to "grant the President discretionary authority to review and act upon foreign takeovers, mergers, acquisitions, joint ventures and licensing agreements which threaten the national security or essential commerce of the United States."[28] The objective of the legislation, he said, was to "encourage the Administration to protect the national interest" and create legal means for the president to block foreign takeovers of domestic companies without having to invoke the IEEPA (Alvarez 1989, 56). While the IEEPA technically empowered the president to take action in

---

26. Executive Order no. 11,858 (1975).

27. See Exon-Florio Amendment, § 18(a).

28. See statement of Senator Exon, *Foreign Investment, National Security and Essential Commerce Act of 1987*, HR 3, 100th Congress, 1st sess. (1987).

the Fujitsu case, or any other foreign acquisition, its language—empowering the president to take measures to prevent "any unusual and extraordinary threat, which has its source in whole or substantial part outside the United States, to the national security, foreign policy, or economy of the United States, *if the President declares a national emergency with respect to such threat*"[29]—rendered a presidential veto of most foreign takeovers of US companies untenable, as it would have been "virtually the equivalent of a declaration of hostilities against the government of the acquirer company" (US Senate 1987, 17, statement by Senator Wilson). Thus the Exon bill was designed, in large measure, to give the president explicit authority to block such takeovers without declaring a national emergency, as the IEEPA required. A similar bill was introduced in the House of Representatives by Congressman James Florio (D-NJ).[30]

The original version of the Exon bill required the secretary of commerce, upon the motion of any head of department or agency, to undertake an investigation to determine how any merger, acquisition, joint venture, or takeover by a foreign person would affect national security, essential commerce, and economic welfare. The bill then gave the president power to block such acquisitions or investments after considering a number of factors, including the domestic production needed for projected national defense requirements; the requirements for growth in such industries; the control of such industries by foreign persons; the impact of foreign control on the economic welfare of individual domestic industries, and any substantial unemployment; or decrease in revenues of government, loss of skills or investment, or other serious effects resulting from foreign control.[31]

Despite Senator Exon's assurances that he was "not trying to block foreign investment" and thought it was "vitally necessary" (US Senate 1987), much of the debate surrounding the Exon amendment revolved around concerns over whether or how the legislation might be used to halt foreign investment that did not threaten national security.[32] Supporters of an open investment policy regarded three aspects of the legislation as particularly troublesome: the "essential commerce" provision, the inclusion of economic factors in the statutory criteria for assessing whether to prohibit a transaction, and the inclusion of joint ventures and licensing arrangements among those transactions subject to review. The legislation also would have placed the lead role in the US government with the secretary of commerce, a provision the Reagan administration resisted.

---

29. *Omnibus Trade and Competitiveness Act*, §§ 1701–1702, emphasis added.

30. *Foreign Investment, National Security and Essential Commerce Act of 1987*, HR 3, 100th Congress, 1st sess. (May 8, 1987), § 905(a); Public Law 100-418.

31. *Foreign Investment, National Security and Essential Commerce Act of 1987*, HR 3, 100th Congress, 1st sess. (May 8, 1987), § 905(b).

32. Members of Congress and business leaders also voiced concerns that the threat of government investigations would increase transaction costs and deter foreign investment.

Essential Commerce

The initial Exon bill required the secretary of commerce to investigate the effects that foreign mergers, acquisitions, takeovers, joint ventures, and licenses would have on "essential commerce" and "economic welfare."[33] This provision drew fierce criticism from the Reagan administration and business leaders, and during the June 10, 1987, hearings held by the Senate Committee on Commerce, Science, and Transportation, a number of administration officials and senators expressed their opposition to it.

The most vocal criticism of the "essential commerce" provision came from then Secretary of Commerce Malcolm Baldrige, who summed up his position by reaffirming Reagan's commitment to "not discourage foreign investment or trade unless it poses a risk to national security." He added, "We are very concerned about the possibility of chilling any investment in the United States." Furthermore, the legislation could potentially undermine the administration's policy of "taking the lead in all kinds of trade, free trade, GATT kinds of policy" (US Senate 1987, 7). Finally, Baldrige criticized the bill's language for being too broad. He acknowledged that the president should have the power to block investments for national security reasons, but he accused Senator Exon of "trying to kill a gnat with a blunderbuss" (US Senate 1987, 17).

US Trade Representative Clayton Yeutter also expressed his disagreement with the "essential commerce" provision. In a letter addressed to the committee, he wrote that

> the notion that governmental review may be necessary to determine the *economic* effects of foreign direct investment in the United States runs directly contrary to our belief that investment flows which respond to market forces provide the best and most efficient mechanism to promote economic growth here and abroad. (US Senate 1987, 70; emphasis in original)

Secretary of the Treasury James Baker struck the heaviest blow to the legislation by hinting at a presidential veto. In a letter to the committee, he declared that "foreign investment brings us capital, jobs, new technology and management skills." He added that "amendments of this nature could cause grave damage to the US economy" and concluded that "if this [trade] provision is in the final bill, I would find it particularly difficult to recommend that the President sign the bill" (US Senate 1987, 68).[34]

---

33. *Foreign Investment, National Security and Essential Commerce Act of 1987*, HR 3, 100th Congress, 1st sess. (May 8, 1987), § 905(a).

34. When asked to clarify Baker's ominous statement, Dick Darman, who had recently left the Reagan administration as deputy treasury secretary, replied, "That is the kind of language you use when you know you want to recommend veto, but you do not have the authority to say that the Administration will stand behind the veto" (US Senate 1987, 57). The chairman of the Federal Reserve, Paul Volcker, also testified in opposition to the amend-

Economic Factors

The original version of the Exon amendment would also have required the secretary of commerce and the president to consider a number of economic factors to assess whether a transaction threatened national security or essential commerce.[35]

In the committee hearings, Secretary Baldrige opposed consideration of any factors that did not directly relate to national security: "The economic welfare of individual industries. Now, that could mean anything to anybody, but to me it would mean that we would have to be concerned about foreign competition coming into the United States, and that is not the right way for us to compete." He added, "When I see words like the President shall consider the economic welfare of individual industries, that sends a shiver up anybody's spine trying to invest here from abroad" (US Senate 1987). He then criticized the provision requiring the president to consider whether the transaction might create substantial unemployment. "How do you know that unemployment is not necessary in order to make the industry competitive and end up with more employment in total after it does become more competitive?" he asked (US Senate 1987, 11; punctuation in original). Finally, he opposed considering loss of skills or investment, concluding that "for us to deny the opportunity for foreign investment based on that is really a major, major step backwards as far as an open investment policy" (US Senate 1987, 12). Baldrige's views did not go unchallenged. Senator John Breaux (D-LA) rebutted Baldrige's arguments by pointing out that these considerations were discretionary: "If you think that those are not important considerations, you can close the books, slam the door, and walk away from it. You are not required to have one single investigation under the Exon Amendment" (US Senate 1987, 15).

The version of the Exon amendment that was eventually signed by the president nonetheless omitted the considerations to which Baldrige objected.[36] As enacted, the Exon-Florio Amendment authorized the president, in reviewing the effects of a foreign investment on national security, to take into account the domestic production needed for projected national defense requirements; the capability and capacity of domestic industries to meet national defense requirements, including the availability of human resources, products, technology, and other supplies and services; and the control of domestic industries and commercial activity by

---

ment. He argued that the term "essential commerce" was too "broad and ambiguous" and worried that including it in the legislation could "lead to the establishment of an approval process for almost any foreign direct investment in the United States." Such a tactic, he argued, "would be contrary to our long-standing national policy of maintaining an open economy" (US Senate 1987, 69).

35. *Foreign Investment, National Security and Essential Commerce Act of 1987*, HR 3, 100th Congress, 1st sess. (May 8, 1987), supra note 105.

36. *Omnibus Trade and Competitiveness Act*, § 5021.

foreign citizens, as it affected the capability and capacity of the United States to meet national security requirements.[37]

Joint Ventures and Licensing

A number of senators and key witnesses at the Senate committee hearings on the original Exon bill objected to including "joint ventures" and "licensing agreements" as transactions under the statute, on the grounds that such transactions did not raise the same concerns as hostile takeovers or acquisitions. Senator Bob Kasten (R-WI) argued, "I do not want anything in this amendment to stop that kind of what I believe is synergistic joint ventures" (US Senate 1987). Robert McNeill, executive vice chairman of the Emergency Committee for American Trade, a protrade business group, objected to covering licensing agreements. He stated that barriers to licensing exchanges would "complicate enormously and immensely the ability of US companies to conduct their business in the international arena" (US Senate 1987, 53). These views carried the day. After the committee hearings, the terms "joint ventures" and "licensing" were omitted from the bill.

Proponents of the bill downplayed the potential adverse effects that the amendment in general, and the essential commerce provision in particular, might have on foreign investment. Senator Exon emphasized that the power granted to the secretary of commerce and the president was discretionary. He pointed out that the decision to block investment rested with the president alone, who was free to allow such mergers after reviewing the requisite determinations. Exon testified that "all that the Exon Amendment does is say that if you, as the Secretary of Commerce, want to use this tool, you can. You can consider using this tool. You do not have to" (US Senate 1987, 12). Senator Breaux was skeptical at the administration's argument that the proposed amendment would adversely affect foreign investment. He remarked: "I get a real kick out of the reason, Mr. Chairman, why they are not supporting the legislation. What we are hearing about is this chilling effect. Do not do this because we are going to have a big chill out there and people are not going to want to invest in the United States' companies." He added that countries around the world grant authority to their governments to "take a look at it [investment] from a national security standpoint, or from a cultural standpoint, or from an economic standpoint" (US Senate 1987, 13), and there was therefore no reason not to allow the US government to conduct a similar review.

No one at the Senate committee hearings disputed the need to protect national security, and excepting Secretary Baldrige, the speakers generally

---

37. *Omnibus Trade and Competitiveness Act.* Note that other factors were subsequently added by the Byrd Amendment.

acknowledged a need to grant the president greater authority to block investments that threatened national security. As a result of the opposition to Exon's original bill, Senator Exon and his supporters on the committee agreed to "tighten" the statutory language, to both avoid a presidential veto and address concerns about the potential chill on desired foreign investment (US Senate 1987, 34, 44, 50, 58, 61).[38]

On June 19, 1987, the Senate Commerce Committee adopted a revised version of the Exon amendment that addressed some of the concerns voiced at the hearing.[39] It changed the review criteria of foreign acquisitions to "national security and essential commerce *which affects national security*."[40] The committee report added that the committee "in no way intends to impose barriers to foreign investment," and that the amendment was not to have "any effect on transactions which are clearly outside the realm of national security" (Alvarez 1989, 71).

These revisions, however, could not overcome the opposition of the Reagan administration and the US business community. After the president took the extraordinary step of threatening to veto the entire trade act—one of the centerpieces of the 100th Congress—if it included the amended Exon amendment, the bill was sent back to the House-Senate Conference Committee. The version of the amendment that Congress eventually enacted amended Section 721 of the Defense Production Act of 1950. The amendment thereafter became known as the Exon-Florio Amendment, recognizing the roles of Senator Exon and Representative Florio, a member of the House Energy and Commerce Committee. Importantly, it omitted any mention of "essential commerce" or "economic welfare."

Subsequent Attempts at Amendment

In the years since Exon-Florio's enactment in 1988, a number of members of Congress have attempted to amend the law to include the provisions in Senator Exon's original proposal that were discarded by the conference committee. These efforts have focused on economic interest as a CFIUS factor, the chairmanship of the committee, technology transfer, and enhanced monitoring. With the notable exception of the Byrd Amendment

---

38. Senator Don Riegle (D-MI) stated, "I certainly support the notion of national security." He cautioned, however, that "if we stick with wording similar to national security or essential commerce, that we in fact create a level of ambiguity that probably does not serve us well" (US Senate 1987, 44).

39. Senate Committee on Commerce, Science and Transportation, *Senate Report No. 100-80 to Accompany S 907 (Technology Competitiveness Act of 1987,* 100th Congress, 1st sess., *Senate Report* 80, 1987, 28).

40. Senate Committee on Commerce, Science and Transportation, *Senate Report No. 100-80 to Accompany S 907.* See also Alvarez (1989, 69).

in 1992, discussed below, these proposals uniformly have been defeated. At the time of this writing, in the wake of the Dubai Ports World controversy, more than a dozen bills had been introduced to reform Exon-Florio, and there seems to be irresistible pressure to amend the law.[41]

Economic Interest

In response to growing concerns that the president had not adequately exercised the powers granted to him under the Exon-Florio Amendment, Representative Mel Levine (D-CA) introduced HR 2386, entitled "The Foreign Investment and Economic Security Act of 1991." The bill reflected frustration that CFIUS had recommended blocking only one merger out of the more than 500 proposed transactions that the committee had reviewed to date. It declared that "while foreign direct investment can generate United States economic growth, such investment in industries central to our national defense and economic security must be carefully evaluated," and proposed amending Section 721 to read: "The President or the President's designees may make an investigation to determine the effects on economic and national security of mergers, acquisitions."[42] Not surprisingly, the bill received little support, given the strong opposition to similar language in Senator Exon's original bill. HR 2386 was referred to several committees but never debated.[43]

Some efforts to amend Exon-Florio on economic interest grounds have focused on particular industries. In 2001, Representative Dennis Kucinich (D-OH) proposed HR 2394, "The Steel and National Security Act," which contained a provision that would amend the Exon-Florio Amendment to require CFIUS to conduct an investigation any time a person or a foreign country "seeks to engage in any merger, acquisition, or takeover that could result in the control by such person of a domestic steel company."[44]

---

41. See *Committee on Foreign Investment in the United States Reform Act*, HR 4915, 109th Congress, 2nd sess., March 2006 (introduced by Congresswoman Maloney); *United States Security Improvement Act of 2006*, HR 4813, 109th Congress, 2nd sess., February 2006 (introduced by Congressman M. Foley); *Smart and Secure Foreign Investment Act*, S 2335, 109th Congress, 2nd sess., March 2006 (introduced by Senator Bayh); and "a bill to transfer authority to review certain mergers, acquisitions, and takeovers of United States entities by foreign entities to a designee established within the Department of Homeland Security," S 2400, 109th Congress, 2nd sess., March 2006 (introduced by Senator Collins, hereinafter referred to as the Collins bill).

42. *Foreign Investment and Economic Security Act of 1991*, HR 2386, 102nd Congress, 1st sess. (1991).

43. On May 17, 1991, the bill was referred to the House Committee on Banking, Finance and Urban Affairs, the House Committee on Foreign Affairs, and the House Committee on Energy and Commerce.

44. *Steel and National Security Act*, HR 2394, 107th Congress, 1st sess. (2001).

This bill was referred to the House Committee on Financial Services and never debated.

A number of members of Congress have advocated including economic factors among the criteria CFIUS considers to assess investment-related risks to national security. Shortly after the statute's enactment in 1988, Senator Exon himself voiced his concern about the "unrelenting purchases of American firms by foreign interests" and encouraged the Reagan administration to use Exon-Florio "to protect the national security when foreign industries try to take over key American industries and technologies."[45] He added that some industries are "so crucial that they must remain under American control."[46] Two years later, Representative Doug Walgren (D-PA) proposed a more expansive definition of national security. He asserted that the "military and economic dimensions of national security are inseparable" and urged that "conditions should be placed on foreign purchasers to protect our national security from the erosion of the industrial base."[47] His bill, HR 5225, would have authorized the president to consider the "control of domestic industries and commercial activity by foreign citizens as it affects the industrial and technological base of the United States."[48] In a similar vein, two separate bills introduced in 1991 by Representatives Cardiss Collins (D-IL) and Mel Levine (D-CA) proposed an additional four factors that CFIUS should consider: the concentration of foreign investment in the industry in question; the US and world market positions of the persons engaged in interstate commerce in the United States, the foreign persons involved in the transaction under investigation, and global concentration in particular industry sectors; the effect on critical technologies; and whether the persons engaged in interstate commerce in the United States had received US government funds by grant or contract in the preceding 10-year period, and if so, the dollar amount of such funds.[49] These bills were referred to various committees but received little or no debate.[50]

---

45. *Congressional Record* 135 (1989): 25352.

46. *Congressional Record* 135 (1989): 25352. In a separate debate, Representative Hamilton Fish (D-NY) noted that these industries may include "technology, telecommunications, semiconductors, robotics, computers, biotechnology, pharmaceuticals, strategic metals, and advanced materials." 100th Congress, 2nd sess., *Congressional Record* 134 (April 21, 1988): H2297.

47. 100th Congress, 2nd sess., *Congressional Record* 136 (1990): 27408.

48. *To Amend the Defense Production Act of 1950 to Clarify and Strengthen Provisions Pertaining to National Security Takeovers,* HR 5225, 101st Congress, 2nd sess. (1990).

49. Representatives Mel Levine (D-CA) and Cardiss Collins (D-IL) introduced HR 2386 and HR 2624 respectively in the 102nd Congress (1991).

50. Both bills were referred to the House Committee on Banking, Finance and Urban Affairs, the House Committee on Foreign Affairs, and the House Committee on Energy and Commerce.

More recently, in June 2005 Representative Donald Manzullo (R-IL) stated in testimony before the US-China Economic and Security Review Commission that Congress should "reform the CFIUS process to consider economic security as part of national security."[51] As discussed below in more detail, in July 2005, in the midst of the debate over the proposed transaction between the China National Offshore Oil Corporation (CNOOC) and Unocal, Senator James Inhofe (R-OK) offered an amendment to the Defense Production Act that would have required CFIUS to consider a transaction's impact on "national economic and energy security."[52]

Transferring the Chair of CFIUS

The Collins and Levine bills would have designated the secretary of commerce as the chair of CFIUS, to transfer power away from the Department of the Treasury. Representative Collins argued that Treasury's chairmanship of CFIUS conflicted with the department's primary responsibility of promoting foreign investment, and therefore CFIUS should be chaired by some other agency.[53] The Levine bill granted authority to the secretary of commerce to annually review whether a foreign person involved in an investment was complying with the assurances provided.[54] Senator Inhofe's recent bill, offered in July 2005, would move the chairmanship of CFIUS to the Department of Defense,[55] even though the Pentagon reportedly told Senator Inhofe that it did not seek the chairmanship of CFIUS. More recently, Senator Susan Collins (R-ME) introduced a bill—another so-called Collins bill—to transfer the chairmanship to the Department of Homeland Security (DHS).

Technology Transfer

The first Collins bill, along with the bill authored by Representative Doug Walgren (D-PA), also contained provisions that would have required the

---

51. Testimony of Donald Manzullo to the US-China Economic and Security Review Commission, *Manufacturing Dragon: China's Emerging Role As A Global Factory and Its Implications for American Innovation*, 109th Congress, 1st sess., June 23, 2005.

52. *National Defense Authorization Act for Fiscal Year 2006*, SA 1311 to S 1042, 109th Congress, 1st sess. (2005).

53. Remarks of Representative Collins, 102nd Congress, 1st sess., *Congressional Record* 137 (1991): 5117–5123. Representative Collins made these remarks in the debate leading up to enacting Public Law 102-99, which extended the expiration date of the *Defense Production Act of 1950*.

54. *Foreign Investment and Economic Security Act of 1991*, HR 2386, § III(i), 102nd Congress, 1st sess. (1991).

55. *National Defense Authorization Act for Fiscal Year 2006*, SA 1311 to S 1042, 109th Congress, 1st sess. (2005).

secretaries of commerce and defense to identify any "essential" or "critical" technology involved in mergers, acquisitions, or takeovers, while authorizing the president to consider the existence of such technology in determining the potential effect of an investment on national security.

HR 5225, the Walgren bill, would have required each member of CFIUS to identify annually the "technologies which are essential to the industrial and technological base of the United States." The secretaries of commerce and defense would have had to request that CFIUS conduct an investigation after determining that a merger, acquisition, or takeover involved an essential technology. In a sweeping provision, the bill would also have authorized the president to consider "the control of domestic industries and commercial activity by foreign citizens as it affects the industrial and technological base of the United States."[56]

Similarly, Representative Cardiss Collins's measure would have required the secretaries of commerce and defense to collect information pertaining to mergers, acquisitions, and takeovers by foreign persons, and identify any plans to transfer technology from the United States. The two secretaries would also have had to conduct an investigation if any critical technology was involved in the transaction. Finally, the Collins bill authorized the president to consider the effect on critical technologies when deciding whether to block a merger. The bill never made it out of committee.

Enhanced Monitoring

Representative Phillip Sharp (D-IN) introduced HR 2631, entitled the International Mergers and Acquisitions Review Act, in 1991. The goal of this bill was to allow Congress to "more logically monitor, and when necessary, regulate transnational mergers, joint ventures and takeovers." Representative Sharp argued that many mergers and acquisitions raise both antitrust and national security concerns. Thus, "it makes sense to provide linkages between the two regulatory domains. In this way, potential threats to our economic welfare and our national security can be monitored and efficiently regulated by either or both sets of competencies, operating independently."[57] HR 2631 would have amended § 721(a) by requiring CFIUS to "make an investigation to determine the effects on national security of

---

56. *To Amend the Defense Production Act of 1950 to Clarify and Strengthen Provisions Pertaining to National Security Takeovers*, HR 5225, 101st Congress, 2nd sess. (1990). Introduced by Representative Walgren.

57. *International Mergers and Acquisitions Review Act*, HR 2631, 102nd Congress, 1st sess., *Congressional Record* 137 (1991): 15575.

58. The Clayton Act (*US Code* 15 (1914), §§ 12–27; *US Code* 29 (1914), §§ 52–53) is one of the United States' principal antitrust statutes. We are not aware of a National Security Liaison Committee, but assume that it was an interagency committee that referred, to the appropriate US government agencies, national security issues that may have arisen in the DOJ's enforcement of the Clayton Act.

any proposed acquisition which the National Security Liaison Committee has referred under section 7B(c)(2)(a) of the Clayton Act"[58] and permitting an investigation of any acquisition referred under 7B(c)(2)(b) of the Clayton Act.[59] The bill also would have broadened the president's powers by allowing him to take action any time "an interest exercising control, *whether foreign or domestic*, might take action that threatens to impair the national security." This bill was referred to several committees, but was never debated.[60]

Enhanced Congressional Involvement

In 2005 Senators James Inhofe (R-OK) and Richard Shelby (R-AL) introduced some of the most sweeping amendments ever offered to the Exon-Florio Amendment during a heated debate in Congress over the proposed acquisition of Unocal by CNOOC. The amendments were swiftly followed by a GAO report that was highly critical of the way that CFIUS was implementing the Exon-Florio Amendment.[61] The most sweeping, and likely unconstitutional,[62] provision in both bills would have given Congress the authority to override a presidential decision to approve a particular transaction.

The Inhofe bill, which the Shelby Amendment sought to amend, would have required the president to notify Congress of all approvals of "any proposed merger, acquisition or takeover that is investigated." It would also have prohibited a transaction, subject to an investigation and approved by the president, from being "consummated until 10 legislative days after the President" provided notice to Congress. In addition, the Inhofe bill required a delay in closing the transaction if the chairman of one of four congressional committees introduced a resolution disapproving of the transaction:

---

59. *International Mergers and Acquisitions Review Act*, HR 2631, 102nd Congress, 1st sess. (1991). Proposed amendment to § 721(a).

60. This bill was referred to the House Committee on Banking, Finance and Urban Affairs, the House Committee on Foreign Affairs, the House Committee on Energy and Commerce, and the House Committee on Judiciary.

61. Inhofe Amendment, SA 1311 to S 1042, 109th Congress, 1st sess. (2005); Shelby Amendment, SA 1467 to S 1042, 109th Congress, 1st sess. (2005); US GAO (2005). As mentioned above, the Inhofe bill would require CFIUS to consider "national economic and energy security" and would have moved the chairmanship of CFIUS to the Department of Defense. Both bills also would have extended the initial 30-day period to 60 days.

62. The proposed amendments would provide that a transaction approved by the president would be blocked if both houses of Congress passed a resolution of disapproval. This provision appears to be unconstitutional. In *INS v. Chadha*, 462 US 919 (1985), the Supreme Court held that Article I of the Constitution requires not only passage by a majority of both houses of Congress, but also presentment to the president for a possible veto.

If a joint resolution objecting to the proposed transaction is introduced in either House of Congress by the Chairman of one of the appropriate Congressional committees during such period, the transaction may not be consummated until 30 legislative days after such resolution.[63]

Finally, if the resolution of disapproval was adopted by both houses, "the transaction may not be consummated."[64] These provisions mirrored a provision in the original Exon bill that permitted Congress to enact a joint resolution to disapprove of a presidential action.[65]

The Shelby Amendment also would have empowered the House and Senate Banking Committees, through the request of the chairman and ranking member, to force CFIUS to investigate, or conduct an extended review of, particular transactions. Both the Inhofe and Shelby amendments would have substantially expanded CFIUS's reporting requirements through either, in the Inhofe amendment, monthly reports on each transaction considered by CFIUS, or, in the Shelby Amendment, the same reports on a quarterly basis.[66]

The Inhofe and Shelby Amendments reflected a growing frustration with what many in Congress perceived as a lack of transparency within the CFIUS process, as well as a growing anxiety generally over the specter of large-scale investments in the United States by Chinese and Gulf State companies. On the issue of transparency, CFIUS has been criticized for limiting the type and amount of information it shares with Congress on particular transactions. CFIUS was heavily criticized for not even notifying Congress about the proposed acquisition of Peninsular and Oriental Steam Navigation Company (P&O) by Dubai Ports World. After all, critics argue, Congress exempted itself from the confidentiality restrictions in Exon-Florio. In the authors' view, however, CFIUS has appropriately withheld from Congress proprietary information supplied by parties that have filed for Exon-Florio approval. We believe that the congressional veto provisions in the Inhofe and Shelby bills, which insert Congress into the CFIUS process, are excessive and unworkable. CFIUS could provide more information to Congress while protecting both the integrity of the CFIUS process and preserving confidential, proprietary information that parties to a particular transaction submit. Chapter 6 discusses ways to improve information sharing with Congress in more detail.

As of this writing, Congress was actively considering legislation to reform CFIUS, but declined to act on the Inhofe and Shelby Amendments,

---

63. Inhofe Amendment, SA 1311 to S 1042, 109th Congress, 1st sess. (2005). Inhofe originally submitted an amendment to S 1042 and later submitted S 1797.

64. Inhofe Amendment, SA 1311 to S 1042, 109th Congress, 1st sess. (2005).

65. See statement of Senator Exon, *Foreign Investment, National Security and Essential Commerce Act of 1987*, supra note 92, sec. (f).

66. See statement of Senator Exon, *Foreign Investment, National Security and Essential Commerce Act of 1987*, supra note 92, sec. (f); and SA 1353.

both of which were originally offered as floor amendments to the 2006 defense authorization bill. However, in that same bill, Congress did pass language expressing the "Sense of the Congress" that the president should develop a comprehensive strategy with respect to China. Among other things, this strategy should include a

> review of laws and regulations governing the Committee on Foreign Investment in the United States (CFIUS), including exploring whether the definition of national security should include the potential impact on national economic security as a criterion to be reviewed, and whether the chairmanship of CFIUS should be transferred from the Secretary of the Treasury to a more appropriate executive branch agency.[67]

It is unclear how and whether the Bush administration will respond to this statutory language.

The Meaning of "National Security" in Practice

As noted above, CFIUS has retained a great deal of flexibility to define and assess national security risks on a transaction-by-transaction basis. This approach has enabled the prism through which US officials assess national security interests to shift with time and circumstances. Predictably, a number of US government agencies shifted their views on the national security implications of foreign investment after September 11. Overall, however, the data available on Exon-Florio reviews indicate that, even with a broader view of national security, Exon-Florio still captures a relatively small percentage of total FDI in the United States.

Assessing National Security Risks

As a general matter, CFIUS uses a risk-based analytical approach to assess the national security risks associated with particular transactions. In recent years, the threshold for what constitutes a risk that might require mitigation has been lowered considerably, with US government officials citing myriad potential national security risks depending on the transaction.

CFIUS agencies have never published a list of risks associated with foreign investment. Below, we offer a summary of the most frequent threats that, in our experience and based on interviews with past and current CFIUS officials, CFIUS agencies have identified with foreign acquisitions of US companies. While some of these threats overlap with the statutorily enumerated criteria discussed above for national security, such as loss of

---

67. *National Defense Authorization Act for Fiscal Year 2006*, Public Law 109-163, 109th Congress, 1st sess., 2005, *Senate Report* 109-069, § 1234(c)8.

US technical leadership in a sensitive sector, many are much broader. The threats most commonly considered by CFIUS include the following potential actions of foreign investors:

- shutting down or sabotaging a critical facility in the United States;

- impeding a US law enforcement or national security investigation;

- accessing sensitive data, or becoming aware of a federal investigation or methods used by US intelligence and/or law enforcement agencies, including moving transaction data and records offshore;

- limiting US government access to information for surveillance or law enforcement purposes;

- denying critical technology or key products to the US government or US industry;

- moving critical technology or key products offshore that are important for national defense, intelligence operations, or homeland security;

- unlawfully transferring technology abroad that is subject to US export control laws;

- undermining US technological leadership in a sector with important defense, intelligence, or homeland security applications;

- compromising the security of government and private-sector networks in the United States;

- facilitating state or economic espionage through acquisition of a US company; and

- aiding the military or intelligence capabilities of a foreign country with interests adverse to those of the United States.

Of course, a number of these reported "threats" reflect certain assumptions, which often may not be true in particular cases. The threat that a foreign acquirer might deny critical technology or key products to the US government assumes a lack of procurement options for the US government or other strategic industries in the United States. For the Department of Defense (DOD) to lack real procurement options, the relevant industry must be tightly concentrated, the number of close substitutes limited, and the switching costs to new products high.[68] In contrast, if there are multi-

---

68. For a more detailed discussion of the factors necessary for a legitimate threat to US national security due to a company denying a product, technology, or service, see statement of Theodore Moran, House Committee on Energy and Commerce, Subcommittee on Commerce, Consumer Protection and Competitiveness, *Hearings before the Subcommittee on Commerce, Consumer Protection and Competitiveness of the House Committee on Energy and Commerce*, 102nd Congress, 1st sess, February 26 and June 12, 1991. Moran cited a number of examples

ple alternative suppliers, it would be hard to argue that a credible national security threat exists, no matter how vital the good or service.

Perhaps most important, virtually all of the examples above assume that there is something inherently less trustworthy, or suspect, about foreign corporations. Meanwhile, most of the largest companies in the world consider themselves to be global entities, rather than companies exclusively affiliated with individual countries. Every company has a home base, and some—particularly those owned and controlled by foreign governments—remain "national." But most truly global companies seek to create a uniquely local identity for each country in which they operate, through branding, hiring local employees, and customization. C. Michael Aho and Marc Levinson (1988, 144) argue that

> questions of corporate nationality have come to possess little relevance. The physical location of a company's headquarters and the place of its incorporation are largely questions of historic accident and legal convenience. . . . Most large firms, whether their headquarters are in Europe, North America, or Japan, operate with global scope, with employees of many nationalities, and produce earnings for shareholders all over the world. To distinguish among them according to the country in which each is based is to place an inappropriate emphasis on factors that simply no longer matter.

Aho and Levinson made this argument before mutual and hedge funds and cross-border portfolio investment substantially expanded.[69] There are, of course, major exceptions, including major corporations, such as Lockheed Martin or Boeing, that need to maintain their American identity for security and marketing reasons. But excluding the universe of companies that for various reasons want to maintain their national identities, the

---

in which governments, including the United States, instructed companies based in their countries to withhold technology from another country. He also cited several industrial segments in which industry concentration was so tight that there was potential to withhold technology from the United States or the US government. Among these industrial segments was "advanced lithography," a highly specialized process used to make detailed patterns in silicon wafers. Moran was prescient, as in 2001, in the first year of the George W. Bush administration, a foreign acquisition of a US company in the lithography sector became highly controversial. See the discussion of the ASML-Silicon Graphics transaction in chapter 5.

69. See also Todd Malan, testimony before the House Financial Services Committee Subcommittee on Domestic and International Monetary Policy, Trade, and Technology, March 1, 2005. Malan states, "When it comes to national security concerns arising from commercial operations of critical infrastructure, why should the nationality of the owners of the capital stock be the principal or sole concern? Certainly, there may be instances of foreign ownership that do raise special concerns as in the case of government ownership of the acquirer—a situation where CFIUS already pays special attention. But the national security risks arising from certain activities—such as infrastructure operations—are present whoever owns the capital stock and should be addressed on their merits, not only in the context of an acquisition. If we agree that there are vulnerabilities in a particular area, the solution is to address the risk comprehensively and not take the view that the risk lies only with ownership."

largest multinational companies, which in turn are the largest global investors, increasingly seek to be branded as global companies.

In turn, the shares of most large public companies are owned by other large institutional investors, which may be US- or foreign-based, or raise capital from the United States, foreign countries, or, more likely, both. Institutional investors or mutual funds own 54 percent of General Electric's shares and 63 percent of DuPont's. In the energy sector, 54 percent of Exxon-Mobil's shares are held by institutional investors or mutual funds. BP (formerly British Petroleum) is 80 percent owned by institutional investors and mutual funds, and is owned by virtually the same number of Americans (approximately 40 percent) as British (approximately 42 percent). Which company should be considered American, BP or ExxonMobil? Under the Exon-Florio Amendment, only BP would be required to obtain CFIUS approval to acquire an American company. In our view, both Exxon and BP operate as global companies, not American or British companies. Other leading executives agree.[70] Even in sensitive sectors, foreign ownership of US assets by global companies based outside the United States does not create national security risks on its own. CFIUS must look at the particular facts associated with the foreign acquirer, its leadership and shareholders, and the asset being acquired to determine whether a particular transaction poses a national security risk.

National Security Assessments under Exon-Florio

Through the end of 2005, 1,593 notices had been filed with CFIUS, representing about 10 percent of all reported FDI in the United States. After an initial burst of filings in the first four years after Exon-Florio was enacted, during which CFIUS received between 106 and 295 filings per year, the number of filings has leveled off to between 40 and 80 annually. The large number of filings early in the amendment's lifetime reflected uncertainty in the business and legal communities about how Exon-Florio would be implemented. As a result, in an abundance of caution, more filings were made than were probably necessary.

Table 2.1 summarizes CFIUS's activities. The 1,593 filings have generated 25 investigations, 13 withdrawals, and 12 decisions by the president. The president has formally rejected only one transaction. Critics of CFIUS point to the small number of transactions that have gone to an investigation, as well as that single rejection, as evidence that the provision is ineffective. In a July 21, 2005, speech on the Senate floor, Senator Inhofe stated, "CFIUS has not demonstrated an appropriate conception of national secu-

---

70. Chad Holliday, chairman and CEO of DuPont, once said, "With DuPont being a global company, we cannot do it the American way everywhere." Cynthia Challener, "Gaining Executive Mindshare: US and European Chemical CEOs; Focus 2003: Chemical Leaders: CEOs and Companies," *Chemical Market Reporter,* May 26, 2003, FR8.

Table 2.1   CFIUS notifications and investigations, 1988–2005

Year	Notifications	Investigations	Notices withdrawn	Presidential decision
1988	14	1	0	1
1989	204	5	2	3[a]
1990	295	6	2	4
1991	152	1	0	1
1992	106	2	1	1
1993	82	0	0	0
1994	69	0	0	0
1995	81	0	0	0
1996	55	0	0	0
1997	62	0	0	0
1998	65	2	2	0
1999	79	0	0	0
2000	72	1	0	1
2001	55	1	1	0
2002	43	0	0	0
2003	41	2	1	1
2004	53	2	2	0
2005	65	2	2	0
Total	1,593	25	13	12

a. Includes the China National Aero Tech (PRC)/MAMCO Manufacturing transaction, which the president ordered divested on February 2, 1990.

Source: Data obtained from the Department of the Treasury.

rity." Inhofe continued by citing the data mentioned above: "Of more than 1,500 cases of foreign investments or acquisitions in the United States, CFIUS has only investigated 24. And only one resulted in actually stopping the transaction."[71] But these data fail to present the full picture. A number of transactions were abandoned after informal consultations with CFIUS led the parties to conclude that CFIUS approval would not be forthcoming. Another 13 transactions were withdrawn after CFIUS began an investigation. Others were withdrawn within the first 30 days of the review process, and CFIUS does not keep or publish data on withdrawals that occur after a filing has been made but prior to an investigation. Even more important, CFIUS has used its power to review transactions to impose strict conditions on foreign acquisitions to mitigate national security concerns. Examples of these mitigation measures are discussed later in this chapter.

Since September 11, 2001, the number of investigations and withdrawals has increased compared with previous years, reflecting the increased level of scrutiny foreign acquisitions receive in the new security environment. Between January 2003 and December 2005, there were six investigations

---

71. 109th Congress, 1st sess., *Congressional Record* 151 (July 21, 2005): S8609.

and five withdrawals, more than during the previous 10 years combined. Adding the DHS to CFIUS in February 2003 also increased the level of scrutiny by CFIUS in this period.

In practice, the question before CFIUS in most transactions is not whether or not to block a particular investment, but how to mitigate any perceived threat to national security that may result from it. As discussed in detail below, CFIUS has pursued mitigation strategies primarily through agreements with, or commitment letters from, the parties to a transaction. These measures are negotiated either before or during the formal CFIUS process. In many circumstances, CFIUS agencies will proceed to the investigation simply because they have not had sufficient time during the initial 30-day review period to reach agreement with the transaction parties, or reach consensus within CFIUS, on appropriate mitigation methods.

Exon-Florio in the Post–September 11 Environment

Since the terrorist attacks of September 11, 2001, transactions requiring CFIUS review have been subjected to greater scrutiny and tougher conditions for approval, as concern about national and homeland security has dramatically increased following the attacks. In February 2003, President Bush added the DHS to CFIUS, shifting the committee's balance of power significantly in favor of agencies prioritizing security over economic policy considerations. Despite the criticism that the Bush administration inadequately scrutinized the Dubai Ports World acquisition, a number of senior officials in the Bush Administration, particularly at the DOD, have not embraced foreign investment in the United States with the same enthusiasm as did their predecessors in the Bill Clinton, George H. W. Bush, and Ronald Reagan administrations.

The heightened emphasis on security within CFIUS has resulted in more investigations and stricter security-related conditions for CFIUS approval. In this new, more uncertain security environment, as discussed in chapter 4, CFIUS also has expanded its focus on protection of critical infrastructure, which the DHS views in broad terms.[72]

---

72. See chapter 4. See also Homeland Security Presidential Directive-7 (HSPD-7), which sets forth government policy for protecting critical infrastructure and key resources, identifies critical infrastructure sectors, and assigns various agency responsibilities for protecting those sectors. Homeland Security Presidential Directive-7 (December 17, 2003) is available at www.whitehouse.gov. The operative legal definition of critical infrastructure is found in *Uniting and Strengthening America by Providing Appropriate Tools Required to Intercept and Obstruct Terrorism (USA PATRIOT) Act,* § 1016(e), codified at *US Code* 42 (2001), § 5195c(e): "The term 'critical infrastructure' means systems and assets, whether physical or virtual, so vital to the United States that the incapacity or destruction of such systems and assets would have a debilitating impact on security, national economic security, national public health or safety, or any combination of those matters."

Telecommunications Transactions under Exon-Florio

The telecommunications sector provides an interesting case study of Exon-Florio for two reasons. First, it is the only sector in which security agreements negotiated pursuant to CFIUS review are made public. As mentioned above, a major focus of CFIUS has been to mitigate the national security impact of a foreign investment, rather than blocking it outright. The security agreements are made public through the US Federal Communications Commission's (FCC) Web site, because CFIUS uses the threat of revoking FCC licenses as an enforcement tool to ensure that foreign acquirers of US telecommunications companies live up to the obligations in the agreements. Second, the telecommunications sector provides plenty of data for analysis because there have been so many foreign acquisitions of US telecommunications companies, both pre– and post–September 11, given the relative openness of the US market to foreign telecommunications companies.

Two events in the mid- and late 1990s opened the US telecommunications market to foreign investors. First, Congress passed the landmark Telecommunications Act of 1996, enhancing competition in multiple telecommunications sectors, including long distance, wireless, satellite, and local service. The act spurred investment in new telecommunications companies (many of which later went out of business), led to innovative new services, and was a major catalyst for the technological revolution of the late 1990s in the United States. Second, and more significantly in its effect on foreign investment in the United States, the United States and 68 other countries reached a landmark agreement in the World Trade Organization (WTO) in 1997 to open markets for basic telecommunications services. This Basic Telecommunications Agreement of the WTO was signed by countries then representing more than 90 percent of global telecommunications revenues. It established principles of nondiscrimination and national treatment for telecommunications providers throughout the world. Most of the countries that signed the agreement made binding commitments to open their basic telecommunications and satellite markets to foreign investments, adopt procompetitive and deregulatory policies, and allow foreign companies to participate in their home markets (Foreign Participation Order).

The United States made broad and deep commitments to ensure that foreign telecommunications providers had access to the US market. To implement these commitments, in November 1997 the FCC adopted two measures, one governing foreign participation in the telecommunications market (hereinafter the Foreign Participation Order), the other providing special rules for the satellite market (together referred to as Orders). These orders sought to "significantly increase competition in the US telecommunications market by facilitating entry by foreign service providers and investors."[73] They created an open entry policy for carriers from WTO member countries.[74] In essence, an investment in the United States from a company based in a WTO member country would be presumed to be procompetitive by the FCC because the WTO Agreement on Basic Telecommunications created more competition in that company's home market, thereby reducing the risk of cross-subsidization from foreign carriers that were monopolies in their home markets.

Since these regulatory changes in 1997, the FCC has considered and approved dozens of transactions involving foreign investors in multiple telecommunications sectors. Today the German telecommunications company Deutsche Telecommunications owns T-Mobile, the fourth-largest US wireless carrier, with more than 17 million subscribers in early 2005. Vodafone, the British mobile operator, owns 45 percent of Verizon Wireless, the largest US wireless carrier. Dozens of other foreign carriers, including NTT (Japan), Telnor (Norway), France Telecom, BT (formerly British Telecom) and Videsh Sanchar Nigam Limited (VSNL, India) own or control US affiliates. Indeed, in the open US market, foreign firms have acquired US-based firms owned by other foreign nationals. In 2005 BT acquired Infonet, a California-based telecommunications provider serving the enterprise market, from six foreign carriers: TeliaSonera (Sweden/Finland), Swisscom AG (Switzerland), KPN Telecommunications B. V. (Netherlands), Telefonica International Holding (Spain), Telstra (Australia), and KDDI (Japan). Thus the WTO Basic Telecommunications Agreements and the Orders have to be considered a huge success, as they accomplished their goal of substantially increasing competition in US and foreign markets.

In adopting the Foreign Participation Order, the FCC had to consider the extent to which it would defer to the executive branch on national security, law enforcement, foreign policy, and trade issues. There was some debate between interested parties over the propriety of the commission's consideration of the latter two areas. However, with the exception of comments from German telecommunications company Deutsche Telecom, there was little debate over whether the FCC should defer to the executive branch on national security issues.

---

73. US FCC press release, "Commission Liberalizes Foreign Participation in the US Telecommunications Market," Report No. IN 97-36. November 25, 1997, available at www.fcc. gov; *Rules and Policies on Foreign Participation in the US Telecommunications Market*, Report and Order, *Federal Communications Commission Record* 12 (1997): 23,891, hereinafter the Foreign Participation Order; *Amendment of the Commission's Regulatory Policies to Allow Non-US Licensed Space Station to Provide Domestic and International Satellite Service in the United States*, Report and Order, *Federal Communications Commission Record* 12 (1997): 24,094.

74. For WTO member countries, the FCC eliminated the "effective competitive opportunity" test, in which the commission, among other things, analyzed the extent to which the home market was open to US carriers as an indicator of whether a particular foreign company's participation in the US market was "procompetitive" (Foreign Participation Order).

When the commission adopted the regulations to liberalize investment restrictions, terrorism was far from the minds of most Americans, the US economy was booming, and the perception that the rise of China posed a serious economic and political challenge to the United States had not yet taken root. The commission did not, and could not, have realized that its decision to defer to the executive branch on national security, law enforcement, foreign policy, and trade issues in determining whether an application was in the "public interest" would create an opening for the DOJ, DOD, and DHS to assert broad rights to regulate foreign investment in telecommunications companies.

In the Foreign Participation Order, the commission noted that "we expect national security, law enforcement, foreign policy and trade policy concerns to be raised only in very rare circumstances. Contrary to the fears of some comments, the scope of concerns that the Executive Branch will raise in the context of [foreign investments] is narrow and well defined." The commission also noted that "during our two years in administering the *Foreign Carrier Entry Order*, with approximately 140 authorizations granted to carriers with foreign ownership, the Executive Branch has never asked the Commission to deny an application on national security or law enforcement grounds." Finally, the commission concluded, "We expect this pattern to continue, such that the circumstances in which the Executive Branch would advise us that a pending matter affects national security, law enforcements or obligations arising from international agreements to which the United States is a party will be quite rare."[75]

The FCC could not have been more wrong. Regularly, if not in all foreign acquisitions, the DOJ, DOD, and DHS, as well as the Federal Bureau of Investigation (FBI), ask the FCC to withhold approval for a transaction until they can complete their security analyses and negotiate security commitments with the parties to the transaction. Since September 11, telecommunications lawyers have grown so accustomed to the security agencies putting a hold on FCC approval for foreign investments pending a security review that, in FCC applications, lawyers now stipulate that the FCC should not process an application for a license until CFIUS security agencies have stated for the record to the FCC that their national security concerns have been satisfied. Given that foreign firms easily achieved FCC approval for acquisitions of US telecommunications firms, one could credibly argue that the only difficult and uncertain regulatory process that foreign telecommunications firms face is Exon-Florio.

Moreover, since September 11, 2001, national security concerns about the telecommunications sector have grown for certain CFIUS agencies.

---

75. In the Matter of Rules and Policies on Foreign Participation in the US Telecommunications Market, IB Docket No. 97-142, Order and Notice of Proposed Rulemaking, *Federal Communications Commission Record* 12 (1997): 7847, paragraph 63.

Before September 11 and the creation of the DHS, security agencies that participated in CFIUS were typically concerned about four national security issues.

First, the DOJ and FBI wanted to make sure that their ability to pursue investigations, conduct wiretaps and other surveillance activities, and gain access to data, such as billing records, would not be impeded by virtue of a carrier's foreign ownership.[76] They did not want to be in the position of needing data quickly from a telecommunications carrier based in the United States, but having acquisition of such data slowed by a foreign national or government that controlled the company.

Second, the DOJ and the FBI wanted to keep sensitive data out of the hands of foreign governments, and were concerned that a foreign company, either private or government owned and controlled, might share such data with a foreign government, through either loyalty to or pressure from that government. They believed that US citizens, or companies owned by US persons, would be less likely to have incentives to share such data.[77] In particular, the DOJ and FBI wanted to avoid foreign governments gaining access to information concerning the targets of US national security and law enforcement investigations, the nature of those investigations, and the sources and methods used, as well as information

---

76. The DOJ and the FBI typically seek three types of data through court-approved subpoenas and other law enforcement processes: subscriber data (customer names, addresses, phone numbers, etc.); transactional data (details on calls, including the call length, number called, etc.; for voice over Internet protocol, or VOIP, calls, the DOJ and the FBI will seek similar data, including the session time, login and logout records, etc.); and communications data (the content of communications, acquired through wiretapping or review of e-mails, voice mails, or other electronic data). See, e.g., statement of Kevin V. DiGregory, Deputy Assistant Attorney General, Criminal Division, Department of Justice, before the US House of Representatives Subcommittee on Telecommunications, Trade, and Consumer Protection, Committee on Commerce, *Foreign Ownership Interests and Foreign Government Ownership Interests in the American Communications Infrastructure*, 106th Congress, 2nd sess., September 7, 2000, available at www.usdoj.gov.

77. Statement of Larry R. Parkinson, general counsel for the Federal Bureau of Investigation, at the same hearing. He stated,

> These [national security] concerns exist regardless of whether the controlling entity is foreign government owned. Even when the foreign entity controlling a US communications network is privately held, there is cause for concern that the foreign-affiliated carrier may be subject to the influence and directives of the foreign government or others to compromise US investigations and carry out or assist in carrying out intelligence efforts against the US Government or US companies. On a continuum of risk, however, a service provider that is directly or indirectly owned or controlled by a foreign government or its representatives falls on the higher risk end of the spectrum.

about the extent to which the US government was aware of a foreign government's intelligence activities.[78]

Third, DOJ was concerned about enforcing US privacy laws and unauthorized data sharing with foreign persons or governments. In testimony to Congress, Kevin DiGregory, a senior DOJ official, articulated a number of questions DOJ considers when reviewing foreign acquisitions of US communications companies:

- Does the proposed ownership interest create an increased risk of espionage, and foreign-based economic espionage in particular, against US companies and persons?

- Does the proposed ownership interest compromise US ability to protect the privacy of US citizens and their communications?

- Will US national security, law enforcement, and public safety capabilities be impaired by the proposed foreign ownership interests?

- Does the company have existing policies for protecting privacy, handling classified information, and complying with lawful process?

- Does the company have a good record of complying with lawful process related to national security and law enforcement capabilities?

- What is the degree and nature of the proposed foreign control?

- If the ownership interest is transferred to a foreign entity, does the United States have adequate assurances that National Security Emergency Preparedness and US Infrastructure Protection requirements are met?

Fourth, the DOD was typically concerned about acquisitions of US companies that held classified or sensitive communications services contracts with the DOD or other national security agencies.

Following September 11, however, CFIUS's security concerns about the telecommunications sector grew. As reported in the *New York Times* and other leading publications, US surveillance activity grew significantly after the attacks, and security agencies ensured that they could access lines owned or controlled by foreign telecommunications companies.[79] As discussed above, when President Bush added the DHS to CFIUS in 2003, an additional national security concern was given unprecedented focus: protection of critical infrastructure. The Clinton administration had pre-

---

78. See statement by Larry R. Parkinson.

79. Eric Lichtblau and James Risen, "Spy Agency Mined Vast Data Trove, Officials Report," *New York Times*, December 24, 2005, A1.

viously identified this as a national priority,[80] but the DHS has made it a major focus of policy with respect to the telecommunications sector.[81]

The greater focus on broader electronic surveillance and protection of critical infrastructure can best be seen through the evolution of network security agreements (NSAs) between foreign carriers and the security agencies within CFIUS. To satisfy national security concerns, the security agencies within CFIUS—the DOD, DHS, DOJ, and FBI—require the parties engaged in the transaction to enter into an NSA. An NSA typically applies to any subsidiary, division, department, branch, or other component of the US telecommunications network receiving foreign investment that provides communications between locations in the United States, or that originates or terminates in the United States. The breadth and depth of an NSA depends on the perceived security risk of a particular transaction. The security assessment, in turn, depends on a number of factors, including the importance of the telecommunications system to US critical infrastructure; the location of tangible and intangible assets; business plans and proposed practices; the organizational structure of the acquirer and target; the degree and nature of foreign control; the level of national and international controls over the system's operations; political risks associated with the acquirer's home country, and that country's security or political relationship with the US government; the existence of classified or otherwise sensitive contracts with the US government held by the target, particularly with respect to US defense, law enforcement, and national security agencies; and relevant historical intercept activity. The greater the risk that the security agencies assign to a particular transaction, the tougher the requirements the acquirer can expect in the NSA.

Before September 11, NSAs negotiated between transaction parties and the US government typically focused on the ability of US law enforcement to conduct electronic surveillance and access data in telecommunications networks through wiretaps; it also involved the service of lawful process (e.g., wiretaps or data production) and preventing foreign governments from accessing data. Pre–September 11 NSAs also permitted calls originating and terminating in the United States to be routed outside the country for bona fide commercial reasons. Likewise, a telecommunications provider subject to an NSA had to maintain data and key network equipment, including network operating centers, routers, and switches, inside the United States, absent a bona fide commercial reason to maintain them abroad. Other pre–September 11 NSA requirements typically included pro-

---

80. Among other actions, President Clinton issued Presidential Decision Directive 63 (PDD 63) on May 22, 1998, which established the national security objective of protecting US cyber and information networks from attack or disruption. The FBI created the National Infrastructure Protection Center, a public-private forum to coordinate critical infrastructure protection among federal, state, local, and private-sector stakeholders.

81. See HSPD-7, supra note 158.

hibiting foreign governments' access to data and content related to calls originated and terminated in the United States. Companies entering into an NSA also had to comply with US law enforcement requests to access data and conduct surveillance.

Since September 11 and the DHS's appointment to CFIUS, NSAs have become tougher, pursuing the much broader US government objectives of expanded electronic surveillance and protecting critical infrastructure. A number of recent NSAs have reduced telecommunications firms' flexibility to route domestic calls and maintain network equipment outside the United States, presumably to enhance US security agencies' ability to conduct electronic surveillance and access data for counterterrorism and law enforcement purposes. Post–September 11 NSAs have also borrowed heavily from security agreements typically utilized by the DOD to mitigate security concerns associated with foreign-owned companies that have classified defense contracts. To varying degrees, these NSAs have

- eliminated the bona fide commercial exception for data storage and call routing outside of the United States;

- eliminated the bona fide commercial exception for critical network equipment located abroad, thereby requiring the network to be controlled entirely from within the United States;

- permitted only US citizens to serve in sensitive network and security positions (e.g., positions with access to monitor and control the network);

- required third-party screening of senior company officials and personnel with access to critical network functions;

- restricted or prohibited the outsourcing of functions covered by the NSA, unless such outsourcing is approved by the DHS or occurs pursuant to approval by the DHS;

- given US government agencies the right to inspect US-based facilities and to interview US-based personnel on very short notice (as short as 30 minutes);

- required third-party audits of compliance with the terms of the NSA;

- required the implementation of strict visitation policies regulating foreign national access (including by employees of the acquiring company) to key facilities, including network operating centers; and

- required senior executives of the US entity, and certain directors of its board, to be US citizens approved by the US government and responsible for supervising and implementing the NSA.

These strict requirements have been applied in a number of transactions across multiple sectors of the telecommunications industry. The first post–

September 11 NSA that included these tough new requirements was signed by Global Crossing and Singapore Technologies Telemedia (ST Telemedia), after a heavily debated CFIUS process requiring a full 45-day investigation and ultimately a personal decision by President Bush.[82] Global Crossing is a large, backbone network based in the United States.[83] ST Telemedia is owned by the Temasek Group, the state-owned investment holding company of Singapore. The DOJ and DHS are believed to consider backbone networks as the most sensitive subsector in the telecommunications industry, because of the significant consequences to the US communications system if a major backbone network were to be disrupted. Similar tough agreements were also required for four much smaller transactions:

- Pacific Telecom's (Philippines) acquisition of Micronesian Telecommunications Corporation (MTC), the local exchange carrier in the Northern Mariana Islands.[84] MTC served approximately 25,000 households and businesses, and provided digital subscriber line (DSL) and wireless services on the islands of Saipan, Tinian, and Rota, each of which are considered territories of the United States and therefore subject to Exon-Florio.

- Telefonica's (Spain) acquisition of NewComm, the fifth-largest wireless carrier in Puerto Rico.[85]

- VSNL's (India) acquisition of Tyco Global Network (TGN), a large, global backbone fiber network.[86] Importantly, however, the TGN, unlike Global Crossing, did not include a fiber network within the United States; it connects to the United States via a cable landing station. Thus, the component of TGN subject to US jurisdiction is extremely small. The Indian government owns approximately 26 percent of VSNL.

- Arcapita's (Bahrain) acquisition of Cypress Communications, a provider of in-building telecommunications and a reseller of telecommunications services.[87]

---

82. David M. Marchick, "Crossing the Line," *Legal Week Global*, December 2003, 16–17.

83. Backbone networks are traditionally considered the part of the Internet or telecommunications system that connects traffic from multiple carriers to each other.

84. In re Bell Atlantic New Zealand Holdings, Inc., Transferor, and Pacific Telecom, Transferee, Order and Authorization, IB Docket No. 03-115, *Federal Communications Commission Record* 18 (November 6, 2003): 23,140.

85. In both the Pacific Telecommunications and Telefonica transactions, the NSAs did not require the appointment of a third party to audit compliance.

86. FCC Public Notice, DA 05-1268 (April 29, 2005).

87. In the Matter of Cypress Communications Operating Company, Inc., Application for Consent to Transfer Control of a Company Holding International Authorizations and a Blanket Domestic Authorization Pursuant to Section 214 of the Communications Act of 1934, as amended, IB File No. ITC-T/C-20041112-00448 (rel. June 28, 2005).

There have been a few exceptions to the recent trend toward tougher NSAs and commitment letters, primarily involving satellite sector acquisitions by the United States' closest allies, in particular the United Kingdom.[88] For Intelsat's acquisition of certain satellite assets from Loral,[89] and News Corp's acquisition of Hughes (which also held satellite assets),[90] the US government required only the appointment of a security or special audit committee, made up of US citizens with authority to supervise implementation of security commitments. These requirements, which were embodied in letters to the US government rather than an NSA, did not include the more onerous restrictions dealing with network control or data storage. In another recent transaction, British Telecom's acquisition of Infonet, a US-based communications company providing telecommunications and information technology (IT) services for multinational companies, BT committed to maintaining strong security policies, creating a "security board" in the US subsidiary (rather than at the board of director level in the parent), confirming the ability to run the US network from the United States in case of national emergency, and adopting broad, third-party screening of employees in sensitive network and security positions.[91]

Only CFIUS agencies are privy to the precise factors determining whether the parties to a given transaction are required to negotiate a broad, Global Crossing–like NSA, or a narrow, Intelsat-like exchange of letters. However, one can observe a few patterns that suggest how CFIUS analyzes the national security risks associated with transactions, and the measures required to mitigate those risks. Backbone and fiber networks seem to be viewed as more sensitive from a national security perspective than satellite or wireless networks are. The acquisitions of Global Crossing, Tyco, and Micronesian Telecommunications Corporation required broad and tough NSAs, even though the Tyco network barely touches the United States, and MTC is a relatively small local exchange carrier. The

88. In the Matter of Intelsat, Ltd., Transferor and Zeus Holdings Limited, Transferee, Consolidated Application for Consents to Transfers of Control of Holders of Title II and Title III Authorizations and Petition for Declaratory Ruling under Section 310 of the Communications Act of 1934, as Amended, IB Docket 04-366.

89. Order, In the Matter of Loral Satellite, Inc. (Debtor-in-Possession), Assignors and Intelsat North America, LLC, Assignee, Applications for Consent to Assignments of Space Station Authorizations and Petition for Declaratory Ruling Under Section 310(b)(4) of the Communications Act of 1934, as Amended, File Nos. SAT-ASG-20030728-00138, SAT-ASG-20030728-00139, ISP-PDR-20030925-00024 (rel. February 11, 2004).

90. Petition to Adopt Conditions to Authorizations and Licenses (submitted by the DOJ and the FBI), Application of General Motors Corporation and Hughes Electronics Corporation, Transferors, and The News Corporation Limited, Transferee, for Authority to Transfer Control, MB Docket 03-124 (November 18, 2003).

91. BT-Infonet Security Letter (January 12, 2005).

MTC and NewComm transaction came on the heels of the Global Crossing transaction. As a result, the security agencies might have felt some constraints in negotiating a more flexible arrangement with MTC and NewComm than they did with Global Crossing. Acquirers based in countries considered to be close strategic and political allies to the United States are likely to be deemed a lower security risk. The BT and Intelsat security requirements seem to confirm that British companies will be seen as a lower national security risk than companies from other countries, consistent with the extraordinarily close US-UK security and political relationship. By contrast, CFIUS scrutinized the Tyco and Arcapita acquisitions very closely, perhaps reflecting the greater security concerns within the US government toward India and Bahrain respectively. Finally, government ownership tends to result in tougher security requirements: Again, witness the tough Global Crossing and Tyco agreements. A company ultimately owned by the government of Singapore acquired Global Crossing, and a company partially owned by the government of India acquired Tyco Global Network.

The recent NSAs demonstrate that the security commitments extracted by the US government through the Exon-Florio review process can impose significant costs on business. Limiting outsourcing, routing of domestic calls, data storage, and the location of network infrastructure can have considerable competitive effects, and raise issues of disparate treatment both between US- and foreign-owned companies and between foreign-owned companies that are similarly situated. While many US telecommunications companies have strong security policies and protocols, and cooperate with the DOJ, DHS, and FBI, none are subject to requirements comparable to the oversight resulting from an NSA. Similarly, foreign telecommunications companies that have made acquisitions in the United States after September 11 may face tougher and more restrictive security requirements than similarly situated companies that cleared CFIUS prior to that date. In the mobile telecommunications sector, in 2004 and 2005 Cingular acquired AT&T Wireless and Sprint merged with Nextel. If either of the acquirers had been a foreign company, the foreign party potentially would have faced a tougher NSA than that signed by Deutsche Telecom, which acquired VoiceStream in 1999, simply because NSAs signed in 2005 tended to be tougher and more comprehensive than those negotiated in 1999.

Ultimately, if the DOJ, DHS, DOD, and FBI are to achieve one of their key goals—enhancing the security and integrity of the domestic telecommunications system—they will need congressional authority to impose tougher security requirements on all telecommunications companies, regardless of foreign ownership and whether a foreign acquisition was made before or after September 11. However, unless Congress authorizes security agencies to impose security requirements across the board, regardless of capital affiliation, disparate treatment will unfortunately remain a fact of life.[92] As the only regulatory hook available to security agencies, Exon-Florio will continue to be invoked to impose requirements, on an opportunistic basis and as individual transactions arise, regardless of any resulting unfairness in the treatment of one company relative to another. In our view, CFIUS needs to identify more precisely the incremental risks that genuinely relate to foreign ownership of US telecommunications companies, and narrowly tailor NSAs to those risks. CFIUS should not, however, be used as a back door way to pursue important yet broader telecommunications security goals but impose restrictions only on foreign-owned companies.

Defense Acquisitions and Exon-Florio

With Exon-Florio's national security focus, the amendment has been used extensively to regulate FDI in the defense industrial sector. As both the principal customer for defense companies and guardian of the nation's military secrets, the DOD has a strong interest in regulating this industry. In practice, however, these two roles frequently pull DOD in opposite directions. As a customer, DOD values the competition and innovation that foreign defense contractors contribute to developing and procuring weapons systems. But DOD's strong interest in maintaining technological superiority over actual and potential enemies, protecting operational security, and guarding against sharing classified technology make it wary allowing classified information to fall into the hands of foreign-controlled companies. Moreover, the efforts of the domestic defense industry to persuade Congress and the Pentagon to "buy American" have historically tipped the balance toward a guarded approach to investment by non-US defense suppliers in research, development, and production facilities in the United States (Adams 2002).

In the late 1990s, the combination of these factors helped stimulate the Clinton administration to break down barriers to transatlantic defense industry collaboration. In 1999, a top DOD official called for "a 'competitive, transatlantic industrial model' characterized by industrial linkages of multiple firms, operating on both sides of the ocean, effectively competing in both the large European and US markets—and sharing technology albeit with, of course, effective external technology controls being applied."[93]

---

92. For example, the Bush administration's attempts, repeatedly rebuffed by Congress, to gain authority from Congress to impose security requirements on domestic chemical facilities have been widely covered in the press. See, e.g., editorial, "Time for Chemical Plant Security," *New York Times*, December 27, 2005.

93. Speech by Jacques S. Gansler, Under Secretary of Defense (Acquisition and Technology) at the Defense Industry Business Forum, Toulouse, France, "International Defense Cooperation: The New Environment," December 6, 1999, available at www.acq.osd. mil (accessed March 7, 2006).

Notwithstanding the US government's declared enthusiasm for closer defense industrial cooperation with its allies, foreign firms to date have established only a modest presence in the United States. Two British firms, BAE Systems and Rolls Royce, have established successful US subsidiaries that compete for defense contracts. Other major European defense companies have made inroads into the US market through joint ventures with American counterparts. Thales (France) has teamed up with Raytheon Systems, and the European Aeronautic Defense and Space Company (EADS), the European consortium, collaborates with Northrop Grumman. Firms from a few select Asian allies, including Australia and Singapore, have also established an important presence in the defense industrial sector.

In addition to the war on terrorism, the growing perception within the DOD that China represents a serious long-term threat to US security has influenced the application of Exon-Florio to the defense sector. As discussed in chapter 4, US concern about Chinese espionage in the early 2000s led to a series of prosecutions of Chinese nationals and US citizens of Chinese origin for illegally transferring defense-related controlled technologies. Washington's violently negative reaction to EU plans to lift its embargo of arms exports to China in 2005 also highlighted differing perceptions of the threat posed by China. Many in the Pentagon, and in the rest of the US national security establishment, view Europe, particularly continental Europe, as a weak link in the control of exports of sensitive technology to China.

Even without Exon-Florio, the US government would possess significant means to control foreign investment in the US defense industry. Under the National Industrial Security Program Operating Manual (NISPOM; US DOD 1995), issued pursuant to executive order in 1995 and amended in 1997 and 2001, all DOD contractors must have a facility clearance to qualify for access to classified material or be awarded a classified contract. NISPOM establishes detailed criteria to determine when US companies cleared or under consideration for a facility clearance are under foreign ownership, control, or influence (FOCI). In some respects, these criteria sweep more broadly than Exon-Florio does. As chapter 6 discusses, NISPOM designates ownership of 5 percent or more of the company's voting securities by a foreign person as one of a number of factors to be taken into consideration in determining whether a company is under FOCI (US DOD 1995).

If a company with a facility clearance is determined to be under foreign control or influence, NISPOM directs the company's facility clearance to be suspended, thereby rendering the company ineligible for classified work. However, NISPOM also specifies a series of possible "methods to negate risk in foreign ownership cases" (US DOD 1995, § 306) that can allow a company under FOCI to receive a facility clearance. These methods are basically the same as those described below as necessary mitigation measures to secure CFIUS approval for foreign investments in the defense sector.

The voluntary notification to CFIUS of a transaction involving foreign investment in the defense sector starts a process similar, in many respects, to what NISPOM requires for companies found to be under FOCI. According to the DOD, "The major difference between CFIUS and FOCI reviews is that the CFIUS review is subject to time limits while FOCI is not" (US DOD 2003). Indeed, the time limits under Exon-Florio are important procedural safeguards for foreign investors and US companies being acquired. They guarantee that a foreign investor will obtain a decision, favorable or not, in a relatively short time. Without them, foreign acquisitions could be held in regulatory limbo for months, or even years, without a decision. Exon-Florio also requires the DOD to make certain specific determinations with respect to transactions notified to CFIUS, and the 1993 amendments to Exon-Florio require the DOD to determine if the company or business unit being acquired possesses critical defense technology under development, or is otherwise important to the defense industrial and technology base.[94] If either criterion is met, the DOD prepares an assessment of the risk of technology diversion, which is circulated to other CFIUS members.

If the DOD believes that the risks it identifies can be managed, it may also negotiate mitigation measures with the transaction parties. These generally fall into four categories (in ascending order of restrictiveness), mirroring the measures available under NISPOM:

- *Board resolution.* A board resolution certifying that the foreign shareholder shall not be given, and can effectively be precluded from, access to all classified and export-controlled information is sufficient when the foreign party to the transaction will not acquire voting stock sufficient to elect directors, and is otherwise not entitled to representation on the US company's board of directors. A board resolution is typically used in cases in which there is limited foreign ownership and control of a company in the defense sector.

- *Limited facility clearance.* When the US government has signed an industrial security agreement with the parent government of the foreign party, a limited facility clearance can be granted, allowing that foreign party access to classified information is limited to performance on a contract or program involving the parent government.

- *Special security agreement (SSA) and security control agreement (SCA).* SSAs are less intrusive than proxy agreements, but still substantial

---

94. *National Defense Authorization Act for Fiscal Year 1993*, Public Law 102-484, *US Statutes at Large* 106 (1992): 2315, codified at *US Code* 10, § 2537(c).

ways of limiting foreign control and influencing foreign companies handling classified contracts with the Pentagon. SSAs and SCAs create a subsidiary, but allow limited involvement in and oversight of the subsidiary by the foreign owner. Under a classic SSA, the US company acquired by a foreign owner must be governed by a board of directors, a majority of whom are US citizens, cleared by the Pentagon, with no ties to the foreign investors. In contrast to a voting trust or proxy agreement, in which the foreign owner is precluded from participating on the board, under an SSA or SCA the foreign owner can participate on the board so long as the directors it names remain in the minority and do not have access to or knowledge of any classified information.

■ *Voting trust agreement and proxy agreement.* Under a voting trust or proxy agreement—two substantially similar approaches—the DOD requires a foreign investor to create a separate subsidiary to handle classified work with the Pentagon. Through a voting trust or proxy agreement, foreign shareholders agree to eliminate completely any rights to control, influence, or direct the operations or strategic direction of the subsidiary. Through these agreements, the foreign owners vest all of their rights and privileges as shareholders—except for receiving aggregated financial information and profits—to board members, all of whom have to be US citizens eligible for security clearances, and are appointed subject to Pentagon approval.

In practice, the other CFIUS agencies typically defer to the DOD on any defense acquisition by a foreign company. The DOD will take the lead in negotiating terms to mitigate foreign control and influence; only with an agreement with the DOD in place will CFIUS approve the transaction. Most defense acquisitions enjoy smooth sailing through CFIUS for three reasons. First, the DOD is not only the potential customer, but also the agency with authority over the NISPOM process, so most foreign acquirers of defense assets consult intensively with the DOD before filing with CFIUS. In many cases, acquirers even have informal consultations with the DOD before making an acquisition. Given that the DOD is a foreign investor's future customer, parties to a transaction are understandably loath to force a decision on it through CFIUS. Second, as mentioned above, the Pentagon has authority independent of Exon-Florio to regulate foreign acquisitions through NISPOM regulations, which are not subject to time constraints. The lack of statutory time constraints to force a DOD decision under NISPOM, and CFIUS agencies' deferral to the DOD on defense matters, make it almost pointless for parties to a transaction to start the CFIUS clock before concluding negotiations with the DOD on a mitigation agreement. Finally, a large percentage of defense acquisitions are by companies that have repeatedly been through the CFIUS process. These repeat customers have such close relations with the Pentagon that they typically know the Pentagon's boundaries for acceptable and unacceptable acquisitions. In certain cases, frequent acquirers negotiate "umbrella" SSAs, under which trusted foreign defense contractors can place future acquisitions without needing to negotiate a new agreement.

Unlike the NSAs that CFIUS imposes on foreign parties in the telecommunications sector, SSAs remain confidential between the US government and the other signatory parties. It is difficult, therefore, to discern trend lines in the DOD's and CFIUS's approaches to foreign investment in the defense sector. Some steps appear to have been taken toward the end of the second Clinton administration to relax somewhat the controls that CFIUS imposes on foreign investors. In 1999 a senior defense official cited three steps to "improve the Department's industrial security policies": issuing an SSA to the Thomson-CSF aircraft training and simulation unit in Arlington, Texas, simplifying the national interest determination process for GEC Marconi's acquisition of Tracor, Inc., and removing a previous requirement for a proxy company so that Rolls Royce/Allison could be governed by a standard SSA.[95] For the most part, the Bush administration appears to have shown flexibility in foreign acquisitions of defense contractors. However, given the broader strategic factors at play since September 11, 2001, it seems reasonable to conclude that there has been some retrenchment compared with the relative liberalization of the late 1990s.

■ ■ ■

As discussed above, the Exon-Florio statute establishes a review process granting the president and CFIUS agencies remarkable flexibility, which CFIUS agencies have fully utilized by broadening their view of national security since September 11, 2001, and negotiating much tougher NSAs in recent telecommunications acquisitions. Notwithstanding the enhanced scrutiny by CFIUS agencies, a number of members of Congress and the GAO have recommended giving security concerns further weight under the Exon-Florio statute. These and other ideas for reforming Exon-Florio are discussed in chapter 6. But what are the economic effects of foreign investment in the United States in the first place? How much does the United States stand to gain or lose through tougher FDI regulations? These questions are taken up in the next chapter.

---

95. Speech by Jacques S. Gansler, Under Secretary of Defense (Acquisition and Technology) at the Defense Industry Business Forum, Toulouse, France, "International Defense Cooperation: The New Environment," December 6, 1999, available at www.acq.osd. mil (accessed March 7, 2006).

3

The Economic Effects
of Foreign Investment
in the United States

As noted in the previous chapter, since the passage of the Exon-Florio Amendment, a number of members of Congress have argued that the Committee on Foreign Investment in the United States (CFIUS) should assess the impact of a foreign acquisition on the "economic security" as well as the "national security" of the United States. These proposals to expand Exon-Florio's criteria seem to presume that foreign direct investment (FDI), or some subset of it, could harm US economic interests. In this chapter, we argue that the vast preponderance of evidence supports the opposite conclusion, that FDI creates benefits for the economy. There might be exceptions to this, but they are rare and difficult to identify. Had the Exon-Florio Amendment required screening measures to protect the "economic security" of the United States, it would most likely have caused, and not prevented, damage to the US economy. We examine the effects of FDI on the US economy, in particular on the US international economic situation overall; US workers; research and development (R&D); long-run US economic growth; and generation of externalities (or "spillovers") that might affect the US economy, either positively or negatively.

Importance of FDI to the US Economy

As mentioned in chapter 1, the effects of FDI on the US economy must be examined in the context of the current international economic position of the United States. The United States is heavily dependent on continuing

Box 3.1   The macroeconomic basis for the US balance of payments deficit on current account

The national income identities are

$$Y = C + I + G + (X - M)$$

where Y is national product on an output basis, C is goods and services produced for consumption, I is goods and services produced for investment, G is goods and services produced for the government, X is exports of goods and services, and M is imports of goods and services; also

$$Y = C + S_{priv} + (T - Tr)$$

where Y again is national product (but on a factor payments basis; but this is the same as national product on an output basis), C is goods and services consumed (again, this must be the same as C in the previous equation), S_{priv} is private savings, T is government revenue, and Tr is net transfers to the public by the government.

Subtract the second of these identities from the first, and note that aggregate national savings S can be defined as $S = S_{priv} - (G - T + Tr)$, to get

$$I = S + (M - X)$$

or, written out more fully,

$$I = S_{priv} - (G - T + Tr) + (M - X)$$

This last identity tells us that domestic investment must be financed by domestic savings (where a government budget deficit counts as a subtraction from this savings) plus a capital inflow or outflow, where the inflow (outflow) is exactly equal to the balance of payments on the current account (essentially, the difference between exports and imports; in practice, this must be adjusted for any net unilateral transfers from the domestic economy to foreign economies).

We can conclude that as long as a nation such as the United States (i) invests more than it generates in private savings and (ii) in net, the government (including federal, state, and local governments) runs a budget deficit, the nation will have to finance the two shortfalls from abroad, and the amount of financing needed from abroad will be equal to the balance of payments on the current account, which will itself be in deficit.

inflows of foreign investment, because US savings, net of the drain on these savings created by public-sector deficits, are insufficient to finance domestic investment. As a consequence, the United States must import savings from abroad, generating net capital inflows—or, equivalently, net foreign investment—into the United States. As shown in box 3.1, the amount of foreign investment required is exactly equal to the US balance of payments deficit. This deficit for 2005 was slightly greater than $800 bil-

Table 3.1   Gross capital inflows into the United States, by type of flow, 2005

Type of inflow	Billions of dollars	Percent of total capital flows
Foreign direct investment in the United States	128.6	9.9
Private foreign purchases of US Treasury securities	196.8	15.2
Private foreign purchases of US securities other than US Treasury securities[a]	489.2	37.8
Increase in liabilities to private foreign persons by nonbanking concerns[b]	62.2	4.8
Increase in US liabilities to private foreign persons by US banks, not reported elsewhere[c]	175.7	13.6
Increase in US currency held by foreign persons	19.4	1.5
Increase in assets held in the US by foreign governments	220.7	17.1
Total	1,292.7	100.0

a. Mostly consist of stocks and bonds issued by US corporations.
b. Mostly increases in accounts payable by US business concerns to foreign creditors.
c. Increases in bank deposits held by foreigners in US banks.

Source: US Bureau of Economic Analysis, US International Transactions, available at www.bea.gov; figures are preliminary.

lion, implying that the United States needed to import in excess of $2 billion per day during 2005 to close the gap between domestic investment and saving. Failing to do so would create the risk of interest rates rising significantly, with the likely consequence of curtailing investment, growth, and productivity.

Capital inflows into the United States take a number of forms, of which FDI is only one. As table 3.1 shows, in 2005, gross foreign investment into the United States was $1.44 trillion, of which FDI was about $128.6 billion or about 9.9 percent of total capital inflow. But also the US government, companies, and individuals expanded their ownership of foreign assets by $801 billion. Thus net foreign investment in the United States was $491.2 billion, not counting a statistical discrepancy of about $9.6 billion, which was the difference between net recorded capital flows and the measured balance of payments on current accounts: As just noted and explained in box 3.1, the balance of payments and net capital flows must be equal.

That the United States is likely to continue to need net foreign investment does not, however, create any guarantee whatsoever that FDI will actually continue to flow into the country. FDI requires both that there be fa-vorable investment opportunities in the United States for foreign firms, and that US policies toward this investment do not deter it. Given that the gap between US investment and savings is unlikely to disappear any time soon, it would be unwise for the United States to take actions that would unnecessarily deter FDI. Policymakers thus must consider the risk of chill-ing FDI when contemplating changes to the Exon-Florio Amendment. While the United States must respond to any national security threat that an investment might create, the nation can hardly afford to invent nonex-istent threats, and by so doing, quite possibly deter or even drive away a significant amount of investment.

The United States is likely to remain dependent upon foreign invest-ment continuing to flow into the economy, irrespective of what form that investment takes. In the remaining sections of this chapter, we argue that, especially in light of this dependence, FDI in the United States is a desir-able form of investment. It would generate net benefits to the United States even if there were no dependence on it; with this dependence, how-ever, the importance of FDI to the US economy cannot be overstated.

FDI's Effects on US Workers

In 2003, US affiliates of foreign investors employed 5,253,000 workers in the United States.[1] This might suggest that FDI in the United States in 2003 created this number of jobs, but it would be something of a reach to claim that without FDI, there would have been 5,253,000 fewer jobs in the country. The overall number of workers employed in the US economy at any one time is largely determined by macroeconomic and fiscal policy; however, actions of the federal government on fiscal policy, and the Fed-eral Reserve on monetary policy, do not directly determine whether jobs are created by domestic or foreign investment. It is entirely possible that, had there been no FDI in the United States, domestic employers would have created jobs in sufficient numbers to offset the loss of US jobs that currently exist in foreign-controlled firms. When one examines the effects of FDI on US workers, largely at issue is not how many jobs are created by investment, but rather, the quality of those jobs. Above all else, job quality can be measured by compensation to workers. Do foreign in-vestors in the United States pay workers higher or lower compensation than similar domestic investors do?

An earlier study of FDI in the United States by Edward Graham and Paul Krugman (1994) noted that, in the manufacturing sector, foreign in-vestors in the United States on average paid higher wages than all US

---

1. US Bureau of Economic Analysis, available at www.bea.gov (accessed March 10, 2006).

manufacturing employers did.[2] But this study also noted that this might be due to a "selection bias" in foreign investment, in that it tends to occur disproportionately in activities for which wages paid, whether by domestic US firms or foreign-controlled ones, are higher than the national average (on selection bias, see box 3.2). This possibility has been borne out by subsequent studies based on less aggregated data than the original study (Doms and Jensen 1998). Within the manufacturing sector, foreign-controlled firms are relatively concentrated in the chemical, computer and electronic equipment, and transportation equipment subsectors. These pay higher wages and salaries than average for the entire manufacturing sector, and thus even if foreign-controlled firms were to pay average wage and salary within these subsectors, they would be above average for the manufacturing sector as a whole.

However, within major manufacturing subsectors in which foreign-controlled firms have a significant presence, those firms pay higher annual wages and salaries than the average firms in the subsector do (table 3.2a). Foreign-controlled firms employ at least 100,000 workers in the United States in eight manufacturing subsectors; in seven out of the eight, foreign firms pay more than the overall US average wage and salary within those subsectors. The sole exception is transportation equipment, the dominant component of which is automotive manufacturing—and even within this subsector, wages and salaries paid by foreign-controlled firms are only slightly below average for the subsector.

The gap between the higher wages and salaries paid by foreign-controlled firms and those paid on average in these subsectors could be accounted for by selection bias within the subsector: Foreign-controlled firms might be more heavily concentrated in those activities within subsectors in which wages and salaries are higher than average anyway. It is not entirely clear from the data whether this is so. What is clear is that the higher wages paid by foreign-controlled firms within the manufacturing sector are not explained fully by selection bias across the entire sector. Moreover, the gap between wages and salaries paid by foreign-controlled firms and the average wage and salary does not disappear if one looks beyond the manufacturing sector (see table 3.2b). In every nonmanufacturing subsector in which there is significant participation by foreign-controlled firms, foreign firms pay higher wages on average.

If these differences are not due to industry selection bias, then why do they exist? There could be biases other than industry selection bias in the data. The data on the entire industry are from the Bureau of the Census, which organizes its data on an "establishment" basis—that is, the data are classified by industry for individual facilities or establishments. The data for majority-owned affiliates of foreign investors are from the Bureau of

---

2. It is appropriate to examine the manufacturing sector because FDI in the United States occurs most heavily in this sector; see chapter 1.

Box 3.2   Selection bias in wage averaging and the distortions it can create

To illustrate what "selection bias" in averaging is, and how this bias can distort results, we use a very simple hypothetical example. Suppose there is a nation (call it "Vidalia") where all manufacturing consists of just two subsectors, "high tech" and "low tech." Suppose that each subsector employs half of the nation's total manufacturing workforce. The average hourly wage in high tech is $30, but in low tech, only $10. Then the average wage in the Vidalian manufacturing industry would be $20 per hour (half the workers make $30 per hour and half make $10 per hour). Low-tech workers cannot easily advance to high-tech jobs because they lack critical technical skills.

Suppose now that a US-based multinational firm acquires a Vidalian firm that operates in high tech and employs half of all high-tech workers. Under US ownership—which, from the Vidalian point of view, is foreign ownership—this firm continues to pay the same wage as under Vidalian ownership.

In one sense, nothing changes. Wages in Vidalia, and in Vidalian high tech, are the same as they were as before the foreign investment. Moreover, the now US-owned firm pays exactly the same wage as Vidalian firms in the same subsector.

But in the foreign-owned portion of the manufacturing sector, the average wage is now $30 per hour, whereas the average wage in all Vidalian manufacturing remains $20. So in Vidalia, foreign-owned firms pay a higher than average wage in the manufacturing sector. Additionally, because the Vidalian high-tech subsector is now only 50 percent domestically owned, the average wage paid by domestically owned manufacturing firms is now $16.67 ($1/3 \times $30 + 2/3 \times 10), so foreign-owned firms on average pay nearly twice the wages domestically owned firms.

These arguably distorted wage averages are then the result of selection bias. In effect, the workers employed by foreign-owned firms are "selected" from a different, and higher paid, subpopulation of workers than the entire population of all manufacturing workers. The distortions disappear when average wages are presented at the relevant subsectoral level. Nonetheless, an overenthusiastic advocate of foreign direct investment in Vidalia might use the averages to claim that foreign-owned enterprises pay better than do domestically owned enterprises.

In chapter 3, we argue that selection bias accounts for some—but not all—of the wage premium that foreign investors apparently pay in the United States. Foreign investors in the United States seem to pay more than do domestic firms, even when operating in the same sectors or activities. However, when selection bias is accounted for, the difference in wages favoring foreign investors is not as great as aggregated averages might suggest.

Table 3.2a   Workforce, wages, and salaries of workers by manufacturing subsector, majority-owned affiliates of foreign investors in the United States and entire subsector, 2003

| | Majority-owned affiliates of foreign investors in the United States | | Entire subsector | |
| | Number of workers (thousands) | Average annual wages and salaries per worker (dollars) | Number of workers (thousands) | Average annual wages and salaries per worker (dollars) |
Subsector				
Food processing	114.7	42,528	1,496.0	31,144
Chemicals	305.4	82,904	841.4	57,680
Plastics and rubber products	120.9	43,011	1,096.6	29,296
Nonmetallic mineral products	153.4	44,902	467.6	38,680
Primary and fabricated metals	144.2	49,570	1,998.0	38,359
Machinery	247.6	54,960	1,129.1	43,392
Computers and electronic products	219.8	67,020	1,189.5	55,976
Transportation equipment (includes autos)	377.1	49,180	1,606.7	49,771

Note: This table includes subsectors where majority-owned affiliates of foreign investors employ 100,000 or more workers.

Sources: Bureau of Economic Analysis, Foreign Affiliate Data, available at www.bea.gov. Entire subsector data from Bureau of the Census, US Employment by Sector, available at censtats.census.gov.

Economic Analysis (BEA), which organizes its data on an "enterprise" basis—that is, the data are classified by industry for affiliates of foreign investors. As a result, the BEA data might include a higher percentage of professional or managerial employees, as opposed to manufacturing production workers, than the Census data do. This makes some sense: If a manufacturing firm has a central headquarters operation, or an R&D facility, separate from its production operations, then on an establishment basis, workers in such an operation would be classified as being in the "professional, scientific, and managerial services" sector rather than in the manufacturing sector. On an enterprise basis, the same workers might be placed in the manufacturing sector. Given that personnel in a central headquarters operation or in an R&D facility are likely to be paid more

Table 3.2b   Wages and salaries paid by majority-owned affiliates of foreign firms operating in the United States and average wages and salaries, selected nonmanufacturing sectors, 2003 (annual wages and salaries per worker in dollars)

	Majority-owned affiliates of foreign firms	Entire sector
Wholesale trade	58,333	46,111
Retail trade	23,728	21,487
Information services (includes publishing and telecom)	60,402	56,675
Professional, scientific, and managerial services	65,340	54,244

Sources: Bureau of Economic Analysis, Foreign Affiliate Data, available at www.bea.gov. Entire sector data: Bureau of the Census, available at censtats.census.gov.

than those in a production facility, the data organized on an enterprise basis will show higher wages in the manufacturing sector than do the same data organized on an establishment basis.

But the differences in the way the data are organized by enterprise are not likely to account for all of the differences in wages and salaries. For one thing, some foreign firms have multiple US affiliates. One affiliate might specialize in manufacturing, while another specializes in R&D. Under this example, data generated on an enterprise basis will be comparable with data generated on an establishment basis. As a result, the biases in the data will be reduced. The BEA data for majority-owned affiliates of foreign investors include a large data category for the professional, technical, and managerial services sector. Thus not all of the professional and managerial personnel employed in foreign-controlled manufacturing firms are classified in the manufacturing sector. Likewise, not all such personnel employed by domestically controlled firms will appear in the professional, technical, and managerial services sector, because some of those personnel work inside production facilities.

Another possibility to explain the wage and salary difference noted in tables 3.2a and 3.2b above is simply that, within the United States, even controlling for distribution of activity by sector or subsector, multinational firms pay higher wages on average than nonmultinational firms do, regardless of whether those firms are ultimately under foreign or domestic control. We can explore empirically whether this bias exists, as the BEA produces the relevant data for the parent firms of US-controlled multinationals. These data are organized on an enterprise basis, as are data for majority-owned affiliates of foreign investors. One would expect the lat-

Table 3.2c Compensation per employee, by manufacturing subsector, US parents of US-controlled multinational firms versus majority-owned affiliates of foreign investors operating in the United States, 2003 (average compensation per employee in dollars)

Subsector	US parents of US-controlled multinational firms	Majority-owned affiliates of foreign investors in the United States
Food products	46,565	57,035
Chemicals	86,652	102,551
Plastics and rubber products	54,623	58,371
Nonmetallic mineral products	55,940	58,904
Primary and fabricated metals	53,841	64,487
Machinery	66,357	68,700
Computers and electronic products	74,723	82,803
Transportation equipment	66,177	64,163

Source: Bureau of Economic Analysis, available at www.bea.gov.

ter to pay lower wages than US parents of multinational firms do, because the parents of US-controlled multinationals would be expected to have a higher percentage of their worldwide managerial and technical persons located in the United States than would foreign-controlled multinationals. But the data show the opposite to be the case.

Table 3.2c presents relevant data. Measures used in this table are no longer average wages and salaries paid to employees, but rather average compensation, which includes wages, salaries, and fringe benefits.[3] These data, however, show almost the same results as the data in table 3.2a: Controlling for industry, affiliates of foreign-controlled firms in the United States pay more than the average compensation paid by US parents of multinationals.

While it is unclear whether domestic investment would replace jobs supported by foreign investment if foreign investment were withdrawn, it is clear that FDI creates desirable US jobs at very good wages. Wages paid by foreign affiliates tend to be at the top of the scale for the sector in which the investment is located, particularly in manufacturing. In a sense,

---

3. Why this difference? The answer lies in the underlying data; in the Bureau of the Census data, we could find information only on wages and salaries, whereas in the BEA data for US multinational parent firms, we could find information only on compensation. Fortunately, for the majority-owned affiliates of foreign investors, we could find data for compensation in wages and salaries.

then, one of the ways to slow the decline in the US manufacturing base would be to attract additional foreign investment.

FDI and US Research and Development

Economists largely agree that the major long-run driver of per capita economic growth is technological progress, which enables goods and services to be produced more efficiently, driving real price reductions. Technological progress also leads to product improvements and new product innovation that, in turn, improve peoples' lives. Does anyone want to go back to driving the automobiles of the 1950s, watch television on receivers of that era, or be limited to 1950s telephone technology or prices?

Corporate R&D is a major source of technological progress, although it is far from being the only such source;[4] the case can be made that technological progress benefits an economy irrespective of where that progress is first achieved, because new technologies diffuse rapidly across the globe. This is particularly true when multinational firms create new technologies, because the firms are capable of very rapid international intrafirm technology transfer. From a US national interest perspective, an important question is whether or not foreign firms that invest in the United States are innovators of new technologies. To a very large extent, the answer to this question rests on the global capabilities of these firms, and not whether or not the underlying R&D is actually performed in the United States.

Recognizing that the United States benefits from technology created overseas, we focus here primarily on how much, and how often, foreign-based multinational firms perform R&D inside the United States. The extent to which this happens might not be as relevant to the long-run economic interest of the United States as the amount of R&D these same firms perform globally. Even so, important benefits are associated with US-based R&D activity. Many economists believe that privately performed R&D creates "spillover" effects—positive effects that are not captured by the firm that performs the R&D, but rather by the community in which the R&D is performed. Scientists or researchers could be part of a team that undertakes important R&D work for a private entity. Those scientists could either move to other firms, bringing their technical knowledge and skills with them, or they could share knowledge with other scientists through formal or informal means of communication. Because of this spillover effect, evidence suggests that large "clusters" of R&D activity that are concentrated in a particular location are more productive than an equal amount of R&D activity spread over a large geographic territory. Thus to the extent that foreign investors perform R&D in the United

---

4. Other sources include universities and government laboratories, and some technological progress is created in private, for-profit corporations, but not in formal R&D facilities.

Table 3.3a   R&D expenditures by majority-owned affiliates of foreign investors in the United States, and by US parents of US-based multinational firms, by sector or subsector, 2003
(billions of dollars)

Sector or subsector	Majority-owned US affiliates of foreign investors	US parents of US-based multinational firms
All sectors	29.52	140.10
All manufacturing	22.02	112.94
Chemicals	9.41	34.65
Of which: Pharmaceuticals	7.97	25.58
Machinery	1.56	8.09
Computers and electronics	5.12	33.52
Of which:		
Computers	0.76	7.06
Communications equipment	1.77	10.34
Semiconductors	0.43	11.52
Transportation equipment	3.52	23.78
Of which: Autos	3.26	17.26
Wholesale trade	5.14	2.72
Information services	0.85	9.91
Professional, scientific, and technical services	1.13	10.74
Of which: Computer systems design	0.19	9.00

Sources: Bureau of Economic Analysis, available at www.bea.gov.

States, they are quite likely to place their facilities in existing clusters and, by doing so, enhance the aggregate output of these clusters.

From a national security perspective, it also matters in certain circumstances where R&D takes place, because if hostilities occur and connections are broken among the component organizations of a large, multinational firm, it may be important to be able to access the R&D capability of that firm. Such access is most assured, of course, if those capabilities are in the United States, and not abroad.

Given its national security importance, it is reassuring that foreign-controlled firms perform a significant amount of R&D in the United States. Table 3.3a indicates, by sector and subsector, total expenditures for R&D by majority-owned US affiliates of foreign investors during 2003, comparing them with similar expenditures by the US parents of US-based multinational firms. The data include those sectors and subsectors that are the most R&D intensive. US parents of US-based multinational firms spent massively on R&D in the United States ($141.1 billion), but majority-owned affiliates of foreign investors spent very large amounts as well ($29.5 billion). In both cases, the amount of R&D performed by companies operating in the manufacturing sector predominates. Parents classified as operating in the manufacturing sector account for 80 percent of all R&D performed by US parents of multinationals. Similarly, 75 percent of all R&D performed by US affiliates of foreign investors is accounted for by affiliates in the manufacturing sector. However, for US affiliates of foreign investors, some $5.1 billion of R&D is listed as being performed in the wholesale trade sector, almost surely by certain large foreign automotive firms, the activities of which include both manufacturing and importing vehicles. Because these data are classified on an enterprise basis, all data are put into the sector category pertaining to the primary activity of the firm, which for certain automotive firms is importing autos (a subset of wholesale trade), even though these same firms also manufacture finished vehicles in the United States. Arguably, the R&D data for these firms would be more properly placed in the manufacturing sector: Assuming that all R&D listed for US affiliates of foreign investors appearing in the wholesale trade category is in fact performed by these automotive firms, if this R&D were to be properly placed in manufacturing, that sector would account for almost 92 percent of all R&D done by US affiliates of foreign investors in the United States.

Although the amount of R&D undertaken in the United States by foreign-controlled firms is very large, as the data show, it is not nearly as large as the amount performed by US-based firms. But the aggregate size of foreign-controlled operations in the United States is also significantly smaller than domestic operations under the control of US-based multinationals. How then, does the amount of R&D performed by foreign-controlled firms in the United States compare with R&D undertaken by US-based multinationals in this country, controlling for overall size of operations? Table 3.3b compares, for the same sectors and subsectors, the amount of R&D performed by each type of firm, divided by US value added by those firms. The value added is the contribution of the firms to US GDP. Normalizing by value added produces what we think is a valid comparison.

Table 3.3b indicates that US parents of US-based multinational firms invest slightly more in R&D as a percentage of overall contribution to US GDP. US firms spend about 7.1 percent of value added on R&D, whereas the majority-owned affiliates of foreign investors spend about 6.1 percent of value added on R&D. A difference exists, but the affiliates of foreign investors do not lag behind parents of US multinationals by very much. It is, in fact, rather surprising that foreign investors' R&D spending as a percentage of value added approximates R&D spending by the parents of US-based multinationals at all, given that most firms tend to concentrate their R&D activities close to their worldwide headquarters, which are typically located in a company's home country. In manufacturing, the gap between R&D divided by value added is somewhat greater than it is in other sectors. US parents spend about 13 percent of value added on R&D, whereas

Table 3.3b   R&D expenditures by majority-owned affiliates of foreign investors in the United States, and by US parents of US-based multinational firms, by sector or subsector, divided by value added, 2003 (ratio)

Sector or subsector	Majority-owned US affiliates of foreign investors	US parents of US-based multinational firms
All sectors	0.061	0.071
All manufacturing	0.097	0.130
Chemicals	0.188	0.251
Of which: Pharmaceuticals	0.283	0.372
Machinery	0.079	0.113
Computers and electronics	0.281	0.301
Of which:		
Computers	0.334	0.294
Communications equipment	0.392	0.346
Semiconductors	0.206	0.376
Transportation equipment	0.100	0.165
Of which: Autos	0.102	0.206
Wholesale trade	0.061	0.029
Information services	0.032	0.038
Professional, scientific, and technical services	0.063	0.106
Of which: computer systems design	0.065	0.210

Source: Bureau of Economic Analysis, available at www.bea.gov.

majority-owned affiliates of foreign investors spend about 10 percent. However, in some subsectors of manufacturing, the results are reversed. In the computer manufacturing and communications equipment subsectors, which include telecommunications equipment, the affiliates of foreign firms spend a greater portion of value added on R&D than US parents do.

In addition, majority-owned affiliates of foreign investors in the United States spend more on R&D, both as an absolute amount and as a percent of value added, than do affiliates of US multinational firms operating abroad. Some relevant figures are contained in table 3.3c.

The data thus show that while majority-owned affiliates of foreign investors spend about $29.5 billion on R&D in the United States, overseas affiliates of US multinationals spend about $22.3 billion. And though R&D expenditure made by US-based firms abroad does not lag behind R&D expenditure by foreign-based firms in the United States by much, the US economy accounts for approximately one-fifth of the global economy. In other words, the United States accounts for a disproportionate amount of R&D activity, further demonstrated by the fact that the R&D expenditures of majority-owned affiliates of foreign investors measured as a fraction of value added (0.061) is about double that of the affiliates of US multina-

Table 3.3c   R&D expenditures by majority-owned affiliates of foreign investors in the United States and by affiliates of US multinationals abroad, 2003

Sector or subsector	Majority-owned affiliates of foreign investors		Affiliates of US multinationals abroad	
	Gross expenditure on R&D (billions of dollars)	R&D as fraction of value added	Gross expenditure on R&D (billions of dollars)	R&D as fraction of value added
All sectors	29.52	0.061	22.33	0.032
Manufacturing	22.02	0.097	19.90	0.057
Of which:				
Chemicals	9.41	0.188	5.07	0.068
Pharmaceuticals	7.97	0.283	4.26	0.113
Computers and electronics	5.12	0.281	4.73	0.134
Transportation equipment	3.52	0.100	6.48	0.131
Wholesale trade	5.14	0.061	0.18	0.002
Information services	0.85	0.032	0.75	0.026
Professional, scientific, and technical services	1.13	0.063	1.04	0.028

Source: Bureau of Economic Analysis, available at www.bea.gov.

tionals abroad (0.032). Moreover, in 2003, total worldwide R&D expenditures of US-based multinationals was about $162.4 billion, including those of US parents and their overseas affiliates. Of this amount, over 86 percent was spent in the United States.

How do other nations fare with respect to R&D done in their territories by foreign-based firms, and R&D done in their territories by US-based firms in particular? It is hard to say, because international data are sparse. However, some relevant, albeit incomplete, data have been published in the most recent United Nations Conference on Trade and Development's *World Investment Report 2005* (UNCTAD 2005, annex table A.IV.1). UNCTAD estimates that in 2002, the amount of R&D expenditures in advanced nations by firms not based in these nations was about $62 billion, or about 15.7 percent of all R&D expenditures in those nations. In that year, foreign-controlled firms spent about $27.5 billion on R&D in the United States; in other words, about 44 percent of the total of such expenditures in advanced nations by nonlocally based firms seemed to take place in the United States. In developing nations, nonlocally based firms expended about $4.1 billion on R&D in 2002, or about 18 percent of all such expenditure in these nations. Worldwide, but excluding the United States, expenditures on R&D by nonlocally based firms was $39.4 billion. This suggests that US-based firms' R&D expenditures outside the United States account for as much as three-fourths of the total of such expenditures worldwide by nonlocally based firms. But, again, one must realize that all of the numbers cited in this paragraph are based on imperfect data, and thus must be interpreted with caution and even skepticism.

FDI and Economic Growth

We have shown that foreign investors pay high wages and salaries, and that foreign-controlled firms contribute significantly to US R&D. We now turn to the question of whether FDI in the United States has a measurable positive effect on US economic growth in the long run. While the preponderance of research on this issue demonstrates a positive link between FDI and long-term growth, there have not been studies on the specific effects of foreign investment on US growth, and for good reason. For technical reasons, it is difficult to measure precisely the effect on growth of the most important determinants of economic growth, and even more difficult to measure precisely the effect of FDI on growth, because economists consider foreign investment to be a minor determinant of growth. Most economists who study the issue agree that the major determinants of long-run economic growth are the total amount of capital available for production; the rate at which this capital stock is augmented; the vintage, quality, and sectoral distribution of capital stock; the levels and composition of the skills of the workforce, including at the technical and managerial levels; the rate at which new workers enter the workforce and old workers exit it; and the rate and direction in which new technology enters the economy. FDI is less important than any of these determinants. In addition, foreign investment can affect several of these determinants to some extent, but is not a dominant force behind any of them. As noted in the previous section, foreign-controlled firms conduct a significant amount of R&D in the United States. These firms are easily able to transfer new technologies developed outside the country into their US operations. Thus the rate and direction of new technology into or out of the US economy is to some extent affected by FDI. As a result, FDI almost surely exerts some positive effect on US growth through technology. But purely domestic sources of new technology are more important determinants of growth than are FDI-related sources. Alas, it is difficult, again for technical reasons, to measure precisely even the exact contribution of all technological advances on economic growth, and virtually impossible to isolate the contribution of foreign-source technology.[5]

---

5. To measure the contribution of technology to economic growth, one must specify a production function for the US economy. There are a number of ways to specify such a function, all of which would be acceptable to an econometrician, and different specifications yield somewhat different results for this contribution. Thus while it is possible to determine a "ballpark" figure for this contribution, we cannot with confidence estimate a very precise figure.

Although we cannot precisely measure the effect of FDI on growth, we should not abandon the question entirely as to whether FDI in the United States helps to generate growth. The question has long been debated by economists, though considerable, but not unequivocal, evidence suggests that there is a positive link. To begin, FDI is associated with higher international trade, which in turn leads to increased efficiency, enhanced competition, and positive externalities, all of which tend to accelerate economic growth. Moreover, a number of studies have appeared in the recent literature on the empirical relationship between FDI and economic growth using various methodologies and datasets. Most of these studies indicate a positive and significant relationship, though a number of the results must be qualified, and one important study concludes that a positive and significant such relationship does not exist (Carkovic and Levine 2005).

Most of the studies use panel data to compare results across both countries and time. Until very recently, such studies were performed using ordinary least squares estimators, a technical matter touched upon below. Blomström, Lipsey, and Zejan (1994), prominent international economics professors at the Stockholm (Sweden) School of Economics, Queens University New York, and the International Monetary Fund, find that FDI positively affects growth if and only if a national wealth threshold is reached. In other words, FDI does not positively affect growth if a country is quite poor. Balasubramanyam, Salisu, and Sapsford (1996), three researchers at the International Monetary Fund, also find a positive relationship, but only if the country is open to international trade. This result is not inconsistent with the results of Blomström et al. (1994) because in recent history poorer countries have tended to be less open to trade than richer countries have. Borensztein, de Gregorio, and Lee (1998), also at the International Monetary Fund, find a positive relationship as well, but only if a country meets a threshold level of education. Again, this finding is generally consistent with the earlier results, as poorer countries tend to have less well-educated populations than do richer ones—although Blomström et al. (1994) consider education as a conditioning variable and do not find it to be significant. Alfaro et al. (2003), researchers at the World Bank, also find a positive relationship but only in countries with well-developed financial markets; again, this is roughly consistent with earlier findings because richer countries have better-developed financial markets than poorer ones do.

Finally, using a later and larger data set than Blomström et al. (1994), Blonigen and Wang (2005), both researchers at the US National Bureau of Economic Research, find that FDI affects growth more in developing (poorer) countries than in developed (richer) ones. This last finding is not wholly consistent with the others, and might be explained by a number of factors, including that the data are more recent, and hence strongly affected by economic growth in China, where there has been considerable FDI. Also, much recent FDI among developed nations, in contrast to earlier times, has taken the form of cross-border mergers and acquisitions (M&As). Blonigen and Wang (2005) speculate that M&As might have a weaker effect on growth than greenfield FDI, discussed in chapter 1. Kumar and Pradhan (2005) use new panel data estimation techniques to adjust for certain shortcomings of ordinary least squares estimators to test whether FDI has had a positive and significant effect on economic growth in the countries of South Asia. They conclude in the affirmative.

However, Carkovic and Levine (2005) find that while FDI has a positive effect on growth, it is not significant. They use the same estimator that Kumar and Pradhan use, but apply it to a larger set of countries. It is possible that the effect of FDI on growth is positive for those countries tested by Kumar and Pradhan, but that this effect disappears when the same estimator is applied to a broader set; the Carkovic-Levine results are of particular importance precisely because they use an improved technique on a broad set of countries. Given this, however, whether or not they actually reach the right conclusion from their own analysis is open to some question. In their analysis, they at one point include an FDI variable in their set of conditioning variables, the set of variables meant to explain economic growth. This variable is positive and significant, which suggests that FDI is in fact a robust explanatory variable. But then they add to the set of conditioning variables a variable to account for openness to international trade. When they do so, FDI, while remaining positive, ceases to be statistically significant.

What can we make of this? The authors themselves conclude that FDI is not a robust determinant of growth. However, Melitz (2005), commenting on Carkovic and Levine (2005), notes that if international trade and FDI are jointly determined and if these two variables move together, then a joint link remains between economic growth and increased trade and investment. Thus Melitz argues that by linking the effects of FDI and international trade, even the Carkovic and Levine results show a positive and statistically significant effect of FDI on growth, consistent with the other six studies mentioned above.

Even leaving econometric matters not wholly resolved, it is safe to say that the majority of empirical studies support a positive link between FDI and economic growth, especially when one considers that FDI in many countries (e.g., China) has led to export growth. As suggested at the outset, and reinforced by Melitz, these gains might owe in part to efficiencies that result from joint interaction between increased trade and FDI. Economists classically see such efficiencies as having three root causes. First, openness to investment and trade enables countries increasingly to specialize in the economic areas in which they have an advantage, and to benefit from importing goods, services, and knowledge in areas in which other countries have an advantage. Second, with open investment and trade policies, countries can focus on producing a narrower range but larger output of goods and services, making production in those goods and services more

Table 3.4   Imports and exports of majority-owned affiliates of foreign investors in the United States, 2003

Sector or subsector	Imports		Exports	
	Billions of dollars	Fraction of value added by affiliates	Billions of dollars	Fraction of value added by affiliates
All sectors	356.66	0.733	150.82	0.310
Manufacturing	138.97	0.610	93.26	0.410
Of which:				
Food	2.05	0.220	7.40	0.795
Chemicals	21.08	0.422	16.07	0.322
Pharmaceuticals	13.21	0.469	6.34	0.225
Plastics and rubber products	4.74	0.527	2.53	0.281
Primary and fabricated metals	6.78	0.550	3.71	0.301
Machinery	9.25	0.466	8.65	0.435
Computers and electronic	24.22	1.060	13.99	0.612
Wholesale trade	206.50	2.463	53.11	0.633
Information	1.06	0.039	1.01	0.038
All other sectors	5.82	0.087	2.24	0.034

Source: Bureau of Economic Analysis, available at www.bea.gov.

efficient though increased economies of scale. Third, increased trade and more open investment policies lead to increases in effective competition, forcing firms to price competitively, thus creating incentives for these firms to reduce costs and improve product quality. Importantly, these benefits are generated by increased trade (both imports and exports) and not by increased exports alone.

Is there a link between FDI in the United States and increased trade? As table 3.4 shows, in both the manufacturing and nonmanufacturing sectors, majority-owned affiliates of foreign investors create substantial exports and imports. The table contains both quantities of imports and exports accounted by these affiliates, and exports and imports as a percent of value added created by the affiliates.

As can be seen, manufacturing affiliates of foreign investors are particularly active in exports and imports. They import goods and services equal to about 61 percent of their domestic value added, and export goods and services equal to about 41 percent of their domestic value added.[6] Both imports and exports of these foreign-controlled firms contribute to US eco-

---

6. For purposes of comparison, for the economy as a whole, the value of imports of manufactured goods is equal to about 83 percent of value added in the US manufacturing sector, while the value of exports of manufactured goods is equal to about 44 percent of value added in this sector.

nomic efficiency and growth: As is also the case with US multinational firms, foreign-based firms tend to manufacture goods where it is most economical to do so. Thus substantial portions of foreign-controlled firms' imports are of parts, subassemblies, and other inputs used in US manufacturing operations. The result of this is that the overall efficiency, and hence overall cost, of the final product is reduced from what would have been the case if the final product had consisted entirely of local content. In some cases, importing inputs is complemented by importing finished goods for which US manufacture would be uneconomically inefficient. But at the same time, these firms are engaged in US production—with substantial US value added—and often, US production is more economical than overseas production is, as the very substantial exports of these firms reflect.

FDI and Spillovers

As noted in the introduction to this chapter, one way FDI can contribute to overall economic growth is by creating beneficial "spillovers" into the economy, the most important of which is technology transfer to external agents resulting from FDI. This spillover of technology can occur in a number of ways. A foreign firm may introduce new technologies or methods of business to local employees, who take the knowledge with them when they leave the foreign firm's employment. A foreign firm also may share new technology or business methods with local companies, which then may use it to serve other companies, including the foreign firm's rivals. Alternatively, the domestic employees of the foreign firm may simply leak the new technology or business method, ultimately benefiting domestic rivals.

In addition to technology transfer, localized R&D can result in important positive externalities. To create a successful R&D operation, it may be advantageous for a foreign firm to locate its operations in close proximity to similar, established operations, to access personnel with the talents and skills that it needs for its R&D activities. Such clusters of innovative activity are often found quite near major universities that supply graduates (or, in some cases, dropouts) who have the necessary talents and skills. The clustering of the R&D activity, coupled perhaps with the local university, creates externalities: R&D specialists, even if employed by different firms or nonprofit organizations, tend to talk to one another in a way that leads to a virtuous and continual exchange of ideas, permitting the firms in the area to partake of and benefit from the ideas that each generates. Silicon Valley, south of San Francisco, is an example of such a cluster, where Stanford University is the premier university.

Spillovers from clustered activities are not necessarily limited to R&D. The clustering of financial institutions in New York has almost surely created an external scale economy that generates positive externalities in the form of financial innovation. In both cases, the generation of positive externalities is doubtlessly enhanced by the fact that a well-established cluster of innovative activity tends to attract many of the best-qualified persons in the relevant field, who seek to live and work near the clusters to maintain close contact with other top specialists in the field. By locating in the cluster, foreign firms can contribute their own ideas and best-qualified people, and possibly facilitate an inward transfer of technology that the firm developed elsewhere, thereby further enhancing the positive externalities associated with the cluster.

Is there any strong evidence that US domestic activity has benefited from positive spillovers created by FDI? The best evidence that we know of comes from the automotive sector. Baily et al. (2005) examine the labor productivity gap between US-owned and foreign-owned firms from the late 1980s, when FDI began to create the so-called transplant operations in the United States of foreign auto producers, to 2002. As recently as 10 years ago, this gap was substantial and favored foreign-owned firms. By 2002, however, the gap had narrowed very considerably, such that now there is very little gap at all. Baily et al. (2005) attribute the near-closing of the gap to new technologies and managerial techniques introduced into US-owned facilities by foreign-owned facilities, especially those of Japanese-owned firms.

International evidence on whether FDI generates spillovers is mixed: Some studies show evidence of it, but others do not. In a recent survey of the literature on this subject, Lipsey and Sjöholm (2005) find that newer studies confirm spillovers more often than older ones do. Two possibilities suggest themselves: Either statistical techniques, along with the needed data, have improved with time, in which case it is possible that the spillovers have been out there for a long time but not properly recorded, or the advance of technology or a more rapid rate of its diffusion has caused an increase over time in the incidence of measurable spillovers. Either way, the evidence seems to support that spillovers occur, and we suspect that additional microanalysis in the United States of sectors other than autos will reveal their existence.

Given that FDI in the United States seems to benefit the US economy, it would follow that the United States should try to limit it to the smaller extent possible. Yet national security issues do not arise from increased levels of FDI generally, but rather when it comes from specific countries or companies that already raise concerns for the US government. As chapter 1 discussed, the United States in the past has sought to protect itself from FDI originating in Germany and Japan. Today similar sentiments are harbored toward Middle Eastern countries for their supposed links to terrorist activities, but more importantly, toward China, which, as a vast and growing economy, could one day challenge the United States in economic might. The implications associated with FDI from China for national security are thus both more fundamental and more complex than FDI from most other nations, and it thus is to China that the next chapter turns.

4

National Security Issues Related to Investments from China

As discussed in earlier chapters, much of the concern in the US Congress and the US media over foreign direct investment (FDI) in the United States during 2005, epitomized by the emotional debate over the China National Offshore Oil Corporation's (CNOOC) proposed acquisition of Unocal, focused on investment from China.[1] Such debates are often heated, emotional, and a topic of conversation throughout the country, not just in Washington.[2] The most recent debate, over the proposed acquisition of the Peninsular and Oriental Steam Navigation Company (P&O) by Dubai Ports World, is a case in point. The proposed acquisition had all of official Washington on the edge of its seat for much of early 2006, blanketed front pages of newspapers, and was the subject of countless hours of talk radio and cable television programming. From time to time, foreign acquisi-

---

1. See, e.g., the Sense of the Congress included in the fiscal 2006 Department of Defense authorization bill, discussed in chapter 1. Congress called on the president to develop a comprehensive strategy toward China, which included considering several changes to Exon-Florio. That Congress framed the possible changes in a China-specific provision of the bill demonstrates Congress's particular concerns with investment in the United States from China.

2. A CNN/Gallup/USA Today poll found that 66 percent of US voters opposed the sale of P&O to Dubai Ports World. Holly Yeager, "Ports Sale Unrest Deepens Bush Political Woes," *Financial Times*, March 9, 2006, A4. Further evidence of the emotional impact of these debates was the *Financial Times'* statement that the transaction presented President Bush with "one of the toughest political battles" in his presidency. Stephanie Kirchgaessner and Holly Yaeger, "Dubai Gets Approaches for Its US Terminals," *Financial Times*, March 9, 2006, 1.

tions of US companies hit a nerve in the United States, a pattern we have seen since the early 20th century.

The debate over investments from China is not the first time that anxiety and opposition have been directed toward a single nation. Both the US Congress and military were greatly concerned about the security implications of German direct investment in the United States during World War I. This concern motivated the passage of the Trading With the Enemy Act (TWEA) in 1917, as well as a number of sector-specific restrictions on FDI enacted during the early 1920s. Hostility toward German FDI in the United States reemerged in the 1930s. As we argued in chapter 1, some of the concern at that time was warranted, even if not all German FDI threatened US national security. Some of the FDI from Germany might actually have been to the military advantage of the United States, and not Germany, when war later broke out. In the late 1980s, Japanese investments were the subject of concern in Congress, the media, and academic circles, ultimately leading to the passage of the Exon-Florio Amendment. In hindsight, much of the furor over Japanese FDI in the United States now seems exaggerated or even downright silly.

Is, then, the present-day concern over possible security threats posed by Chinese direct investment in the United States warranted, as was concern over German FDI during the 1930s, or will it prove as exaggerated as that over investment from Japan in the 1980s? We seek to answer this question in this chapter.

China: A New Player in FDI

Throughout most of its long existence, China has been organized as a kingdom or an empire.[3] It has never been a fully functioning democracy, although a nominal democracy and, by most counts, ineffective one existed in the early 1900s. Chinese history is usually represented as falling into a series of powerful and advanced dynasties, interspersed with periods of weakness, internal chaos, and even civil war.

China has alternated between being a strong and relatively weak power. China arguably reached its apex as a world power during the Tang Dynasty, which lasted from 618 AD to 907 AD. An earlier period of strength occurred during the Han Dynasty, from 206 BC until 221 AD, coinciding to a large extent with the period during which the Roman Empire dominated in the West. A third period of significant Chinese power was the Song Dynasty (1127–1279), during which technology and industry rapidly advanced in China. Another high point was the early part of the Ming Dynasty, which lasted from 1368 AD until 1644 AD. Early in the Ming Dy-

---

3. Sources for information pertaining to the pre-1979 history of China in this section include Huang (1997), Levathes (1994), and Morton (1980).

nasty, China possessed what was by far the world's strongest navy, employing ships of advanced design and firepower that were not equaled in the West until the late 18th century. China also was relatively powerful during the early days of the Qing Dynasty (1644–1911).

However, at the end of the Han Dynasty, China splintered into three separate kingdoms that warred with each other. China was reunited under the Sui Dynasty, which was followed by the Tang Dynasty. The collapse of the Tang Dynasty was followed by another period of internal strife, during which China splintered into 15 separate entities. This ebb and flow continued until the 20th century, when China was ravaged by both internal strife and foreign intervention. This prolonged period of weakness ended only after the Communist victory in the civil war of 1947–49 and the establishment of the modern Communist state in China.

Even during periods of strength, China has often experienced internal problems. The Uighur, an ethnic minority in China but the dominant group in the western part of the Tang empire, staged a successful rebellion in 755 AD that resulted in the western lands becoming independent. The Uighur rebellion is still active in modern China. Likewise, during the Song Dynasty, the Han Chinese majority battled an ethnic minority, the Xia tribes, that occupied the upper reaches of the Yellow River valley. Defeated by the Han, many of the Xia migrated to what were then mostly unpopulated lands in the region now known as Tibet—part of China today, but also home to an active independence movement.

Thus one very important historical lesson is that the overthrow of incumbent dynasties in China, shifting borders, and ebbs and flows in the level of centralized control have often been precipitated by popular uprisings, and accompanied by bloody civil wars or periods of high social instability and economic downturn. The current Communist government was established in 1949 after a very prolonged period of internal strife, civil war, and foreign intervention. Mindful of both ancient and recent history, the Chinese leadership today constantly fears another period of popular uprising, social instability, and economic deprivation, especially if the currently high rates of growth and rising prosperity ends. These fears drive China's leaders to tightly control economic and political activity, and are invoked to justify undemocratic policies.

A second lesson is that, during periods of internal weakness and instability, China has on several occasions been subject to foreign domination and even conquest. As noted, Mongol invaders conquered a divided China in 1279–80 and established the Yuan Dynasty, which ruled until 1368. A rebellion in that year, leading to the Ming Dynasty, returned Chinese rule to China. But civil war in Ming Dynasty China in the early 1600s led to conquest by Manchurians, who created the Qing Dynasty, which stayed in power, at least nominally, until 1911. The internal weakness of the Qing Dynasty by the early 19th century led to China succumbing to British, Russian, and other foreign control or influence. Almost a century later, this lengthy period of internal turmoil and sporadic civil war within China culminated in the Japanese takeover of Manchuria in 1937, war with Japan until 1945, and the civil war of 1947–49.

A major goal of the Chinese state under the Communist Party is to never again be controlled, let alone conquered, by foreign interests. All national governments hold similar goals, of course, but recent Chinese history lends a greater urgency to these goals than is found in most nations. To Americans, the idea of the United States coming under foreign control is repugnant, but also only remotely likely. The Chinese, by contrast, take the possibility of foreign takeover seriously. Foreign intervention, including military invasion, occurred frequently in China in the 20th century. Many living Chinese remember Japanese troops occupying major Chinese cities 60 years ago, and even more can recall American troops lined up along the Yalu River bordering North Korea, under the command of a US general who talked openly of bombing and invading China. Almost all Chinese of adult age can remember the massive deployment of Soviet troops on or near China's northern borders.

These lessons must be borne in mind today, as China seeks to build its military capacity and continues to stifle domestic dissent. In the United States, we might not like either development. But we must be cognizant of the historical factors and environment driving Chinese decision making.

The xenophobia kindled by foreign intrusion into China in the latter half of the 19th century and the first half of the 20th doubtlessly contributed to the insular policies that the Communist government pursued from its rise to power in 1949 until the late 1970s. These policies closed China to all foreign commercial presence, with the exception of some Soviet and Eastern bloc trade and investment that ebbed and flowed depending on Sino-Soviet relations. The Chinese government allowed little trade with the external world, had virtually no outward direct investment, and was almost completely closed to inward direct investment. Under Mao Zedong, the economy of China was, by almost any measure, among the most closed on the planet. Rather than trade or invest with the rest of the world, China attempted to become autarkic. By any objective account and measure, the attempt at autarky was unsuccessful.[4] In spite of its past power and wealth, in 1949 China was one of the poorest countries on earth on a per capita basis, and this was still the case more than 25 years later, when Mao Zedong died.

Shortly after Mao's death in 1976, Deng Xiaoping emerged as China's new head of state. Almost from the outset, he set about implementing major changes to Chinese economic policy that would eventually reorient China toward being a more open economy. In 1978 he initiated the "open door policy," allowing limited foreign investment in the country (Jia 1994). However, this legislative change was narrow in scope, reflecting concerns

---

4. The economic history of the Maoist period in China is summarized in Lardy (1994).

that FDI entering into the country would create competition with state-owned enterprises (SOEs). As a result, the reform achieved little; almost no FDI actually came into China (Rosen 1999).

In 1979, China passed a law to create special economic zones in which foreign investors could operate export-oriented manufacturing activities free from most Chinese regulations then in force. The special economic zones had two objectives: first, to expand exports and thus overcome what had been a major constraint to development under Mao, a shortage of foreign exchange; and second, to help China upgrade its technological capabilities in certain designated sectors.

The pace of growth in inward investment to and exports from the economic zones during the late 1980s was staggering. In 1980 total FDI inflows to China were only $57 million. By 1990, FDI to China had increased more than 60 times over, to almost $3.5 billion. Approximately 70 percent of overall direct investment into China in 1990 flowed to the economic zones. Similarly, in 1985, China generated about $27 billion in worldwide exports. By 1990, exports had more than doubled to over $62 billion, with almost $8 billion, or more than one-fifth of the increase, produced by "foreign-invested enterprises," to use the Chinese term. Most of the growth in Chinese exports came from the special economic zones.[5]

In 1992, in the course of what become known as his "trip to the South," Deng visited several of the zones, noted that activity there was booming, and asked rhetorically, but in a way that signaled a change of policy, why the rest of China should not emulate this success by ending many of the restrictions that foreign investors faced.[6] Accordingly, Chinese authorities lifted most of the restrictions limiting export-related privileges to firms located in the zones, and implemented other measures liberalizing policies with respect to FDI into China. These measures were followed in 1995 by the publication of comprehensive regulations on foreign investment in China that were more transparent than those they replaced, but still much more opaque than standards for regulations in the United States and other western countries (Rosen 1999). China continued to liberalize its rules on foreign investment, and joined the World Trade Organization (WTO) in 1999, resulting in new sectors and regions being opened to foreign investment.

FDI in China exploded in the 1990s, as did exports resulting from this investment.[7] As noted, in 1990 FDI inflows into China were a bit less than

---

5. For more detailed information on the history and performance of the SEZs, see Graham (2004).

6. Todd Lappin and Orville Schell, "China Plays the Market: Capitalist Leap," *The Nation*, December 14, 1992, 727.

7. Source of FDI data: *China Statistical Yearbook 2005* and *China Statistical Yearbook 1991* (both published by Beijing, China Statistical Press), tables 18-13 (2005) and 15-10 (1991). For a more comprehensive assessment of the effects of the 1991 reforms on FDI in China, see Wei (1996) and Graham (2004).

$3.5 billion; 15 years later, in 2005, inflows were over $60.3 billion. The stock of FDI in China, about $19 billion in 1990, grew to over $562 billion in 2005. Exports generated by foreign-invested firms were, as noted, slightly under $8 billion in 1990; by 2005 these exports had grown to $444.2 billion.[8] China's total exports grew from $62 billion in 1990 to almost $762 billion in 2005. Thus the increase of $543 billion in exports of foreign-invested enterprises accounted for almost 78 percent of total growth in exports. Foreign investment in China became the main "engine" propelling China's remarkable rise as an exporter and contributed significantly to overall Chinese economic growth.[9]

In the high-income countries of Western Europe and the United States, the vast majority of inward FDI is in the form of mergers and acquisitions (M&As). By contrast, in China, M&As account for only a small fraction of total inward FDI, in part because M&As have been and continue to be largely prohibited in China, although recently there have been some moves by Chinese officials to allow acquisitions, including hostile acquisitions.[10] In 2003, the reported value of takeovers of firms within China by foreign investors was slightly over $1.6 billion, or about 3 percent of reported inward FDI flow—and 2003 was a banner year for such takeovers. Only in 1998 has the reported value of takeovers of Chinese firms been higher, at $1.28 billion. In both 2002 and 2004, the reported values of M&As in China were only slightly more than $1 billion.

Whereas the Chinese government first fostered and later embraced large amounts of inward FDI, policies supporting outward foreign investment have only recently been put in place. In its "Tenth Five-Year Plan Outline on National Economy and Social Development of the People's Republic of China," the Chinese government in 2001 officially adopted a policy encouraging Chinese companies to invest abroad.[11] Since issuing this "going out" strategy, Chinese officials have amplified the policy is speeches. For

---

8. Source for export data: General Administration of Customs, PRC, *China's Custom Statistics*, December, 2005, tables 1 and 6. For more detailed information and analysis on FDI and Chinese exports, see Lemoine (2000) and Lemoine and Ünal-Kesenci (2004).

9. See, e.g., Dayal-Gulati and Husain (2000).

10. One reason for the liberalization might be that research within the Chinese government (the Development Institute of the State Council) has concluded that existing restrictions might in fact be counterproductive for China. See Long (2005).

11. Article 4 of this five-year plan states (translated from Chinese):

Carrying Out "Going Out" Strategy

Fourth, we need to implement a "going out" strategy, encouraging enterprises with comparative advantages to make investments abroad, to establish processing operations, to exploit foreign resources with local partners, to contract for international engineering projects, and to increase the export of labor. We need to provide a supportive policy framework to create favorable conditions for enterprises to establish overseas operations. We also need to strengthen supervision and prevent the loss of state assets. (ILO 2001)

example, Wu Bangguo, the vice premier responsible for Chinese economic policy, encouraged Chinese companies to "go global" in a 2001 speech at the Xiamen Investment and Trade Fair. In his speech, Wu stated that China's "outbound investment strategy will be integrated with the continuous effort to promote foreign capital inflow to boost China's overall involvement in global economic cooperation."[12] The "going out" policy has now started to show results. In 2005, Chinese companies invested about $5.5 billion abroad. Recent overseas investments have included TCL Group's acquisition of the television and DVD operations of Thomson, a French company; Lenovo's acquisition of IBM's personal computer division; and, the largest foreign investment to date, China National Petroleum Corporation's $4.2 billion acquisition of PetroKazakhstan. For the first time, Chinese brands have also started to see success in the globalized market, including Haier (home appliances), Konka (color televisions), Jianlibao (beverage), Tsingtao (beer), and Galanze (microwave ovens) (see Hongand Sun 2004). Chinese companies have made major acquisitions of mining and other natural resource companies in Australia, Canada, South America, and Africa. As discussed earlier and also in detail in chapter 5, the largest proposed acquisition of a US company by a Chinese company, CNOOC's $18.5 billion bid for Unocal, was withdrawn amid strong opposition in Congress during the summer of 2005. One report suggests that there have been approximately 900 Chinese investments in small US companies, worth a total of approximately $1 billion (Hildebrandt International 2005, 43). While outward investment from China has grown, it still pales compared with inward investment. Table 4.1 indicates yearly outward FDI flows from China from 1997 to 2004. As can be seen, the outward flow in 2004 ($1.81 billion) was less than 3 percent of the inward flow ($60.6 billion) and, even in 2001, when outward FDI from China was relatively high, it was only about 15 percent of inward FDI. The total stock of FDI in China was $ 562.1 billion, while the total stock of Chinese FDI abroad was about $44.8 billion. China's overseas direct investment thus represents less than 8 percent of the total direct investment in China.

Unique National Security Issues Associated with Chinese Investment

The growth in outward Chinese investment, including into the United States, has forced agencies in the Committee on Foreign Investment in the United States (CFIUS) to confront its national security implications. This section explores why investments from China have become a particularly difficult national security issue for CFIUS, resulting, in some cases, in controversial and contentious reviews.

---

12. " 'Go Global' Investment Strategy Needed for Chinese Enterprises," *People's Daily*, September 12, 2001.

Table 4.1 Outward and inward direct investment, China, 1997–2004 (millions of dollars)

Year	Outward FDI flows	Inward FDI flows
1997	2,563	45,256
1998	2,634	45,463
1999	1,775	40,319
2000	916	40,715
2001	6,884	46,878
2002	2,518	52,743
2003	152	53,505
2004	1,805	60,630
	Outward FDI stock at year end	Inward FDI stock at year end
2004	44,777	562,105

Note: For reasons not wholly clear to the authors, the FDI stock numbers for China are not the sum of the flow numbers. Flow numbers as reported above are on a balance of payments basis.

Source: China Statistics Press, *China Statistical Yearbook 2005,* tables 3.5 and 18.13.

In practice, Chinese acquisitions of US firms have received heightened CFIUS scrutiny. Of the six CFIUS "investigations," or extended reviews, between January 2003 and December 2005, two—Hutchison Whampoas' proposed investment in Global Crossing and Lenovo's acquisition of IBM's personal computing business—involved acquisitions by companies based in Hong Kong or China.[13] The proposed acquisition of Unocal by CNOOC in the summer of 2005 certainly would also have required a full investigation. The authors are aware of at least two other planned acquisitions abandoned by Chinese companies, after informal discussions with CFIUS agencies or US lawyers suggested that approval would be difficult, if not impossible, to obtain. China National Aero Tech's 1990 attempt to acquire a US aerospace company is the only transaction that the president has formally blocked using his powers under Exon-Florio, although a number of other transactions have been withdrawn to avoid a negative presidential decision.

From a broad, strategic perspective, Chinese acquisitions present CFIUS with different issues and concerns than do acquisitions by companies of other major trading partners. To begin (see table 4.2), of the United States' 10 largest trading partners, China is the only one not considered a strate-

---

13. Some CFIUS agencies reportedly treated Hutchison Whampoas as a Chinese company, even though it was based in Hong Kong.

Table 4.2   Ten largest trading partners of the United States

Country	Strategic/political relationship with the United States
Canada	The United States' largest trading partner by far, with major investment flows in both directions. Like the United States, a member of NATO, Group of Seven (G-7), North American Free Trade Agreement (NAFTA), Organization of American States (OAS), Organization for Security and Cooperation in Europe (OSCE), Organization for Economic Cooperation and Development (OECD), and Asia Pacific Economic Cooperation forum (APEC).
Mexico	Large-scale human exchanges in tourism and immigration; recent rapid economic integration via NAFTA. Also a member of the OECD and OAS.
China	Now the United States' third-largest trading partner. But no friendship, commerce and navigation treaty or bilateral investment treaty; classified by the United States as a nonmarket economy; political and security relationship remains tenuous at best. Member of APEC.
Japan	Broad political and economic cooperation between the two countries. Close security relationship: US-Japan Mutual Security Treaty (1951); US-Japan Missile Defense Agreement (2004); approximately 40,000 US troops based in Japan. Member of G-7, OECD, and APEC. US-Japan Friendship, Commerce & Navigation Treaty signed 1953.
Germany	Major economic partner and European ally. Member of NATO, G-7, OECD, and OSCE, as well as an important player in the EU-US relationship. US-Germany Friendship, Commerce & Navigation Treaty signed 1954.
United Kingdom	Close defense and intelligence ally and important economic partner. Member of NATO, G-7, OECD, and OSCE, and an important player in the EU-US relationship. US-UK Commerce & Navigation Treaty signed 1815.
Korea	Significant economic partner and long-standing Asian ally. US-Republic of Korea Mutual Defense Treaty (1954); approximately 30,000 US troops based in Korea. Friendship, Commerce & Navigation Treaty signed 1956. Member of OECD and APEC.
France	Important trading partner and European ally. Member of NATO, G-7, OECD, and OSCE, and an important player in the EU-US relationship. US-France Navigation & Commerce Treaty signed 1822.
Taiwan	Significant economic partner and regional ally. United States is a major arms supplier to Taiwan, pursuant to Taiwan Relations Act of 1979. US-Taiwan Friendship, Commerce & Navigation Treaty signed 1946 (administered on nongovernmental basis by American Institute in Taiwan since 1979).
Italy	Important trading partner and European ally. Member of NATO, G-7, OECD, and OSCE. Significant voice in EU-US relationship. US-Italy Friendship, Commerce & Navigation Treaty signed 1948.

gic or political ally. Five of the United States' top 10 trading partners are members of the North Atlantic Treaty Organization (NATO), the United States' principal security alliance. In Asia, the United States has strong security ties—including mutual defense treaties and the stationing of tens of thousands of troops—with both Japan and Korea. Finally, while the United States does not maintain formal relations with the government of Taiwan, it has been Taiwan's major arms supplier for two decades.

By contrast, the United States not only lacks a strategic or military partnership with China, but the US Department of Defense (DOD), other US national security agencies, and important opinion leaders in Congress view China with great suspicion (US DOD 2005). China stands out among the United States' largest trading partners in several respects relevant to CFIUS's review of proposed inward investments. Among the United States' largest trading partners, China is alone in its level of state ownership and control of companies, and in the espionage threat assigned to it by the Federal Bureau of Investigation (FBI) and other intelligence agencies.[14] Only China is regarded as a major proliferator of sensitive technologies, including nuclear weapons technologies.

Table 4.2 highlights the gulf between the United States' weak security ties to China, its third-largest trading partner, and the otherwise close relationships with the remainder of its top 10 largest trading partners.

For these reasons, investments from Chinese companies will continue to draw scrutiny from CFIUS agencies, particularly its national security agencies. We examine these issues more deeply, discussing whether tougher scrutiny of investments in the United States by Chinese corporations is warranted.

Chinese State Control of Corporations and the Byrd Amendment

As discussed in chapter 2, the 1993 Byrd Amendment to Exon-Florio, adopted in the wake of Thomson's failed acquisition of LTV, requires an "investigation"—an extended review—for transactions "in which an entity controlled by or acting on behalf of a foreign government seeks to engage in any merger, acquisition or takeover which could result in control of a person engaged in interstate commerce that could affect the national security of the United States."[15] Although the title of this subsection is "Mandatory Investigations," CFIUS has construed the language in the

---

14. Jay Solomon, "US Sees a Big Threat from Chinese Spies, but Businesses Wonder—FBI Builds Cases, but Vague Laws, Charges of Profiling Hinder Progress—Executives Fear Chilling Effect," *Wall Street Journal*, August 10, 2005, 10.

15. Exon-Florio Amendment, § 2170(b).

Byrd Amendment as requiring more than just state control. CFIUS considers two elements when evaluating whether an investment requires an investigation under the Byrd Amendment: whether there is state control, and whether the transaction could affect US national security.[16]

For China, the question of state control can be particularly complicated. Public information about ownership of Chinese companies listed on a stock exchange is opaque, so CFIUS agencies will likely, and perhaps erroneously, presume that virtually all Chinese companies investing in the United States are controlled by the Chinese government. A Chinese company seeking CFIUS approval will likely have the burden of convincing the committee that it is not controlled by the Chinese government. Notwithstanding CFIUS's presumption, whether the Chinese government controls a particular Chinese company is not always a straightforward or simple question in reality. Many Chinese companies are at least partly owned by the state, but frequently at a provincial or local level. Alternatively, several provinces can separately own pieces of a Chinese company and, because of bureaucratic rivalries or other reasons, resist cooperation or coordination. The Exon-Florio Amendment does not distinguish between national and local control by a foreign government.

The question of state ownership and control has been complicated further by rapid changes in the way Chinese companies are governed. Since 1978, the transformation of China's SOEs has occurred in three successive phases: devolution of managerial responsibilities from the central government to SOE managers, creation of state-owned corporations, and privatization of certain corporations at both the local and central government levels (Green and Liu 2005). To grasp the nature of state ownership of Chinese public corporations, it is important to understand first how company shares are classified and allocated.

In 1992 the Chinese government created three categories of shares that a restructured SOE could issue: state shares, legal person (LP) shares, and individual shares.[17] State shares are "nontradable" shares held by the government.[18] Since early 2003, the State-Owned Assets Supervision and Administration Commission (SASAC) has managed nontradable shares for many large Chinese companies (Green 2005, 125, 126–27). LP shares are owned by domestic institutions, which are defined as stock compa-

---

16. See also the discussion of the Byrd Amendment in chapter 2.

17. For a description of share classifications, see Green and Black (2003) and Xu and Wang (1997). Company shares are owned by five types of agents: the state, LPs (institutions), tradable A–share holders (mostly individuals), employees, and foreign investors. The first three groups of owners are the main shareholders, controlling roughly 30 percent each, with employees and foreign investors together holding only 10 percent (see Xu and Wang 1997, 3).

18. Nontradable shares can only be transferred among institutions with government approval, but are not traded on either of China's two stock exchanges. See Green and Black (2003), Liu and Sun (2005, 113), Liu and Sun (2004, 403).

nies, nonbank financial institutions, and SOEs not wholly government owned; like state shares, they cannot be traded on the stock market (Xu and Wang 1997, 7). Individual shares are the only type of shares that can be owned by individuals and openly traded.

By controlling the issuance of different classes of shares, the Chinese government has prevented large-scale and rapid privatization of large, publicly traded SOEs. In the initial stages of the privatization process, only one-third of most SOE shares were sold to the public; the remaining two-thirds were nontradable and state owned (Green 2003a). Chinese authorities have recently been selling additional shares to the public (Green 2003b). Despite this apparent move toward greater privatization, however, most large publicly traded enterprises in China still remain subject to substantial control by various parts of the Chinese state government. By contrast, there has been large-scale privatization of small and medium enterprises (SMEs) in China, particularly SMEs formerly owned by provincial, town, or village governments (TVEs, or town and village enterprises). Moreover, while there has been substantial privatization of SOEs in certain sectors, such as building materials, chemicals, forestry, food processing, textiles, and other light manufacturing, the state has strengthened its control over strategic sectors, including energy, defense, financial services, and telecommunications. Green and Liu (2005, 4–9) have called this the "retreat and retain" strategy, in that the government has retreated from ownership and control of sectors exposed to foreign competition, but retained control of strategic and monopoly sectors.[19]

Academics and researchers have used two models to assess the extent of government control over Chinese public corporations. The first model relies on the official share classification to determine the extent of state control, while the second traces the chain of control back to the state through the pyramid of state shareholding entities. The official share classification system is easier to use because of the greater availability of required data. However, the pyramid approach assesses the level of state ownership of corporations more realistically, in part because it pierces the veil of indirect ownership, focusing instead on the ultimate owner.

Using official Chinese government share classification data, in 2001 state-owned shares comprised 46 percent of all nontradable shares (state and LP shares) in China's publicly listed companies (Liu and Sun 2004, 114). Although multiple studies evaluating corporate performance distinguish between state shares and LP shares (e.g., Chen 2001; Sun, Tong, and Tong 2002; Xu and Wang 1997), Green and Black (2003) argue that many LP shares are ultimately owned either by the state or by state-controlled entities (Green and Black 2003, 3). Assuming that the state ultimately

---

19. Green and Liu (2005) argue that the Chinese government has strengthened its control in strategic sectors—energy, telecommunications, and financial services—despite high-profile foreign investments in these SOEs.

owns all LP shares, state ownership increases to 65 percent of all available shares in Chinese publicly listed corporations (Liu and Sun 2004, 114).[20]

Analyzing state ownership of corporations through "pyramid controlling mechanisms"[21] results in an even higher figure of state control of Chinese corporations. One recent study estimates that by the end of 2001, the Chinese government employed a pyramidal holding company strategy to exert ultimate ownership control over 81.6 percent of the 1,136 publicly listed Chinese companies (Liu and Sun 2005, 7). Although the state exerted direct control over only 9.0 percent of listed firms, it indirectly controlled a further 72.6 percent. The state exercised its indirect control through state-controlled publicly listed firms (2.6 percent), SOEs (58.9 percent), state-controlled unlisted firms (10 percent), and state-owned academic institutions (1.1 percent) (Liu and Sun 2004, 121). Other academics and analysts concur. Pieter Bottelier of Johns Hopkins University estimates that, of approximately 1,300 publicly listed companies in China in 2004, only about 20 were genuinely private; the rest were all ultimately controlled by the state.[22] No matter which method is used to assess state ownership of public companies, the state remains strongly involved in China's economic sector.

In addition to controlling a company through owning shares, the central or local government, or frequently the Communist Party of China, can control publicly traded corporations by influencing the composition of corporate boards and the corporation's management team (Tenev and Zhang 2002; Xu and Wang 1999). In 1997, a World Bank study found that in 80 percent of incorporated SOEs, the original managers and party officials continued to occupy key positions on the boards and supervisory committees of new stock companies (Xu and Wang 1997, 11). Similarly, a 1995 survey of 154 Chinese corporations found that government officials held 50 percent of available board seats, though the government owned in aggregate only 30 percent of the companies' stock (Xu and Wang 1997, 12).[23] When the study split firms into state-dominated and LP-dominated

---

20. In reality, the LP classification does not identify the entity that owns the shares, so the LP shareholder could be the state or a completely private entity. Recently, a Beijing-based investment consulting company found that the state controls "64 percent of the 1,379 companies that have raised funds by selling A shares" on Chinese stock exchanges. Matthew R. Miller, "Defying Risks to Invest in China," *International Herald Tribune*, April 5, 2005, available at www.iht.com (accessed March 14, 2006).

21. See La Porta, Lopez-de-Silanes, and Shleifer (1999). Their model looks beyond the official share-based ownership classification described above, by following the corporate ownership path back to the ultimate shareholder.

22. See testimony of Pieter Bottelier before the US-China Economic and Security Commission, April 16, 2004.

23. Moreover, "[t]he management actually has a greater influence on decision making if we include lower ranking officers such as general managers of subsidiaries in calculating the manager/board ration" (Xu and Wang 1997, 12).

firms according to share ownership, government officials filled more than 70 percent of board seats in state-dominated firms, but only 20 percent in LP-dominated firms (Xu and Wang 1997, 13). In either scenario, individual stockholders held no more than 0.3 percent of board seats on average, despite owning roughly one-third of the companies' stock (Xu and Wang 1997, 12).

A more recent survey of 257 companies listed on the Shanghai Stock Exchange reached similar conclusions about the extent of state control over the governance of China's public corporations. The state maintained "absolute control" over companies by directly or indirectly selecting roughly 70 percent of all directors appointed by shareholders (Tenev and Zhang 2002, 83). The study also showed that parent companies controlled the boards of publicly listed subsidiaries (Tenev and Zhang 2002, 85). Most telling was the study's finding that 73 to 76 percent of the companies' executive and nonexecutive directors were formerly employed by SOEs, and 12 to 24 percent of them had served in a government ministry (Tenev and Zhang 2002, 90).

Thus it is clear that the state, at a minimum, controls a very large number of publicly listed Chinese corporations. But the nature of ownership and frequency of listings by Chinese corporations is changing rapidly.[24] China is making important moves to reform state-owned and publicly listed enterprises. On August 24, 2004, the China Securities Regulatory Commission, the agency that regulates China's securities markets, authorized the 1,300 Chinese listed companies to sell, over time, large amounts of stock currently owned by the state.[25] In July 2005 the first privately owned petroleum company, Great United Petroleum Holding Co. Ltd. (GUPC), was formed without government support or involvement.[26] GUPC's creation was authorized by a February 2005 decision of the State Council, China's highest executive and policy-making organ, to allow pri-

---

24. China has two stock exchanges: the Shanghai Stock Exchange (SHSE), established in 1990, and the Shenzhen Stock Exchange (SZSE), established in 1991 (see Xu and Wang 1997, 6). The number of listed companies has grown 62 percent annually, from 53 publicly listed companies in 1992 to 1,380 in 2005 (839 listed on SHSE, 541 listed on SZSE) (see Tian 2001). An aggregate dataset of publicly listed companies found that the average total assets of these corporations was $180 million, including current, fixed, and other asset classes. The average fixed asset was $50 million (see Tian 2001, 5). The average age of these corporations was fourteen years, with a median of seven years, as most listed companies were newly formed or restructured during the reform period (Tian 2001, 4). Note that the data sample excludes fund-managed companies and firms that do not issue shares for domestic investors. The dataset includes 287 companies in 1994, 311 in 1995, 517 in 1996, 719 in 1997, and 826 in 1998.

25. Peter S. Goodman, "China to Allow More Stock Sales: $270 Billion of State Assets Put in Play," *Washington Post*, August 25, 2005, D1.

26. "China's First Private Oil Group Established," *Asia Times Online*, July 8, 2005, available at www.atimes.com (accessed March 8, 2006).

vate companies to be formed in "crucial industries like power, telecommunications, railways, civil aviation and oil exploration."[27]

Despite these recent positive moves toward more meaningful privatization of SMEs, until there has been substantial further reform in China, most publicly traded Chinese companies seeking approval from CFIUS will face a strong presumption of state control.[28] Another complex question that CFIUS will need to consider for Chinese acquisitions of US entities is whether privately held Chinese corporations are still under state control. At both central and regional levels, the Chinese government has an extraordinarily strong hold on many aspects of society, and certain agencies within CFIUS might argue that a company owned by private Chinese citizens, with no government ownership, still might be under government control. As one China expert told the authors, "The strong working presumption has to be that even 100 percent privately owned companies in China are very, very 'responsive' to the Chinese government."[29] The authors are unaware of specific cases in which CFIUS has made a control determination about a privately held Chinese corporation acquiring a US entity. We can, however, anticipate an active debate on the subject.

Failure to overcome this presumption of control will mean, in effect, that the company in question has satisfied the first prong of CFIUS's test for applying the Byrd Amendment. CFIUS next analyzes whether the acquisition "could affect the national security of the United States."[30] Included in this analysis is the traditional evaluation that Exon-Florio requires, including an assessment of the acquisition's impact on the US defense industrial base—particularly if the target company has contracts with the DOD and other security agencies—and the likelihood of transfer of export-controlled technologies. At the time of this writing, Congress was actively debating whether to eliminate any discretion for CFIUS in the second prong of the Byrd Amendment. If it does, most Chinese companies should expect to face a full 90-day review. In its traditional security analysis, CFIUS is also likely to consider a number of issues unique to Chinese acquisitions, including the risk that sensitive technologies will be transferred to third countries, the potential for the Chinese government to conduct espionage through the acquiring company, and the possibility that a particular acquisition will strengthen the capabilities of the Chinese government and military. We turn to these issues next.

---

27. "China's First Private Oil Group Established," *Asia Times Online,* July 8, 2005.

28. CFIUS regulations do not distinguish between the thresholds for determining control in general and the threshold for government control. As discussed below, the CFIUS control test is very broad. CFIUS is likely to determine that a government controls a corporation any time the government owns or controls 10 percent or more of a Chinese corporation.

29. Interview with China expert in Washington. The expert preferred to remain anonymous.

30. Exon-Florio Amendment, § 2170(b).

Export Controls

The possibility of sensitive, export-controlled technology being transferred to countries that raise national security concerns for the United States is a factor in virtually all CFIUS reviews,[31] regardless of the home country of the acquirer. It tends to be a particular concern for acquisitions by Chinese companies, however, in large part because of a series of high-profile breaches of US export control laws and regulations by Chinese companies in the late 1990s and early 2000s. China has improved its internal export control mechanisms significantly—by publishing new export control regulations, making agreements with other countries on end-use verification procedures, and training Chinese companies on the subject—but China's exports of technology to Iran, Libya, Pakistan, and North Korea trouble US officials (US CIA 2003, US Department of State 2003). Chinese companies have been subjected to import, procurement, and other sanctions by the US government on several occasions over the past few years. Among others, the United States imposed sanctions against Xinshidai, a firm that handles exports for Chinese military contractors, because it exported missile technology to sanctioned countries in 2004; Norinco, China's largest military conglomerate, for aiding Iran's long-range missile program in 2003; and nine small Chinese entities for exporting technology and goods to Iran in 2002.[32]

CFIUS scrutiny of potential transfers of sensitive and dual-use technology is also consistent with the US government's heightened concern with the transfer of such technologies to China.[33] Recent testimony by Acting Undersecretary of Commerce Peter Lichtenbaum before the US-China Economic and Security Review Commission concisely summarized the Bush administration's position:

> From a security standpoint, the US Government remains concerned about China's modernization of its conventional military forces and the risk of diversion of sensitive dual-use items and technology to Chinese military programs. For example, building state-of-the-art semiconductor plants could increase China's ability to apply this technology and equipment in military programs. Advanced telecommunications equipment—if illegally diverted to military end-users—could provide the Chinese missile, nuclear weapons and other military programs with the means to enhance performance capabilities in military radar applications.[34]

---

31. The Exon-Florio Amendment requires the president or his designee to consider, as a factor, "the potential effects of the proposed or pending transaction of sales of military goods, equipment, or technology to any country" to which the United States controls exports of particular goods, services, and technologies. Exon-Florio Amendment, § 2170(f)(4).

32. "US Sanctions Chinese Weapons Supplier," Associated Press, September 23, 2004. See also Jennifer Lee, "US Officials Complain That Chinese Companies Supply Rogue Nations," *New York Times*, November 12, 2001, C2.

33. Dual-use items are those that have both commercial and military uses.

34. See statements of Acting Undersecretary of Commerce for Industry and Security Peter Lichtenbaum before the US-China Economic and Security Review Commission, *Hearing on US-China Trade Impacts on the US Defense Industrial Base*, June 23, 2005.

Because of these concerns, and consistent with aspects of the so-called Tiananmen Square sanctions that have been in place since 1990,[35] the Bush administration has adopted a blanket policy against approving licenses to export controlled technology or goods for "military end users or end uses within China."[36] Further, the administration will not issue licenses for sales of "dual-use items and technology to China if the item or technology will make a direct and significant contribution to the People's Republic of China's (PRC) electronic and anti-submarine warfare, intelligence gathering, power projection, or air superiority."

Decisions to approve a license to export controlled technology to China are distinct from CFIUS's evaluations of risks associated with a particular transaction. CFIUS typically evaluates the sensitivity of the export-controlled technology that a target company owns or controls, but those agencies with responsibility for regulating the export of such technologies have made it clear that CFIUS does not make decisions on export license applications. Even if CFIUS approves an acquisition by a foreign company, US government agencies with export-control responsibilities—the Departments of State, Commerce, Defense, and Energy—could still deny that company a license to export a particular technology from the United States to China, including the release of technology in the United States to Chinese nationals (so-called deemed exports). Conversely, the US government could approve an application to export a particular technology to China, but CFIUS could block an acquisition by a Chinese company involving the same technology.

While CFIUS does not make decisions on specific export license applications, it does evaluate the risk of allowing an acquisition of a US company that owns export-controlled technology. This evaluation turns on the sensitivity of the technology involved, and the likelihood, in CFIUS's view, that the acquirer will abide by US export control laws and regulations if the transaction in question is approved. CFIUS is likely to have significant reservations about approving a transaction in which a foreign company that previously violated US export regulations seeks to acquire a US company with sensitive, controlled technology. CFIUS agencies scour the records of Chinese companies acquiring US companies with controlled technologies to determine whether the acquirer or its affiliates have previously run afoul of US export control laws and regulations. CFIUS also reviews the target company's record of compliance. Since Chinese com-

---

35. Following the events in Tiananmen Square, Congress imposed a number of restrictions on technology export licensing to China subject to presidential waiver. See *Foreign Relations Authorization Act, Fiscal Years 1990 and 1991*, Public Law 101-246, codified at *US Code* 22, 2151 (1990), note § 902.

36. Testimony of Acting Undersecretary of Commerce for Industry and Security Peter Lichtenbaum before the House Armed Services Committee and the House International Relations Committee, *EU Arms Embargo Against China, Hearing on the European Union's Plan to Export Arms to China*, 109th Congress, 1st sess., April 14, 2005, 2.

panies have been subjected to multiple enforcement actions or retaliatory sanctions in recent years, Chinese acquisitions of US companies with export- controlled technologies will continue to receive extra scrutiny.[37]

Espionage

In recent years, China's espionage activities have become an increasing concern and a higher priority to the relevant US government agencies involved in counterintelligence activities, including the Department of Justice (DOJ), the DOD, the Department of Homeland Security (DHS), and the FBI. The specter of significant, targeted Chinese espionage activities in the United States first hit public consciousness in the late 1990s with a widely publicized and controversial report by a select committee of the House of Representatives, chaired by Christopher Cox (R-CA)—the so-called Cox Report—and the allegations that Wen Ho Lee, a scientist working at Los Alamos National Laboratory in New Mexico, shared nuclear secrets with the Chinese.[38] The espionage charges against Wen Ho Lee were ultimately dropped, although he did plead guilty to a lesser charge of mishandling classified information. The Cox Report found, among other things, that China had stolen design information on the United States' most advanced thermonuclear weapons, and that Chinese penetration of US national laboratories reached back several decades (US House of Representatives 1999, overview section ii). The report concluded that the United States did not have adequate safeguards against Chinese espionage at US national laboratories. China had mounted a "widespread effort to obtain US military technology by any means—legal or illegal" and US counterintelligence efforts had been "complicate[d]" because China conducted espionage activities in a "less centralized" manner than did the Soviet Union during the Cold War (US House of Representatives 1999).

Subsequent reports and articles suggest that Chinese espionage activities are receiving increased attention from the US counterintelligence community. In an August 10, 2005, front page *Wall Street Journal* report, entitled "FBI Sees Big Threat from Chinese Spies," David Szady, the FBI's top counterintelligence official, stated, "China is the biggest [espionage] threat to the US today." The FBI had "sent hundreds of new counterintelligence agents" throughout the United States, many with "a specific focus on China." Further, the perceived threat was much different from that posed previously by the Soviet Union. Unlike the Soviets, literally "thousands of Chinese nationals" come every year to the United States as "stu-

---

37. China is not alone. CFIUS has also demonstrated similar concerns with other countries, including Israel.

38. See US House of Representatives (1999); James Risen, "US Fires Scientist Suspected of Giving China Bomb Data," *New York Times*, March 9, 1999, A1.

dents and businessmen." These Chinese nationals, the story continued, are contacted by Chinese government officials, who press them into service to "acquire military or industrial technology illegally."[39]

The *Wall Street Journal*'s coverage echoes public reports by the Central Intelligence Agency (CIA). In their 1999 *Report to Congress on Chinese Espionage Activities Against the United States*, the CIA and FBI conclude that "much of China's intelligence collection in 1998 continued to be accomplished by a network of nonprofessional individuals and organizations acting outside the direction and control of the intelligence services." Further, "some of the thousands of Chinese students, scientists, researchers, and other visitors to the United States also gather information, working mostly for the benefit of government-controlled, end-user organizations and other scientific bureaus, research institutions, and enterprises." Finally, "China's commercial entities play a significant role in the pursuit of proprietary US technology. According to the CIA, the vast majority of Chinese commercial entities in the United States are legitimate companies; however, some are a platform for intelligence collection activities" (US CIA and FBI 1999). It seems clear that US officials involved in counterintelligence activities view China as a real threat, and have identified Chinese companies, students, and researchers as a conduit for state-sponsored commercial and military espionage activities.

How does this affect a CFIUS analysis of a Chinese acquisition in the United States? We suspect that, at a minimum, the potential for espionage almost certainly will be a factor in many CFIUS reviews of acquisitions of US companies by Chinese entities. CFIUS agencies will also likely scrutinize a Chinese company's leadership and their ties, or alleged ties, to Chinese intelligence agencies and the military. If CFIUS agencies have concerns about the increased risk of espionage because of a transaction, they may block the transaction, or impose safeguards to mitigate the risk.

Strengthening the Chinese Military

The Pentagon's 2005 report to Congress on China's military power (Pentagon Report) states in unequivocal terms that the growth and strengthening of China's military threatens US interests (US DOD 2005). In the executive summary, it states, "If current trends [toward strengthening of China's military] persist, PLA [People's Liberation Army] capabilities could pose a credible threat to other modern militaries operating in the region." In addition to describing what it regards as worrying trends in China's force structure, strategies, and defense procurement budgets, the Pentagon Report makes clear that the DOD views the development of

---

39. Jay Solomon, "FBI Sees Big Threat from Chinese Spies," *Wall Street Journal*, August 10, 2005, A1.

China's economy and technology base, and the strengthening of its military, as intertwined. It quotes Chinese President Hu Jintao as saying, "It is necessary to establish a mechanism of *mutual promotion* and *coordinated development* between national defense building and economic development," inferring from President Hu's statement that "China's modernization indicates a buildup of armaments that reinforces this notion of coordinated, integrated civilian and military development" (US DOD 2005, 11). The report also asserts that China is actively seeking dual-use and military technologies from the European Union, Israel, Russia, and other countries (US DOD 2005, 23) and that China seeks to "accelerate its military development by using more of its civil production capacity for military hardware" (US DOD 2005, 13).

To illustrate how CFIUS might distinguish between acquisitions of the same US entity by companies based in three different countries, assume that either a Chinese or Pakistani entity were buying a small US company that owned sensitive, export-controlled technologies. If CFIUS was concerned that the technology or manufacturing within this company was critical to US defense capabilities, and that the technology would be transferred offshore, CFIUS would either reject the acquisition, or use a mitigation agreement to prohibit the transfer of technology or movement of manufacturing offshore. If CFIUS was concerned that there would be no way to control technology transfer, or have assurances that it would not happen, CFIUS would likely reject the acquisition by both the Chinese and Pakistani entities. However, if the sole concern of the sale was that its acquisition would strengthen the military capabilities of the acquirer, then the Chinese company might be turned down while the Pakistani company was allowed to proceed, since Pakistan's military is not seen as a threat to the United States.

As long as the Pentagon takes such a negative view of China, CFIUS will likely assess Chinese acquisitions of US companies in part on their impact on China's military strength. This approach turns the traditional CFIUS approach on its head. Rather than focusing on whether an acquisition threatens to reduce the DOD's and other national security agencies' access to goods and services for US national defense, CFIUS instead will consider whether an acquisition strengthens the Chinese military's access to goods and services. Thus weakening the United States and strengthening our enemies can be seen as two sides of the same national security coin.

CFIUS will therefore likely analyze not only the sophistication of dual-use technologies owned or developed by a target company, but also the ties of the Chinese acquirer to the Chinese military-industrial complex. Recent testimony by Evan Medeiros, an expert on China's military at the Rand Corporation, a think tank influential with the Pentagon, identifies 11 SOEs that "have historically always been involved in production of military goods."[40] These SOEs are the China National Nuclear Group Corporation (www.cnnc.com.cn), China Nuclear Engineering and Construction Group Corporation (www.cnecc.com.cn), China Aerospace Science and Technology Group Corporation (www.cascgroup.com.cn), China Aerospace Science and Industry Group Corporation (www.casic.com.cn), China Aviation Industry Group Corporation I (www.avic1.com.cn), China Aviation Industry Group Corporation II (www.avic2.com.cn), China State Shipbuilding Group Corporation (www.cssc.net.cn), China Shipbuilding Industry Corporation (www.csic.com.cn), China North Industries Group Corporation (www.norincogroup.com.cn), China South Industries Group Corporation (www.chinasouth.com.cn), and China Electronics Technology Group Corporation (www.cetc.com.cn).

If the Pentagon agrees with Medeiros's assessment, these 11 companies (and other companies on DOD's own list) could face additional challenges in clearing CFIUS, depending on the sensitivity of the target company in the United States.[41] Any Chinese acquirer must accordingly account for and, if necessary, rebut perceptions about its relationship with the Chinese military to navigate the CFIUS process successfully.

State Subsidies

The issue of Chinese government subsidies, in the form of low- or no-interest loans, became a hotly debated topic in the context of the proposed acquisition of Unocal by CNOOC. Members of Congress, the financial press, and other analysts criticized the CNOOC transaction for being heavily subsidized by the Chinese government. Allan Sloan, an economics columnist for *Newsweek,* suggested that CNOOC "is counting on $7 billion in ultra cheap loans from its parent to help fund its $19 billion Unocal offer." Sloan pointed to a $2.5 billion no-interest loan and a $4.5 billion, 3.5 percent 30-year loan from CNOOC's parent company, observing that CNOOC would not have had access to these loan terms in the commercial financial markets. All told, Sloan concluded, the preferential loans provided CNOOC with a $400 million annual subsidy, representing a value for CNOOC of approximately $9.50 per Unocal share.[42]

---

40. Testimony of Evan S. Medeiros before the US-China Economic and Security Review Commission, *Analyzing China's Defense Industries and the Implications for Chinese Military Modernization,* 108th Congress, 2nd sess., February 6, 2004.

41. Norinco has also been the subject of US sanctions for violating the Iran Nonproliferation Act of 2000, available at www.state.gov (accessed March 8, 2006).

42. Allan Sloan, "Lending a Helping Hand: The Math Behind CNOOC's Rich Offer to Buy Out Unocal," *Newsweek,* July 18, 2005, available at www.newsweek.com (accessed March 12, 2006).

In the past, CFIUS's review of the national security impact of inward investment has not focused on state support in the form of financial subsidies. Of course, no one knows how CFIUS would have analyzed the alleged CNOOC subsidies because, as discussed in chapter 5, it never reviewed the CNOOC-Unocal transaction. We anticipate, however, that favorable loans or other state-supported subsidies could affect CFIUS reviews of future Chinese acquisitions in two ways.

First, to the extent that any ambiguity exists over whether a Chinese company is controlled by the Chinese government, direct state subsidies or favorable loan terms will add weight to the argument that a particular firm is government-owned or -controlled. After all, to determine control, the CFIUS regulations contemplate review of, among other things, "contractual arrangements" and "pledge or other transfer of any or all of the principal assets of the entity."[43] Since a loan agreement is a "contractual arrangement," and presumably such loans require the "pledge" of certain of the acquirer's assets as collateral, favorable or subsidized state-supported loans will likely be scrutinized as a factor in determining whether a company is controlled by the Chinese government.

Second, the reaction to CNOOC's bid for Unocal suggests that favorable, noncommercial loan terms in transactions involving Chinese companies are likely to be a significant factor in determining whether a particular transaction is politicized in Congress. In the proposed CNOOC transaction, Senators Charles Grassley and Max Baucus, the highly respected chairman and ranking member of the Senate Finance Committee respectively, wrote jointly to the president:

> The offer by CNOOC Ltd. for Unocal raises an important question; namely, whether it is appropriate for state-owned enterprises to subsidize investment transactions to acquire scarce natural resources that are in high demand. When government subsidies are directed toward the acquisition and development of scarce resources, any ensuing market distortions should be of particular concern. Such subsidies may facilitate the allocation of scarce resources to inefficient or less-efficient producers. Any review by CFIUS should take into account the impact this type of subsidized acquisition may have on the US economy and its potential threat to our national security interests.[44]

In the wake of the CNOOC transaction, as well as the Dubai Ports controversy, it is likely that both CFIUS and Congress will scrutinize the financial terms of transactions to determine whether they suggest state ownership and control. In our view, such scrutiny is warranted and appropriate for CFIUS to determine whether a foreign acquirer is actually controlled by a foreign government, and, if so, whether that control raises specific national security issues for a particular transaction. We also be-

---

43. *Code of Federal Regulations*, title 31, § 800.204.

44. Senators Charles E. Grassley and Max Baucus, "Grassley, Baucus Express Concern Over Potential CNOOC-Unocal Deal," press release, July 13, 2005, available at grassley.senate.gov.

lieve that the US government should continue its policy of actively encouraging foreign governments to privatize state-owned entities.

Policy Implications for Future CFIUS Reviews of Chinese Acquisitions

How should the United States deal with Chinese investment, given the
unique issues that such investments potentially raise from a national security perspective? First, there is the overarching question of whether Chinese investment should be viewed as a benefit or detriment to the US
economy. It is our view that the United States should continue to support
China's integration into the global economy, and that Chinese outward
foreign investment should be viewed as a natural and positive evolution
in China's economic development. For close to two decades, through Republican and Democratic administrations, the United States has encouraged China to lower tariffs, eliminate nontariff barriers to trade, privatize
SOEs, and participate in—and play by the rules of—the global economy.
The United States has also continually pressed China to eliminate barriers
to FDI by US and other foreign companies. Successive US administrations
have correctly pursued these policies, not only for the economic and commercial benefit of US companies and workers, but also in the belief that
adopting market-based economic policies will facilitate democratic reform
in China.

But the United States cannot have it both ways. A US policy that encourages investment by American companies in China while frowning
upon Chinese investment in the United States is neither sustainable nor
sound from an economic perspective. Rather, the United States should simultaneously encourage China to allow FDI and make clear that Chinese
investment in the United States is not only welcome but encouraged. Enhanced FDI from China would bring substantial economic benefits to the
US economy, just as investment from other countries already does (see
chapter 3). Chinese investment in the United States will create jobs, promote research and development (R&D) in the United States, and enhance
US exports to China, including through intracompany trade.

Additional investment from China would also produce important ancil-
lary benefits for the United States consistent with broader US strategic and
political objectives. China has already bought a substantial number of US
Treasury notes, helping the United States to finance its large and growing
current account deficit; it is one reason why the federal government's sustained deficit has not triggered significant increases in interest rates. Further, while a strong and growing US economy is already in China's economic interest, given that the United States is China's largest export market,
large-scale ownership of US Treasury securities further aligns China's eco-

nomic interests with US objectives. China played a stabilizing role in the Asian financial crisis in the late 1990s by not devaluing its currency.

Some experts and commentators (not including the authors) believe that the large-scale ownership of Treasury securities gives China leverage over the United States.[45] If Chinese authorities wished to express their displeasure with the United States, some argue, they would need only to signal that they would either refrain from buying additional Treasury securities or sell existing holdings. By doing so, China could potentially destabilize US financial markets, cause interest rates to increase, and possibly lead other governments to shun US Treasury notes. The mere possibility of China using its ownership of US debt to wreak havoc on the US economy creates leverage for the Chinese government, and undermines the US government's freedom of action for fear of offending China.

We do not subscribe to these arguments, but if they are correct, then it follows that additional Chinese direct investment—as opposed to investment in Treasury securities—would reduce any incentive the Chinese government may have to disrupt US financial markets. If Chinese companies owned substantial fixed assets and publicly traded US equities, China would be shooting itself in the foot by dumping Treasury securities on the market for political purposes. Chinese FDI in fixed assets and US companies would further align Chinese and US economic interests, and provide a disincentive to politically driven Chinese government sales of US Treasury instruments.

Greater Chinese ownership of and investment in US companies, as well as involvement in the world economy, would have the additional benefit of exposing Chinese companies to global legal norms, including requirements for enhanced transparency. Partnerships, supply relationships, and joint ventures would enable Chinese management to access and develop international management skills. Travel to the West would increase, as would Western travel to China. Interactions between Chinese and Western businesspersons would further integrate China into the global economy, creating greater pressure within China for democratic reform, the rule of law, and cooperation with the United States and the West. Chinese companies successfully operating in the United States would help create a new constituency within China for open trade, just as the US business community consistently presses Washington to liberalize trade and investment in the United States because of its substantial commercial interests abroad. The United States stands to benefit substantially, both directly and indirectly, from increased levels of Chinese direct investment within its borders.

---

45. See, e.g., William Pesek Jr., "Forget Unocal. Real China Risk Is Treasuries," *Bloomberg News*, July 7, 2005, available at www.bloomberg.com; Floyd Norris, "Who's in Charge of Determining US Interest Rates? It May Be Beijing," *New York Times*, May 13, 2005, C1; and Liam Halligan, interview with Paul Krugman, "China Is the Financial Nexus," *Sunday Telegraph*, June 19, 2005, available at www.telegraph.co.uk (accessed March 10, 2006).

In sum, Chinese investment in the United States creates clear economic benefits, and will ultimately move China toward the West. At the same time, the US government is still obliged to protect US national security, including through implementation of the Exon-Florio Amendment. Where should CFIUS strike the balance in its scrutiny of Chinese investments in the United States?

We believe that, proceeding on a transaction-by-transaction basis, CFIUS should focus solely on the incremental risk associated with particular investments. Notwithstanding the serious and legitimate policy concerns relating to espionage, technology transfer, and state control of many Chinese corporations, CFIUS should focus on the marginal increase in risk to US national security, if any, that a particular transaction creates. It should not try to resolve the broad set of problems associated with the US-China economic relationship by regulating individual transactions.

For discussion purposes, let us take two examples at opposite ends of the national security spectrum. In the first example, a Chinese-controlled private equity firm, with no involvement with or ties to the Chinese government, decides to acquire a major US ice cream company. The ice cream company has no special technology and does not directly supply the US government. Hard-liners could argue that the acquisition provides a vehicle for Chinese espionage to each one of the company's major ice cream factories located near a US military base, or an R&D center for a US technology company. It would be absurd for CFIUS to be concerned about this investment. Any legitimate concerns about espionage risks should be dealt with through other laws, and through prudent security practices by the military bases and R&D centers near the ice cream factories. For similar reasons, we suspect that the proposed (but ultimately abandoned) 2005 acquisition of Maytag, the white good manufacturer, by the Chinese company Haier would have easily cleared CFIUS. Arguably, the transaction should not have even been filed with CFIUS.

At the other end of the spectrum, suppose Lockheed Martin, the United States' largest defense contractor, decided to spin off a division involving sophisticated, state-of-the-art precision guidance systems for missiles. Obviously, CFIUS would never, nor should they, allow a Chinese company to access the most sophisticated weapons technologies in the United States, or to own a company that sells unique, sophisticated, and controlled technologies to the DOD. These were doubtless the reasons that President George H. W. Bush rejected the proposed acquisition of a US aerospace company by a Chinese company in 1990.

Transactions that fall in the middle of the spectrum are, perhaps not surprisingly, harder to judge. As discussed in chapter 5, the DHS has identified 12 sectors, including energy and telecommunications, as "critical infrastructure" worthy of special protection. CFIUS has approved telecommunications transactions from dozens of other countries, including many European countries, Korea, Singapore, Taiwan, India, and, most recently,

Bahrain. Certain of these telecommunications acquisitions were made by state-owned companies (Deutsche Telecommunications of Germany, Telnor of Norway, and Singapore Technologies Telemedia). Some of them required negotiating extraordinarily tough network security agreements (NSAs) to get CFIUS approval, even when the assets being acquired were insignificant from a critical infrastructure perspective (see the discussion of NSAs in chapter 3).

But should CFIUS allow Chinese companies to acquire US telecommunications companies? What about Chinese state-owned companies? In our view, CFIUS should ensure that the DOJ and the FBI can pursue sensitive criminal investigations without the knowledge of foreign nationals or governments. If the US telecommunications company being acquired is sufficiently large or sensitive to be considered "critical infrastructure," appropriate safeguards can and should be put in place. But there should not be a blanket ban on Chinese ownership of US telecommunications assets, nor should NSAs for Chinese companies be so onerous as to effectively amount to the same thing.

In the energy sector, it is apparent from CNOOC's failed bid for Unocal that Chinese acquisitions of US energy assets also potentially raise national security concerns, at least in the view of members of Congress. The importance of protecting energy infrastructure was painfully evident in the aftermath of Hurricane Katrina, which ravaged the Gulf Coast, flooded 80 percent of New Orleans, and temporarily reduced 10 percent of US refining capacity, causing substantial energy price increases and gas shortages in the South. Yet it is unclear how Chinese ownership of oil and gas assets in the Gulf of Mexico would have had any negative impact on efforts to restart drilling and repair rigs, pipelines, and refineries. Foreign-owned firms have just as much incentive to get their idle assets running again as American-owned firms do. At the same time, there are legitimate national security questions surrounding the acquisition of US energy assets by Chinese companies, including whether Chinese energy firms will seek to supply gas and oil exclusively to China, as opposed to selling to global markets. When Gazprom, the Russian state-owned natural energy giant, cut off natural gas supplies to the Ukraine in the middle of the winter in 2006, the action was widely seen as ordered by the Russian government to express displeasure with Ukrainian policies.[46] Widely condemned in the United States and Western Europe, the incident will likely lead CFIUS to cast a more critical eye on future acquisitions of US energy assets by certain foreign state-owned energy companies, including those in China and Russia. In addition, certain US energy companies possess dual-use technologies, which may be too sensitive to sell to China, particularly if there are concerns in exporting or sharing technologies with the Chinese military.

---

46. "Gazprom Halts Gas Shipments to Ukraine," *Reuters*, January 1, 2006, available at www.iht.com (accessed March 10, 2006).

Notwithstanding these caveats, in general, Chinese investment should be welcomed. Chinese investments in sensitive sectors such as telecommunications and energy will make for difficult CFIUS cases, and Chinese companies would be wise to invest in less sensitive sectors and build a good track record, allowing CFIUS to gain comfort, before moving on to more sensitive areas. There should, however, be a very high threshold before the president moves to block a particular transaction. If national security issues do arise in relation to a transaction, CFIUS agencies have a wide array of tools, including security agreements, to mitigate their concerns. Further, the United States has other laws at its disposal, including comprehensive export control and counterespionage laws, to protect US national security interests. Indeed, often forgotten in discussions of CFIUS is the statutory requirement that authorizes the president to block a transaction only if (1) there is credible evidence that leads the president to believe that the foreign interest exercising control might take action that threatens to impair the national security, *and* (2) provisions of law, other than Exon-Florio and the International Emergency Economic Powers Act, do not in the president's judgment provide adequate and appropriate authority to protect national security.[47]

In other words, if a particular transaction raises export control concerns, the president can block the transaction only if he finds that existing US export control laws are inadequate to address those concerns.

In sum, we believe that increased Chinese investment in the United States would bring important benefits to both the United States and China. The US should thus make clear to China that it welcomes FDI so long as such investments do not compromise US national security. Undoubtedly, however, Chinese investments create issues for CFIUS that do not frequently arise for investments from other major trading partners. For transactions that raise specific national security concerns, CFIUS should work with the involved parties to craft narrowly tailored arrangements to mitigate the incremental risks created by a particular transaction. Finally, the president should only block Chinese acquisitions of US companies in which unique and significant national security issues arise, and other laws or measures cannot adequately mitigate the risk.

CFIUS reviews, however, do not take place in a bureaucratic vacuum, but amid a political process, and they are not, and perhaps cannot be, immune to politicization. Through congressional pressure, corporations and politicians can pressure CFIUS to reject acquisitions that it might otherwise accept, adding tension to CFIUS's already difficult mandate of balancing what is good for the economy against the needs of national security. The next chapter deals with these issues.

---

47. Exon-Florio Amendment, § 2170(e).

5

Politicization of the CFIUS Process

While no decision-making process in Washington can be entirely immune from political influence, a number of factors can conspire to make Exon-Florio reviews especially inviting targets for manipulation by competing corporate interests. First, the very nature of an Exon-Florio review involves two highly sensitive political issues: foreign ownership and national security. Each of these issues independently can grab the attention of individual constituents, and each certainly also receives attention from interest groups with particular worldviews and varying degrees of influence. As evident in the Dubai Ports World controversy, when these factors combine, they can produce an especially combustible political mix. Second, while most transactions subject to an Exon-Florio review occur in relative anonymity, it is not uncommon for a review by the Committee on Foreign Investment in the United States (CFIUS), much like an antitrust review, to involve a large-stakes or otherwise high-profile transaction. Public scrutiny of such a transaction, and the attendant publicity that may accrue to a politician who takes a noteworthy position on the transaction, increases the transaction's susceptibility to political meddling. Third, and perhaps most important, rival suitors for the US company being acquired may seek to politicize the Exon-Florio process to raise costs for the potential foreign acquirer, or to reopen the bidding process.

As discussed in chapters 1 and 2, each of these factors contributed to the enactment of the Exon-Florio law in 1988, and have motivated subsequent proposed amendments to the law. It should not be surprising, then, that from time to time, Congress has sought to be involved in CFIUS reviews. In the past few years, the CFIUS process has become increasingly politicized for commercial rather than national security reasons, not only because of stronger internal divisions between security and economic agencies, but also because of increased involvement from external parties, including Congress. Companies seeking to manipulate the CFIUS process for commercial gain have frequently drawn congressional attention to specific cases, and a US bidder may seek to eliminate or reduce competition for a particular asset from foreign bidders by creating political opposition to a foreign acquisition of a particular company. The following are a few examples of such attempted congressional involvement in the CFIUS process, as well as one example of highly politicized congressional action that occurred even before a formal CFIUS review was initiated.

BTR-Norton and Global Crossing

In 1990, only two years after Exon-Florio became law, 119 members of Congress wrote to the president asking for an investigation of the UK firm British Tire and Rubber's (BTR) proposed hostile acquisition of the Norton Company, based in Massachusetts. The letter stated that "we do not believe that any take over of Norton would be in our economic security or national security interest" (Karim 1995). These members of Congress, encouraged by Norton, suddenly changed their tune when a French company, Compagnie de Saint Gobain, offered Norton $15 more per share. Clearly, Norton manipulated the CFIUS process to its advantage, because no one raised any national security concerns over the French acquisition. It is hard to imagine how a British acquisition of Norton raised national security issues while a French acquisition did not. There were no national security issues with the proposed British acquisition; Norton simply did not want to be acquired by BTR, and used a political campaign toward CFIUS to prevent it.

More recently, in 2002 the famed corporate raider Carl Icahn tried to use pressure from Congress on the CFIUS process to break up the proposed acquisition of Global Crossing by ST Telemedia, a Singaporean company. After shoring up opposition in Congress to the transaction, Icahn later challenged, in US bankruptcy court, the Global Crossing board of directors' business judgment for sticking with ST Telemedia. Icahn claimed that the ST Telemedia acquisition was unlikely to gain CFIUS approval, and therefore the bankruptcy judge should force a new auction for Global Crossing. Icahn was unsuccessful, but his efforts cost the eventual acquirer time, money, and effort to preserve its transaction.

ASML and Silicon Valley Group

In October 2000, ASML Holding N.V. (ASML), a Netherlands-based manufacturer of silicon equipment announced its intention to acquire Silicon

Valley Group (SVG), a semiconductor equipment manufacturer, for $1.6 billion. The merger would create the world's largest maker of lithography equipment, the powerful machines used to etch microscopic patters onto silicon wafers. SVG, after informal consultations with CFIUS agencies, formally filed its notice with CFIUS on December 13, 2000, in the waning days of the Clinton administration, starting the initial 30-day clock. ASML later decided to withdraw its CFIUS filing, and refile after the Bush administration took office, in part because of Pentagon opposition, but also to avoid problems associated with running a regulatory process during a political transition.[1] The parties refiled their petition on February 5, 2001, expecting a smooth 30-day review.

SVG and its subsidiary, Tinsley Laboratories, manufactured leading optical equipment used for spy satellites, but according to SVG's CEO, they had not done direct work for the Pentagon for years. Close to the end of the 30-day review, the parties appeared to be on the verge of an agreement with CFIUS, under which ASML committed to invest millions of dollars over a multiyear period. ASML would not, however, be forced to divest its subsidiary, Tinsley Laboratories. Instead, it would commit to making Tinsley products available for Pentagon use, and would require ASML not to transfer Tinsley's technology and employees abroad for a number of years.[2]

Just before the end of the initial 30-day review period, close to a dozen influential members of Congress, including then Senate Majority Leader Trent Lott (R-MS), then chairman of the House Armed Services Committee Bob Stump (R-AL), and future chairman of the House Armed Services Committee Duncan Hunter (R-CA), objected to the acquisition and called on CFIUS to extend its review into the 45-day "investigation period." Senator Lott, in a letter to Secretary of Defense Donald Rumsfeld and National Security Adviser Condoleezza Rice, stated that precision optics and semiconductor technologies "will remain critical to the development of new systems that will allow us to preserve our national security."[3] Further, Lott wrote, "Considering the critical and proprietary nature of the technologies associated with the proposed sale, I believe the full 45-day investigation . . . would provide you with a greater opportunity to fully evaluate and deliberate the impact of the proposed sale on US technological leadership and in areas affecting national security."[4] According to

---

1. "ASM Lithography Holding N.V. and Silicon Valley Group, Inc. Announce Intent to Withdraw and Refile Their Petition for Exon-Florio Review," *Business Wire,* January 7, 2001.

2. Peter Spiegel, "Rival Accused after Security Fears Block High-Tech Sale," *Financial Times,* March 9, 2001, The Americas, 12.

3. Glenn Simpson, "Pentagon Moves to Postpone Dutch Deal for Silicon Valley Group," *Wall Street Journal,* March 8, 2001, B6.

4. Glenn Simpson, "Pentagon Moves to Postpone Dutch Deal for Silicon Valley Group."

press reports, with multiple congressional letters streaming in, the Pentagon became even more energized, and forced the review to move to the investigation stage. The Pentagon, and particularly then Deputy Secretary of Defense Paul Wolfowitz, toughened the terms of the security agreement with ASML and continued to oppose the transaction. Ultimately, President Bush approved the transaction, but at one point, it was so perilously close to being rejected that Intel's then CEO, Craig Barrett, an influential figure in Washington, wrote to the secretaries of defense, treasury, and commerce, and met with Vice President Cheney, among others, to lobby for the deal.[5] Intel relied on SVG for critical inputs, and was worried that without a healthy backer like ASML, SVG's viability was in doubt. That the Pentagon forced an investigation into an acquisition from a leading company based in a friendly country,[6] of a US technology company without classified contracts with the Pentagon, signaled a sea change in how the Bush administration would handle CFIUS reviews.

It is not unusual for members of Congress to weigh in on important regulatory matters, but the circumstances surrounding the sudden congressional interest in the ASML-SVG transaction were unusual. Congressional interest was stoked by another Silicon Valley–based competitor of SVG—Ultratech Stepper—which sought to acquire part of SVG but was outbid by ASML,[7] and hired lobbyists to generate opposition on Capitol Hill. In many similar cases, a domestic company seeks to avoid being in the public eye. In this case, Ultratech's CEO was vocal, calling on CFIUS to force ASML to divest Tinsley Laboratories, which CFIUS did. Ultratech also contributed to and activated an antiglobalization group, the US Business and Industrial Council, which circulated fact sheets and videos to hundreds of congressional offices raising national security concerns about the transaction.[8]

The transaction was approved, albeit after an interagency fight and with tougher conditions imposed on ASML: It was forced to commit to significant investments in research and development (R&D), maintain certain R&D functions within the United States, and make good faith efforts to try to sell Tinsley Laboratories to a US owner within six months.[9] The trans-

---

5. Toby Sterling, "ASML/SVG Merger Closes, But Deal Once Hung by a Thread," May 23, 2001, available at www.ofii.org (accessed March 10, 2006).

6. The Netherlands cooperates extensively on military and political matters with the United States, and is an active member of NATO.

7. Peter Spiegel, "Rival accused after security fears block high-tech sale," *Financial Times*, March 9, 2001, The Americas, 12.

8. Toby Sterling, "ASML/SVG Merger Closes, But Deal Once Hung by a Thread," May 23, 2001, available at www.ofii.org (accessed March 10, 2006).

9. ASML sold Tinsley Laboratories to Richmond, California–based SSG Precision Optronics Inc. in December 2001. Sarah Cohen, "ASML Sells Tinsley to SSG Precision Optronics," *The Daily Deal*, December 20, 2001, available at www.TheDeal.com (accessed March 10, 2006).

action was troubled to begin with, in large part due to concerns within the Pentagon. But the involvement of Ultratech, a competitor interested in buying Tinsley Laboratories, added fuel to the fire. Had Ultratech not unleashed such a political firestorm, the ASML-SVG transaction might have been approved within 30 days and with fewer conditions. While Ultratech ultimately could not force the deal to be blocked, it successfully politicized the process, extending the review and forcing tougher conditions on a competitor.

VSNL and Tyco Global Network

One of the most unusual attempts by a competitor to politicize the Exon-Florio process occurred in early 2005, when Crest Communications, an Alaska-based company, raised national security concerns about the acquisition of the Tyco Global Network (TGN) by Videsh Sanchar Nigam Limited (VSNL), a telecommunications company based in India and partially owned by the Indian government. TGN was built by the then-high-flying company Tyco in the late 1990s. Its main asset was an undersea cable network connecting the United States to Europe and Japan. TGN did not include a fiber network within the continental United States.

Tyco conducted an auction for TGN in 2004. Although a number of companies expressed interest in TGN, only VSNL's bid was viable. After five months of consultations and negotiations with the Department of Justice (DOJ), Department of Defense (DOD), Department of Homeland Security (DHS), and the Federal Bureau of Investigation (FBI), VSNL and those agencies signed an extraordinarily tough network security agreement (NSA), particularly considering that TGN only connected to the United States, as opposed to operating within it.

In a 47-page filing to the Federal Communications Commission (FCC), unprecedented for the vigor with which it publicly argued that the transaction posed national security risks, Crest argued that the transaction would severely compromise the DOD's net-centric warfare plans and threaten the security and integrity of military, intelligence, and other sensitive communications in the cable network.[10] Crest also claimed that the acquisition was forced by the Indian government, because it has an interest in ensuring India's self-sufficiency and national security, both of which can be better achieved if "VSNL controls such a significant portion of the critical, global submarine cable infrastructure."[11]

---

10. Petition to Deny of Crest Communications Corporation, In the Matters of Tyco Telecommunications (US) Inc., Assignor, VSNL Telecommunications (US) Inc., Assignee, et al., Applications for Modification, Assignment and Transfer of Control of Cable Landing Licenses for the Tyco Atlantic and Tyco Pacific Submarine Cable Systems, File Nos. SCL-ASG-20050304-0003; SCL-MOD-20050301-0004; SCL-T/C-20050301-0005, at 3 (March 31, 2005).

11. Petition to Deny of Crest Communications Corporation, 12.

In response, Tyco claimed that Crest's claim before the FCC "serves only to further Crest's ongoing corporate 'greenmail' and retaliation strategy against Tyco Telecommunications (US)."[12] According to Tyco, Crest and Tyco had engaged in business negotiations involving another segment of Tyco's business. When Tyco refused to grant Crest a substantial discount on Tyco's services, "Crest followed through on its explicit threat . . . to oppose the TGN sale."[13]

Hyperbolic claims and counterclaims by attorneys are common at the FCC; this transaction was unusual in that competitive carriers placed national security issues before the FCC, even though the FCC, as discussed in chapter 2, defers to the executive branch on matters of national security.

Crest's national security claims received attention in the press and Congress. Fortunately, however, it does not appear that CFIUS agencies paid much attention because Crest's complaints were obviously based on a commercial dispute. On April 7, 2005, only a few weeks after Crest filed its national security arguments with the FCC, the DOJ, DHS, DOD, and FBI signed an NSA with VSNL.[14] On April 11, these same agencies notified the FCC that they had no national security objections to the FCC granting VSNL the licenses it requested.

CNOOC's Proposed Acquisition of Unocal

When the China National Offshore Oil Corporation (CNOOC) announced on June 23, 2005, that it was making a "friendly" bid of $18.5 billion for Unocal, the US-based oil and gas company, it touched off a firestorm in Washington and put the previously obscure CFIUS onto the front pages of newspapers around the world.[15] Rumors of CNOOC's potential interest in Unocal had swirled around New York and other financial centers earlier in the year, and CNOOC had considered but later decided not to formally bid for Unocal in the spring of 2005. After taking bids from a number of interested parties, in April 2004 Unocal's board of directors accepted the Chevron Corporation's offer to acquire Unocal for $16.4 billion in cash and

---

12. Joint Opposition to Petition to Deny, In the Matters of Tyco Telecommunications (US) Inc., Assignor, VSNL Telecommunications (US) Inc., Assignee, et al., Applications for Modification, Assignment and Transfer of Control of Cable Landing Licenses for the Tyco Atlantic and Tyco Pacific Submarine Cable Systems, File Nos. SCL-ASG-20050304-0003; SCL-MOD-20050301-0004; SCL-T/C-20050301-0005, at 1 (April 11, 2005).

13. Joint Opposition to Petition to Deny, In the Matters of Tyco Telecommunications, 2.

14. Joint Opposition to Petition to Deny, In the Matters of Tyco Telecommunications, 22.

15. CNOOC press release, "CNOOC Limited Proposes Merger with Unocal Offering US$67 per Unocal Share in Cash," June 23, 2005, available at www.cnoocltd.com (accessed March 10, 2006). See also Stephanie Kirchgaessner, "Chinese Case Puts Secretive Panel in Spotlight: US Vetting of Foreign Takeovers Is Hot Topic," Financial Times, August 4, 2005, 22.

stock.[16] CNOOC then decided to seek to supplant Chevron's bid with a sweeter offer.[17]

With nominal oil prices at record levels, strong anti-China sentiment in Washington, and a domestic company interested in preserving its agreement with Unocal, CNOOC's attempt to acquire Unocal set the stage for a "perfect storm" in Congress for a debate on the national security implications of foreign investment in the United States. The negative reaction against the CNOOC bid came quickly and with force. Even before CNOOC formally announced its bid, congressmen Duncan Hunter (R-CA) and Richard Pombo (R-CA) sent a letter to the Bush administration asking it to review and potentially block the bid.[18] Outside of Congress, Mikkal Herberg, director of the Asian energy security program at the National Bureau of Asian Research, a Seattle-based think tank, predicted that the CNOOC bid would "feed the fear that the Chinese are coming, the Chinese are coming."[19] C. Richard D'Amato, chairman of the US-China Economic and Security Review Commission, a congressional advisory panel, said, "When we're so dependent on foreign suppliers, giving away American sources of petroleum and hydrocarbons doesn't make sense to me."[20] Congressman Richard Pombo (R-CA) stated, "I do not believe it is in the best interest of the United States to have Unocal owned by the Chinese national government. . . . I am afraid that such an acquisition would come with disastrous consequences for our economic and national security."[21] Sam Bodman, the US secretary of energy, stated that the US government's review of a CNOOC-Unocal transaction, presumably under CFIUS, would be a "truly complex matter."[22] Further fanning the flames, Liu Jianchao, Chinese foreign ministry spokesman, warned the United States to "allow normal trade relations to take place without political interference."[23] This

---

16. Chevron press release, "Chevron Texaco Announces Agreement to Acquire Unocal," April 4, 2005, available at www.chevron.com (accessed March 10, 2006).

17. Chevron is a client of Covington & Burling, the law firm in which David Marchick, one of the authors of this book, is a partner.

18. Russell Gold, Matt Pottinger, and Dennis K. Berman, "China's CNOOC Lobs in Rival Bid to Acquire Unocal—Oil Firm's $18.5 Billion Offer Aims to Knock Out Chevron; Concerns in Washington," *Wall Street Journal*, June 23, 2005, A1.

19. James F. Peltz, Elizabeth Douglass, and Evelyn Iritani, "Chinese Oil Firm Bids for Unocal," *Los Angeles Times*, June 23, 2005, A1.

20. Peltz, Douglass, and Iritani, "Chinese Oil Firm Bids for Unocal."

21. David R. Baker, "Chinese Oil Firm Trumps Chevron Bid for Unocal," *San Francisco Chronicle*, June 23, 2005, A1.

22. David Greising, "China Bids for Oil Giant Unocal; State-Owned Company Offers $18.5 Billion," *Chicago Tribune*, June 23, 2005.

23. David Barboza and Andrew Ross Sorkin, "Chinese Oil Giant in Takeover Bid for US Corporation," *New York Times*, June 23, 2005, A1.

statement was measurably softer than an unusually tin-eared statement a few weeks later from the Chinese foreign ministry: "We demand that the US Congress correct its mistaken ways of politicizing economic and trade issues and stop interfering in the normal commercial exchanges between enterprises of the two countries."[24] Members of Congress typically do not react well to such warnings from a Chinese government official.

Opponents of the CNOOC acquisition focused on a number of distinct arguments. First, they argued that, given high oil prices and tight supplies, ownership of key global energy assets by a Chinese state-owned firm would put global energy sources at risk, as CNOOC might hoard Unocal's oil and gas reserves for China's exclusive use, taking important supplies off the global market. Since the United States' national and energy security depended on secure supplies of oil and gas, a sale to CNOOC would compromise US national security interests. Second, opponents argued that the proposed CNOOC acquisition was an attempt by the Chinese government to control critical oil and gas supplies, and such supplies and the accompanying revenues would strengthen the Chinese government and state.[25] Third, opponents argued that preferential loans to CNOOC by Chinese state-owned banks and CNOOC's state-owned parent put US companies at a competitive disadvantage.[26] Fourth, opponents argued that a CNOOC acquisition of Unocal would potentially facilitate the transfer of sensitive technologies to China.[27] Fifth, opponents maintained that, since the Chinese would never allow a US company to acquire a major Chinese oil company, the United States should block the transaction on reciprocity grounds.

Supporters of the transaction, including one of the authors of this book, argued that since oil and gas are fungible, and oil markets are global, there would be no national security issues associated with the transaction (Graham 2005b). Second, supporters argued that, given the relatively small size of Unocal's global oil and gas holdings, a CNOOC acquisition would have a negligible impact on global energy markets. Third, supporters maintained that Chinese companies already possessed, or could easily acquire from other companies, the type of sophisticated dual-use technol-

---

24. Peter S. Goodman, "China Tells Congress to Back Off Businesses; Tensions Heightened by Bid to Purchase Unocal," *Washington Post*, July 5, 2005, A1.

25. Statement of C. Richard D'Amato, chairman, US-China Economic and Security Review Commission, *National Security Dimensions of the Possible Acquisition of Unocal by CNOOC and the Role of CFIUS: Hearing Before the House Committee on Armed Services*, 109th Congress, 1st sess., July 13, 2005.

26. Allan Sloan, "Lending a Helping Hand: The Math Behind CNOOC's Rich Offer to Buy Out Unocal," *Newsweek*, July 18, 2005, available at www.newsweek.com (accessed March 12, 2006).

27. Statement of C. Richard D'Amato, US-China Economic and Security Review Commission, *National Security Dimensions of the Possible Acquisition of Unocal by CNOOC and the Role of CFIUS*.

ogy that Unocal allegedly held. Thus, a CNOOC acquisition would not give Chinese companies access to technologies that could potentially undermine US security interests. Fourth, supporters argued that the United States had a strong interest in maintaining open markets and encouraging open investment policies around the world; blocking the CNOOC-Unocal transaction would lead to protectionism and ultimately hurt US interests.[28] Finally, CNOOC itself made it clear that it would be willing to sell Unocal's assets based in the Gulf of Mexico if Chinese ownership of such assets created national security concerns.[29]

In the six weeks that followed before CNOOC ultimately abandoned its bid, hardly a day went by in Washington without another attack on the transaction:

- 41 members of Congress sent a letter to Treasury Secretary John Snow in late June 2005, asking that the potential transaction "be reviewed immediately to investigate the implications of the acquisition of US energy companies and assets by CNOOC and other government-controlled Chinese energy companies."[30]

- On June 30, 2005, the US House of Representatives voted 333-92 to prohibit the Treasury Department's use of funds for recommending approval of the sale of Unocal to CNOOC.[31] On the same day, the House also approved, by a vote of 398-15, a nonbinding resolution urging an Exon-Florio review of the bid, stating that CNOOC in control of Unocal "could take action that would threaten to impair the national security of the United States."[32] The language of the resolution mirrored the statutory test in the Exon-Florio Amendment. In other words, the House of Representatives went on record with the view that CFIUS should block the transaction.

- On July 11, 2005, Senators Kent Conrad (D-ND) and Jim Bunning (R-KY) wrote a letter to United States Trade Representative Rob Port-

28. Editorial, "No Way to Treat a Dragon," *New York Times*, August 4, 2005, A18.

29. Fu Chengyu, "Why Is America Worried?" *Wall Street Journal*, July 6, 2005, A14.

30. Letter to Treasury Secretary John W. Snow from Representative William J. Jefferson et al. (undated).

31. H Amdt. 431 offered to HR 3058 by Representative Carolyn Kilpatrick of Michigan, approved in roll call vote no. 353, 109th Congress, 1st sess., 151 *Congressional Record* H5515 (daily ed. June 30, 2005).

32. Expressing the Sense of the House of Representatives that a Chinese State-Owned Energy Company Exercising Control of Critical United States Energy Infrastructure and Energy Production Capacity Could Take Action That Would Threaten to Impair the National Security of the United States, HR 344, 109th Congress, 1st sess., 151 *Congressional Record* H194 (daily ed. January 25, 2005): § 1, 4. The resolution was offered by Representative Pombo and approved in roll call vote no. 360.

man and Secretary of Commerce Carlos Gutierrez suggesting that CNOOC's proposed acquisition "is inconsistent with China's WTO commitments."[33] The letter took aim at the financing arrangements CNOOC had made to support the acquisition, stating "the proposed acquisition is not being conducted on commercial terms and has little commercial justification. CNOOC's bid for Unocal will require CNOOC to secure $16 billion in funding from outside sources. Of this $16 billion, $13 billion will be provided by entities owned by the Chinese government; and $7 billion of this funding will be in the form of no-interest or low-interest loans from its state-owned parent company."[34]

- On July 13, 2005, the House Armed Services Committee held a hearing on the proposed CNOOC acquisition. Among the witnesses was former CIA director Jim Woolsey, who called the proposed deal a "takeover attempt of a US company by the most powerful communist dictatorship in the world. . . . Oil can be used as a weapon of war."[35]

- Also on July 13, 2005, Senators Charles Grassley (R-IA) and Max Baucus, the chairman and ranking member of the powerful Senate Finance Committee, wrote to the president expressing concerns about funding for the CNOOC bid, stating: "The offer by CNOOC Ltd. for Unocal raises an important question; namely, whether it is appropriate for state-owned enterprises to subsidize investment transactions to acquire scarce natural resources that are in high demand. When government subsidies are directed toward the acquisition and development of scarce resources, any ensuing market distortions should be of particular concern. Such subsidies may facilitate the allocation of scarce resources to inefficient or less-efficient producers. Any review by CFIUS should take into account the impact this type of subsidized acquisition may have on the US economy and its potential threat to our national security interests."[36]

- On the same day, representative Richard Pombo wrote to congressman Joe Barton, chairman of the House Committee on Energy and Commerce, asking Barton to amend the draft energy bill moving through Congress. The proposed amendment would limit CFIUS's ability to

---

33. Letter to the Honorable Carlos M. Gutierrez and Ambassador Rob Portman from Senators Kent Conrad and Jim Bunning (July 11, 2005), available at conrad.senate.gov (accessed March 10, 2006).

34. Letter to the Honorable Carlos M. Gutierrez and Ambassador Rob Portman from Senators Kent Conrad and Jim Bunning (July 11, 2005).

35. See statements of Representative James Woolsey before the House Armed Services Committee, *Hearing on the National Security Implications of the Possible Merger Between the China National Offshore Oil Corporation (CNOOC) and the Unocal Corporation* (July 13, 2005).

36. Senators Charles E. Grassley and Max Baucus, "Grassley, Baucus Express Concern Over Potential CNOOC-Unocal Deal" press release, July 13, 2005.

review the proposed CNOOC transaction until the Departments of Energy and State completed a wide-ranging study of the proposed transaction. Among other things, the study, which according to the amendment would need to be completed within 180 days, would require assessments of the type, nationality, and location of energy assets sought for investment by companies in the People's Republic of China (PRC); an assessment of the extent to which China's investment in energy assets was on market-based terms, free from government subsidies; the effect of such investment on the United States' control of dual-use and export-controlled technologies; and the relationship between the PRC and energy-related businesses such as CNOOC.

- On July 15, 2005, Senator Byron Dorgan introduced a bill in the US Senate that would block, through legislation, the CNOOC acquisition of Unocal. The bill, after reciting various findings that argued against the transaction, simply stated, "Notwithstanding any other provision of law, the merger, acquisition or takeover of Unocal by CNOOC is prohibited."[37]

- Also on July 15, five senators wrote to Senator Peter Domenici, chairman of the Senate Committee on Energy and Natural Resources, opposing the CNOOC acquisition. The five senators also asked Domenici to include the same amendment that Congressman Pombo had previously written about to Congressman Barton.[38]

- On July 20, Senator Charles Schumer offered an amendment to an appropriations bill that would prevent a foreign government-owned entity from acquiring a US company until 30 days after the secretary of state had delivered an assessment as to whether there were reciprocal laws allowing for similar transactions in that foreign country. The amendment passed the Senate by a voice vote.[39]

- On July 29, Senate and House negotiators agreed to adopt, with slight changes, the amendment authored by Congressman Pombo requiring that the secretaries of energy, defense, and homeland security conduct a study of China's growing energy requirements and the implications of "such growth on the political, strategic, economic, or national security of the United States."[40] The amendment prohibited CFIUS from

---

37. Bill to prohibit the merger, acquisition, or takeover of Unocal Corporation by CNOOC Ltd. of China. S 1412, 109th Congress, 1st sess., 151 *Congressional Record:* S 8386–8387 (daily ed. July 15, 2005).

38. Letter to Senator Pete V. Domenici from Senators Conrad Burns, Byron Dorgan, Mary Landrieu, Lindsey Graham, and Mel Martinez (July 15, 2005).

39. S 8522, 151 *Congressional Record* (daily ed. July 20, 2005): S 8574. Amendment introduced by Senator Schumer, later became SA 1304 to HR 3057.

40. *Energy Policy Act of 2005*, § 1837, Public Law 109-58, *US Statutes at Large* 119, 594.

concluding its national security review of an "investment in the energy assets of a United States domestic corporation by an entity owned or controlled by the government of the People's Republic of China" until after a period of 141 days. In other words, once the amendment became law, CFIUS could not complete its review of a potential CNOOC-Unocal transaction for 141 days, or 51 days longer than the maximum of 90 days established under the Exon-Florio Amendment.

Six days after the Senate and House conferees for the Energy Policy Act adopted the Pombo Amendment, CNOOC announced that it was withdrawing its bid for Unocal. In a statement, CNOOC's Chairman Fu Chengyu said, "CNOOC has given active consideration to further improving the terms of its offer, and would have done so but for the political environment in the US."[41] Mr. Fu called the negative political reaction to CNOOC's bid "regrettable and unjustified." Despite bidding almost $1 billion more than Chevron, the political backlash against the proposed acquisition created too much risk for both CNOOC and Unocal.

Indeed, while the focus of congressional opponents to the CNOOC bid was squarely on the CFIUS process, the ultimate decision makers would have been the boards of directors of Unocal and CNOOC, and Unocal's board needed to assess the likelihood that a CNOOC acquisition of Unocal would ultimately gain CFIUS approval. According to press reports and a Unocal Securities and Exchange Commission (SEC) filing, Unocal's board of directors would have sided with CNOOC if the Chinese company had further increased its bid in light of the regulatory risk the transaction would face.[42]

The CNOOC-Unocal case was also unusual in CNOOC's decision to file a formal notice with CFIUS, thereby asking CFIUS to commence consideration of its national security review, even though Unocal was formally and contractually committed to be acquired by Chevron. Simultaneous with the filing, CNOOC issued a press release saying that the company made the filing so "the Committee can begin to review CNOOC's proposal to merge with Unocal Corp. CFIUS regulations provide that the Committee will ask Unocal to respond to its questions with respect to the transaction within seven days of the Committee's request."[43] CNOOC further stated that "we have given Unocal certainty with regard to our proposal, which is all cash, and assurances with regard to the regulatory approval process."

41. Fu Chengyu, press release, "CNOOC Announces That It Has Withdrawn Its Offer for Unocal," August 2, 2005, available at www.cnooc.com.cn (accessed January 12, 2006).

42. Russell Gold and Kate Linebaugh, "CNOOC Pressured Unocal on Deal, Derailing Progress," Wall Street Journal, July 26, 2005, A2.

43. CNOOC press release, "CNOOC Limited Files CFIUS Notice," July 1, 2005, available at www.cnoocltd.com/press.

The CNOOC move to file with CFIUS was unusual because, typically, both parties to a transaction file a joint voluntary notice with CFIUS. CNOOC filed alone, triggering a process in which CFIUS, at its discretion, could ask Unocal for information to complete the filing.[44] CFIUS regulations do allow one "party," acting alone, to file a notice,[45] and they authorize CFIUS to seek information from other parties to a transaction or potential transaction.[46] Nevertheless, according to the Department of the Treasury, there have been only three cases out of more than 1,600 in which CFIUS has accepted a filing from only one of the parties. Given the politically charged atmosphere surrounding the CNOOC case, one could expect that CFIUS agencies would not want to break new ground and accept a unilateral filing, particularly since it was unclear whether a CNOOC-Unocal transaction would ever materialize.

Throughout the congressional debate over the CNOOC proposal, the White House and CFIUS agencies, as appropriate, scrupulously tried to stay out of the fray. When asked about the transaction, Scott McClellan, the White House press secretary, demurred, stating, "There are procedures in place, and if a bid goes through then we would expect the appropriate procedures to be followed."[47] Responding to a reporter's question about CNOOC's unilateral CFIUS filing, Tony Fratto, a Treasury spokesman, stated, "A CFIUS review may begin when the necessary information from a potential acquiring company and target company is filed with the Com-

---

44. See Regulations Pertaining to Mergers, Acquisitions, and Takeovers by Foreign Persons, *Code of Federal Regulations,* title 31, sec. 800.402(a)(2). If CFIUS chooses to delay acceptance of the notice and the beginning of the review to obtain any information that has not been submitted by the notifying party, it may inform the nonnotifying party that a notice has been submitted with respect to a proposed transaction involving the party, and request that the information required by the regulations be forwarded within seven days.

45. Regulations Pertaining to Mergers, Acquisitions, and Takeovers by Foreign Persons, sec. 800.401(a).

46. Regulations Pertaining to Mergers, Acquisitions, and Takeovers by Foreign Persons, sec. 800.402(b), which reads,

If fewer than all the parties to an acquisition submit a voluntary notice:

(1) Each notifying party shall provide the information set out in this section with respect to itself and, to the extent known or reasonably available to it, with respect to each non-notifying party.

(2) The Staff Chairman may delay acceptance of the notice, and the beginning of the 30-day review period, in order to obtain any information set forth under this section that has not been submitted by the notifying party. Where necessary to obtain such information, the Staff Chairman may inform the non-notifying party or parties that notice has been initiated with respect to a proposed transaction involving the party, and request that certain information set forth in this section, as specified by the Staff Chairman, be forwarded to the Committee within seven days after such request by the Staff Chairman.

47. Jad Mouawad, "Unocal's Chinese Suitor Wants U.S. Review," *New York Times,* June 28, 2005, C6.

mittee, and the Committee determines that a transaction is likely to be successful. . . . CFIUS does not provide 'advisory opinions.' "[48] CFIUS never acted on the CNOOC filing, as congressional pressure ultimately led CNOOC to withdraw.

It is unknown how CFIUS would have ultimately ruled on the proposed CNOOC-Unocal transaction if the transaction had gone forward. The only detailed public statement ever offered by the Bush administration was made by Deputy Treasury Secretary Robert Kimmit, in testimony before the Senate Committee on Banking, Housing and Urban Affairs. In response to a question by Senator Richard Shelby, the chairman of the committee, about whether the proposed CNOOC acquisition would be subject to a mandatory investigation pursuant to the Byrd Amendment to Exon-Florio, Kimmit stated:

> Let's talk about the public facts. The fact is it was a state-owned company . . . receiving concessional financing, according to reports, wanting to make an investment into a sensitive sector, sensitive by [China's] definition, since they will not let US companies invest in that [sector] in China . . . it would seem to me that it falls squarely within Section B, which was the Byrd Amendment in 1992.[49]

In other words, according to Kimmit, CFIUS would have subjected a CNOOC-Unocal transaction to extraordinary scrutiny.

The Dubai Ports World Controversy

Of all of the cases in which Exon-Florio reviews have become politicized, the Dubai Ports World (DP World) acquisition of Peninsular and Oriental Steam Navigation Company (P&O) stands out in several ways. Statements by congressional leaders from both parties denouncing the deal were unusually strong, so strong that defenders of the deal could have credibly argued that anti-Arab sentiment was a factor in the statements. As a perfect example of the hyperbole, Senator Frank Lautenberg (D-NJ), a leading opponent of the transaction, stated, "Don't let them tell you this is just the transfer of title. Baloney. We wouldn't transfer title to the Devil; we're not going to transfer title to Dubai."[50] Senator Charles Schumer (D-NY) denounced the transaction at a press conference that included families of vic-

---

48. Matt Pottinger and John M. Biers, "To Secure Unocal, Timing May Be Key. Vote on Chevron Bid Nears, and CNOOC Works to Hasten US Regulatory Review," *Asian Business News*, July 4, 2005, available at http://online.wsj.com (accessed March 9, 2006).

49. Senate Committee on Banking, Housing and Urban Affairs, *Implementation of the Exon-Florio Amendment and the Committee on Foreign Investment in the United States: Hearing Before the Senate Committee on Banking, Housing and Urban Affairs*, 109th Congress, 1st sess., October 20, 2005.

50. John Cranford, "Defining 'Ours' in a New World," *CQ Weekly*, March 6, 2006, 592.

tims of the September 11, 2001, attacks on the United States, a clear emotional appeal to the hearts and minds of the American public.[51] The controversy was played out on the front pages of newspapers, in Congress, and even on Air Force One (President Bush issued his veto threat on Air Force One), over a period of three weeks in the spring of 2006.[52]

DP World, a firm based in Dubai, the United Arab Emirates, manages container terminals and other port-related operations in 14 countries. At the end of 2005, it was the seventh-largest port operator in the world. It is owned by the government of Dubai via the Ports, Customs, and Free Zones Corporation, a Dubai governmental agency. P&O was founded in 1837 and historically was known as a steamship operator, as its name implies. However, in early 2005, P&O sold its remaining oceangoing ship-operating business (it retains a ferry service) so that the firm became mostly a ports operator. These activities account for about 80 percent of its profits.[53] Thus, at the end of 2005, P&O was the fourth-largest port operator in the world. It operated 27 container terminals and over 100 logistics services in 18 countries, including the United States.

In October 2005, P&O received a buyout overture from DP World, which led to a bidding war between DP World and a Singapore-based port operator. The buyout offer was reported in the *Wall Street Journal* on October 31; thus, the possibility of DP World taking over port operations of P&O was public knowledge.[54] On November 29, P&O announced that it would accept the DP World offer. The deal would be subject to scrutiny under Exon-Florio, because P&O owned a US subsidiary, P&O Ports North America, which managed operations at six US ports, in Newark, Philadelphia, Baltimore, Miami, New Orleans, and Houston. Following standard procedures, representatives of DP World met with CFIUS staff on October 17, and with representatives of the most relevant CFIUS agencies, specifically the DHS, Customs and Border Protection, the US Coast Guard, the DOJ, and Department of Commerce.[55] During this informal

---

51. Will Lester, "Lawmakers Decry Takeover of U.S. Ports," *Associated Press*, February 20, 2006, available at www.forbes.com (accessed March 10, 2006).

52. David E. Sanger and Eric Lipton, "Bush Would Veto Any Bill Halting Dubai Port Deal," *New York Times*, February 22, 2006, A1.

53. In 1994, P&O sold its remaining passenger ship business (by then, mostly cruise ships) to Carnival Cruise Lines. In 1996, P&O placed its container (cargo) operations into a joint venture with Royal Nedlloyd (then renamed P&O Nedlloyd), in which P&O retained a 25 percent interest. P&O Nedlloyd, including the P&O interest, was sold to A. P. Moeller-Maersk of Denmark in early 2005.

54. Jason Singer, "P&O Attracts Buyout Overture Amid Shipping-Industry Boom," *Wall Street Journal*, October 31, 2005, A3.

55. See testimony of H. Edward Bilkey, COO of Dubai Ports World, before the US Senate Committee on Commerce, Science and Transportation, *Hearing on Security of Terminal Operations at U.S. Ports*, February 28, 2006.

prefiling period, CFIUS and the relevant member agencies began a preliminary review and analysis of the proposed transaction, and upon request, DP World provided additional information to the relevant officials. A meeting of representatives of DP World and P&O Ports North America with the full CFIUS was held on December 6, 2005. Shortly after, on December 15, DP World filed formal notification to CFIUS, triggering the statutory 30-day CFIUS review of the proposed transaction.

During the 30-day review, the DHS negotiated with DP World to provide a "letter of assurances," a common form for a security agreement negotiated under the CFIUS process. This letter was finalized and submitted to CFIUS on January 6.[56] The letter stipulated that DP World would maintain "no less" than current levels of membership and cooperation by P&O Ports North America in existing security arrangements and that DP World would provide the DHS with 30 days advance notice of any change in membership or cooperation in these security arrangements. It also agreed to operate all US facilities to the extent possible with US management, to designate a corporate officer with DP World to serve as point of contact with the DHS on security matters, to provide any relevant information to DHS upon request, and to assist US law enforcement agencies in any matter related to port security, including disclosing information as agencies requested.[57] Comforted that the letter of assurance satisfied their security concerns, CFIUS cleared the transaction on January 17, 2005, without requiring it to be subject to the more extensive 45-day review.

Despite this clearance, the case became highly politicized, but not until mid-February, about a month after the initial CFIUS decision to clear it. Thus, this case stands out among the cases discussed in this chapter for four reasons. First, of all of these cases, the polemics surrounding the DP World–P&O case were especially raucous, even more so than in the CNOOC-Unocal case. Second, the case did not involve a direct foreign purchase of a US firm, but rather an indirect purchase of US assets through one foreign firm acquiring another foreign firm. Because P&O is a British firm and the takeover by DP World would give the latter control over a number of British firms, the takeover was also subject to a security review by authorities in the United Kingdom. These authorities, like their American counterparts at CFIUS, concluded that the transaction would not compromise port security in the United Kingdom. Curiously, in the United Kingdom—a country that, like the United States, has been subject to terrorist attacks at the hands of Islamic extremists—no objections were raised,

---

56. This letter was initially meant to be confidential; however, on February 21, the Ports, Customs, and Free Zone Corporation of Dubai gave permission for the letter to be publicly released. See Defendants' Response to Order to Show Cause at Exhibit C, *Corzine v. Snow et al.*, No. 06-833 (D.N.J.).

57. Defendants' Response to Order to Show Cause at Exhibit C, *Corzine v. Snow et al.*, No. 06-833 (D.N.J.).

either in the press or in Parliament, to this clearance. Third, the sound and fury surrounding the DP World case in the United States erupted only in mid-February 2006, following an article published in the *New York Times* critical of the deal, and subsequent public denunciations by Schumer, Hillary Clinton (D-NY), and Robert Menendez (D-NJ) regarding the transaction—five months after the *Wall Street Journal* had made the deal public knowledge.[58] Never before had an Exon-Florio case become so highly politicized only after the underlying transaction had been cleared. Fourth, after almost three weeks of nonstop news coverage and commentary by members of Congress, including leaders of both parties and mostly adverse to the investor, the investor asked that the case be reopened and subject to the extensive 45-day review.[59] To our knowledge, never before have parties that have already cleared CFIUS requested an additional, more rigorous review.

The catalyst for the political controversy appears to have been a small stevedoring firm based in Miami, Eller & Co. Eller had a long-standing commercial dispute with P&O, and sought to block the deal to increase its leverage in its negotiations with P&O. Eller first sought to intervene with CFIUS, which, appropriately, decided not to factor a commercial dispute into its national security analysis. When Eller could not make its case before CFIUS, it began to stoke the flames on Capitol Hill in late January through a Washington lobbyist, Joe Muldoon. Israel Klein, a spokesperson for Senator Schumer, the leading opponent of the transaction, stated that "Eller was really the canary in the mineshaft for many people on the Hill" regarding the DP World–P&O deal.[60]

With the benefit of hindsight, we can confidently say that it is not a surprise that the DP World case became politicized; indeed, it was highly likely from the outset. The only real surprise is that it took so long for the politicization to happen. The politicization had two causes. First, the deal involved ports, which were already concerns for homeland security. Second, it involved an investor based in a Middle Eastern nation, and ever since September 11, Americans have been skittish about almost anything involving the Middle East. The United Arab Emirates has been an ally and friend of the United States throughout the post–September 11 period, but many persons critical of the DP World–P&O deal seemed quite unaware of this fact.

A recent report by the National Commission on Terrorist Attacks upon the United States (2004)—the so-called 9/11 Commission—has questioned

---

58. See timeline described in David Sanger, "Under Pressure, Dubai Company Drops Port Deal," *New York Times*, March 10, 2006, A1.

59. David E. Sanger, "Threats and Responses: Port Security; Dubai Deal Will Undergo Deeper Inquiry into Security," *New York Times*, February 27, 2006, A15.

60. Neil King Jr. and Gregg Hitt, "Small Florida Firm Sowed Seed of Port Dispute," *Wall Street Journal*, February 28, 2006, A3.

the adequacy of security measures in US ports. It did not cite foreign ownership of operating companies at US ports as a factor in US port security shortcomings;[61] instead it focused on real deficiencies in US port security. Nonetheless, the report doubtlessly created jitters in both the US public and Congress about port security. Thus, when the DP World acquisition of P&O's US port operations became widely known, it was not entirely unreasonable that some public concern regarding security implications of this acquisition might arise.

As the administration, and especially Treasury Deputy Secretary Robert Kimmit, was later to acknowledge publicly, one major failure in this case was that of the administration to recognize that the DP World–P&O acquisition might become highly politicized, or evoke an emotional response from the US public. Thus, the case catalyzed many in Congress to argue for greater transparency in the CFIUS process. The administration admitted that it would have been well served to brief congressional leaders on the case during the CFIUS investigation. Even with such briefings, however, the facts of the case created a second, even more "perfect storm" than CNOOC/Unocal for a political controversy in Congress—an investment in US ports operations by a company owned by an Arab government, at a time when President Bush's popularity was lagging. These facts, combined with a domestic company eager to fan the flames (Eller), created a witches' brew in Congress.

As the controversy developed, Congress was abuzz. Close to a dozen congressional committees held hearings on the subject, and at most of these, members of Congress excoriated CFIUS officials for their supposed lapse in judgment. When Senate Majority Leader Bill Frist (R-TN) and other leaders stated their intent to block the deal, President Bush threatened to veto legislation that blocked the transaction.[62] DP World's request for a 45-day full investigation failed to mollify critics in Congress. On March 8, members of the powerful House Appropriations Committee voted by a whopping 62-2 margin to block the transaction.[63] The next day, Senate Republicans lost a procedural vote offered by Senator Schumer to close debate on a lobbying reform bill, thereby creating the opportunity for Schumer to force a Senate vote on whether to block the transaction. That same day, congressional leaders, including Frist and Speaker of the House Dennis Hastert (R-IL), informed President Bush that they could not garner the votes to sustain a presidential veto of a bill blocking the DP World ac-

---

61. In addition to the six port facilities managed by P&O, the majority of other US ports were managed by firms of foreign nationality, including those in New York and Los Angeles.

62. David E. Sanger and Eric Lipton, "Bush Would Veto Any Bill Halting Dubai Port Deal," *New York Times*, February 22, 2006, A1.

63. Edward Alden, Stephanie Kirchgaessner, and Demetri Sevastopulo, "Dubai Cedes Control in US Ports Battle," *Financial Times*, March 9, 2006, 1.

quisition. According to news reports, the White House contacted the government of the United Arab Emirates with the news, and DP World announced that it would "transfer fully the US operations" to "a United States entity."[64] On March 15, DP clarified its intentions, announcing that it would sell its US operations within four to six months.[65] Hours later, the US House of Representatives voted by a 377 to 38 margin to reject a motion to strike language in an appropriations bill blocking the transaction. *Congress Daily*, a Capitol Hill newsletter, appropriately closed the saga with the headline, "House Puts a Bullet in Port Deal's Corpse."[66]

■ ■ ■

What can we conclude from these cases? Certainly, politicizing the CFIUS process creates costs for the United States. It increases uncertainty for foreign investors, employees, and customers of the transaction parties. Moreover, if the trend toward politicization of the process continues unabated, foreign investors could shy away from acquiring US companies, creating a chill in the investment market and lowering values for US companies. A politicized regulatory review for a foreign investor could create higher risk for foreign investors than for domestic investors, because of the uncertainty associated with the CFIUS process. As a result, in highly politicized transactions, foreign investors could be forced to pay more for an asset than would domestic investors. Alternatively, if a domestic company seeks to be acquired by another company, and the only interested parties are foreign, the domestic company might see the value of its assets diminished because of the CFIUS process. A failed foreign transaction would also hurt the United States if the foreign investor would have brought an acquired US company improved technologies and new capital that would have enhanced productivity and job creation. All of this translates into higher costs for the US economy and, in some cases, diminished benefits.

Until the Dubai Ports controversy, the formal CFIUS process had stayed, based on anecdotal data and interviews with CFIUS officials, fairly immune to political pressure from competitors or from Capitol Hill. This insulation has been particularly effective for the substance of CFIUS's national security analyses and measures to mitigate national security concerns. CFIUS officials from the key security agencies—the DOJ, DHS, and

64. Greg Hitt and Neil King Jr., "Dubai Firm Bows to Public Outcry—Under Pressure, DP World to Shed U.S. Holdings; Fears of Political Fallout—Putting Off Foreign Investors?" *Wall Street Journal*, March 10, 2006, A1.

65. Christopher S. Rugaber and Heather M. Rothman, "DP World Pledges to Sell U.S. Holdings In 4–6 Months; House Votes to Block Deal," *BNA International Trade Daily*, March 16, 2006.

66. *Congress Daily a.m.*, March 16, 2006, available at http://nationaljournal.com/pubs/congressdaily.

FBI—pride themselves on the seriousness and rigor with which they conduct a national security analysis of a transaction. The CFIUS services acted appropriately in staying out of the competition between Chevron and CNOOC over Unocal. CFIUS should not review a transaction unless it is clear that the transaction is highly likely to be consummated subsequent to regulatory approval. Career civil servants, not political appointees, conduct most of the analytical work in the key agencies, and typically are not personally exposed to calls or intervention by members of Congress or their staff. Unfortunately, in the wake of the Dubai case, Congress has criticized the apolitical nature of CFIUS, including the fact that decisions are not made at sufficiently senior levels in the US government.

Members of Congress can have an influence on the process, particularly a CFIUS decision to proceed beyond the initial 30-day review to an investigation. Anecdotal evidence and interviews with CFIUS officials suggest that those officials are more willing to respond to congressional pressure to extend the time frame of an investigation than to change their underlying national security analysis for a particular transaction. By ceding ground on process, CFIUS can reduce the pressure on the substance of their work—determining whether a transaction threatens US national security. After the DP World controversy, it is clear that Congress will be more involved in the CFIUS process, and the extent of that involvement is still playing out at the time of this writing.

On the other hand, some congressional and public input into the CFIUS process can create benefits. One benefit might be better information brought to bear on a CFIUS determination. CFIUS cannot and should not refuse to receive information from the public or Congress that may be useful to its national security analysis. Thus, an alert member of Congress, or a whistle blower in a company, could create a benefit by telling CFIUS if one of the parties intentionally misrepresents the information provided in its CFIUS notice, or if CFIUS is unaware of a national security issue related to the acquisition. At the same time, the CFIUS process should not be used to "blow up" a transaction so another bidder can acquire the same company at a lower cost, nor should it be used as leverage for negotiations or other business matters unrelated to national security, as in the Tyco-Crest and DP World–Eller examples. To that end, both to inspire confidence in the integrity of the process and to deter competitors or members of Congress from intervening with CFIUS for commercial, as opposed to national security, reasons, it would be useful for CFIUS to issue a public statement through the Department of the Treasury that it will frown upon attempts by competitors or their representatives to interfere in the national security review process. Such a statement will only be hortatory, and whether CFIUS can effectively distinguish between commercial and national security considerations depends on the desires of leaders of each CFIUS agency to do so. Congress did not set up CFIUS, however, to block transactions that were politically difficult or unpopular. Rather, the statute intends for the president to block only those transactions that create national security risks to the United States. The potential for domestic companies to exploit the CFIUS process against foreign investors is yet another reason, discussed in chapter 6, why Congress should not expand the criteria for CFIUS reviews to include "economic security." If economic security were added to the statute, the CFIUS process would likely become even more politicized, because it would be much easier for domestic bidders to fashion arguments based on economic security, justifying the need for a particular company to have American rather than foreign owners.

Yet even an unpoliticized CFIUS review can have its flaws, and some of them arise from the way that the CFIUS's mandate is structured. The next chapter offers recommendations for meaningfully reforming CFIUS, by clarifying standards, perhaps implementing new ones, and avoiding existing attempts at reform that would chill investment that the United States wants.

6

Policy Recommendations: Improving the Implementation of Exon-Florio

Does Exon-Florio need changing? As discussed in chapter 2, members of Congress have attempted to amend the Exon-Florio Amendment a number of times, including in 2005. Moreover, at the time of this writing, in the wake of the Dubai Ports World (DP World) controversy, there has been a flood of more than 20 bills introduced in Congress that would reform the Committee on Foreign Investment in the United States (CFIUS), prohibit DP World from acquiring Peninsular and Oriental Steam Navigation Company (P&O), or prohibit foreign ownership of ports and other critical infrastructure. Some earlier reform efforts have been successful, such as the Byrd Amendment in 1993, but most have never been considered or debated even in a congressional committee. Just as Fujitsu's attempt to acquire Fairchild and Sir James Goldsmith's attempt to buy Goodyear led to the adoption of the original Exon-Florio Amendment, a high-profile transaction often catalyzes members of Congress to seek changes to the amendment. The Byrd Amendment, which, among other things, requires mandatory investigations for acquisitions by foreign government-controlled firms, was introduced in the wake of the controversy over the 1992 attempt by Thomson-CSF, a French firm, to take control of LTV Aerospace and Defense Corporation, then a world leader in missile technology. At the time, the French government owned 60 percent of Thomson-CSF's shares, and controlled 75 percent of its voting stock.[1]

---

1. *National Defense Authorization Act*, 102nd Congress, 2nd sess., *Congressional Record* 138 (September 18, 1992): S 14052.

Congressional pressure related to the case led Congress to pass the Byrd Amendment.[2]

Two events preceding the Dubai Ports controversy—the IBM sale of its personal computer division to the Chinese firm Lenovo, the China National Offshore Oil Corporation (CNOOC) offer to buy Unocal—similarly inspired a number of members of Congress to amend Exon-Florio. Responding to the CNOOC transaction, in August 2005 senators James Inhofe and Richard Shelby each offered sweeping amendments. The Inhofe Amendment would have transferred the chairmanship of CFIUS to the Department of Defense (DOD), broadened the criteria CFIUS considers to include "economic security," and given Congress broad powers to override presidential approval of specific transactions. The Shelby bill retained many of the elements of the Inhofe Amendment but preserved the Department of the Treasury as the CFIUS chair and maintained "national security" as the sole criterion CFIUS should consider.[3]

The Dubai Ports controversy has led members of Congress to propose even broader legislation that would not only reform CFIUS but also make broad sections of the US economy off-limits to foreign ownership. Duncan Hunter (R-CA), chairman of the House Armed Services Committee, and 15 other members of the House of Representatives introduced a bill that would prohibit foreign ownership of a broad array of assets defined as "critical infrastructure" by the DOD, expand the criteria CFIUS would need to consider when evaluating transactions, and require broad notification of Exon-Florio reviews by CFIUS, including publication in the *Federal Register* of any transaction that moves to the "investigation stage."[4] As discussed below, if the Department of Homeland Security's (DHS) current list of "critical infrastructure" activities were used to define what would be off-limits for foreign investment, we estimate that the criteria would cover more than 24 percent of the US economy. This would be a huge segment of the economy to bar to foreign investment. Moreover, in some sectors considered critical infrastructure, there is already a large foreign presence that has created no security concerns.

If Congressman Hunter's bill were to become law, foreign firms might be forced to sell their US subsidiaries, with no apparent gain to US secu-

---

2. The Byrd Amendment was actually passed in two stages. Its provisions are found in the *National Defense Authorization Act for Fiscal Year 1993*, Public Law 102-484, *US Statutes at Large* 106: 2315; and *Defense Production Act Amendments of 1992*, Public Law 102-558, *US Statutes at Large* 106: 4198.

3. For a general discussion of these issues, see David M. Marchick and Edward M. Graham, "A Misplaced Curb on Investment," *Financial Times*, October 5, 2005.

4. *To Promote the National Defense by Establishing Standards for the Ownership, Operation and Management of Critical Infrastructure in the United States, and for Other Purposes*, HR 4881, 109th Congress, 2nd sess., March 2006. Introduced by Representative Duncan Hunter (R-CA) (hereinafter, Hunter bill).

rity and almost sure harm to the US economy. (Details on US employment, and employment by foreign-owned firms, in those sectors and subsectors that correspond to the critical infrastructures list prepared by DHS are provided in an appendix to this chapter.) Similarly, Senators Menendez (D-NJ), Clinton (D-NY), Lautenberg (D-NJ), Boxer (D-CA), and Nelson (D-NJ) introduced a bill that would prohibit any mergers, acquisitions, or takeovers by companies owned or controlled by a foreign government of any US company involved in leasing, operating, managing, or owning real property or facilities at a United States port.[5] Senator Norm Coleman (R-MN) introduced a bill that would require any foreign government-owned entity to establish a separate US corporation, with a majority of US citizens on the board of directors, for any investment in "critical infra-structure."[6] Senator Coleman's bill gave existing foreign government-owned companies in sectors considered "critical infrastructure" six months to comply with the new corporate restrictions.[7] In light of the active consideration of proposals to reform CFIUS, or restrict foreign investment in the United States, we discuss and analyze a number of ideas, some good and some bad, for improving or reforming the CFIUS process.

While a number of the bills mentioned above would have extremely negative implications for the United States, several improvements to the CFIUS process should be considered. The national security criteria that CFIUS considers should be expanded to cover critical infrastructure; CFIUS's interactions with Congress, particularly regarding information sharing, should be more clearly defined; and its definitions of what constitutes control of a firm should be clarified. All of these changes can and should be made without compromising CFIUS's ability to maintain confidentiality in the process.

---

5. *Port Security Act of 2006*, S 2334, 109th Congress, 2nd sess., February 2006. Introduced by Senator Robert Menendez.

6. *The Foreign Investment Transparency and Security Act of 2006*, S 2374, 109th Congress, 2nd sess., February 2006 (introduced by Senator Norm Coleman). See also *To Prohibit Entities Owned or Controlled by Foreign Governments from Carrying Out Operations at Seaports in the United States*, HR 4817, 109th Congress, 2nd sess., February 2006 (introduced by Congressman J. D. Hayworth). The Hayworth bill prohibits an entity that is owned or controlled by a foreign government from operating or entering into contract to operate US seaports. See also *Foreign Investment Security Improvement Act*, HR 4833, 109th Congress, 2nd sess., February 2006 (introduced by Congressman J. Doolittle). The Doolittle bill requires that only US persons may control security operations at seaports in the United States or enter into agreements to conduct such security operations. Finally, see *To Prohibit Entities Owned or Controlled by Foreign Governments from Conducting Certain Operations at Seaports in the United States, and from Entering into Agreements to Conduct Such Operations*, HR 4839, 109th Congress, 2nd sess., March 2006 (introduced by Congressman C. Shaw).

7. *Foreign Investment Transparency and Security Act of 2006*, S 2374, 109th Congress, 2nd sess., February 2006 (introduced by Senator Norm Coleman).

Covering Critical Infrastructure

As noted in chapter 2, the Exon-Florio Amendment identifies five factors that the president, or the president's designee, may take into account in determining "the requirements of national security."[8] These factors cover

- domestic production needed for projected national defense requirements;

- the capability and capacity of domestic industries to meet national defense needs;

- the control of domestic industries and commercial activity by foreign citizens, and its effects on the capability and capacity of the United States to meet national security requirements;

- the potential effects of a proposed or pending transaction on sales of military goods, equipment, or technology to any country to which restrictions should apply under various export control and nonproliferation laws, as deemed by the secretary of state;

- the potential effects of a proposed or pending transaction on US international technological leadership in areas affecting US national security.[9]

Omitted from this list is the primary focus of the DHS in CFIUS reviews: protection of critical infrastructure. Because of the flexibility of the Exon-Florio Amendment, and particularly since "national security" is not defined in the statute or regulations, CFIUS began to focus on critical infrastructure during the Clinton administration. It has intensified this focus since President Bush added DHS to CFIUS in March 2003. A number of recent bills, including the Hunter bill, the Collins bill, and a bill introduced by Congresswoman Carolyn Maloney, would require CFIUS to consider the impact of foreign investment on critical infrastructure in the United States.[10] We endorse these efforts. But simply stating that CFIUS should consider the national security impact of foreign investment on critical infrastructure is not enough. There has been little to no policy guidance in the form of speeches, testimony, or official policy pronouncements from any of the most involved agencies on how the US government believes "critical infrastructure" should be protected.

The DHS has identified 12 sectors that it considers to be critical infrastructure: agriculture and food, water, public health, emergency services,

---

8. Exon-Florio Amendment, App. § 2170(f).

9. Exon-Florio Amendment, App. § 2170(f)(1–5).

10. *Committee on Foreign Investment in the United States Reform Act*, HR 4915, 109th Congress, 2nd sess., March 2006.

the defense industry, telecommunications, energy, transportation, banking and finance, chemicals, postal services and shipping, and information technology.[11] Together, these sectors account for 24.4 percent of US nonfarm civilian workers, a huge swath of the US economy.[12] But beyond specifying these sectors, the DHS has not identified the types of companies, or even subsectors, for which acquisition by a foreign firm would be deemed a high risk to national security, nor has DHS explained why foreign ownership of these sectors would create a national security risk. In the energy sector, it would seem fairly clear that foreign acquisitions of US nuclear energy companies could likely raise concerns about the security of critical infrastructure, so it would be appropriate to notify CFIUS of such an acquisition. Would the same apply to foreign acquisitions of US firms operating in other segments of the energy sector? Many foreign companies own electric distribution companies. Do these raise national security issues? What about foreign ownership of a wind farm? Similar questions certainly apply in the other sectors, including the food, transportation (including ports), and financial sectors, where foreign ownership of US firms is common, and where, in many cases, this ownership has been created via takeover of a previously US-owned firm.

Even though the federal government has committed significant time and resources to identifying "critical infrastructure" and developing a "national strategy" to protect it, policy pronouncements discussing the risks and ways to protect critical infrastructure have been shallow. In February 2003, amid much fanfare, the DHS issued a glossy, 100-page report entitled *The National Strategy for the Physical Protection of Critical Infrastructure and Key Assets*. This document identifies the sectors considered critical infrastructure, and makes bold statements about the importance of protecting it. However, a reader looking for details finds only bland generalities and few concrete policy or security prescriptions. The strategy identifies eight bland "guiding principles": ensuring public safety, public confidence, and services; establishing responsibility and accountability; and encouraging and facilitating partnering among all levels of government, and between government and industry (US DHS 2003).

If protection of critical infrastructure is going to be a high priority for the federal government, which it should be, the DHS has an obligation to clarify exactly how it would protect critical infrastructure. In doing so, the DHS must specifically identify what risks are created by foreign investment in critical infrastructure activities. On this identification, however, persons experienced with CFIUS reviews know that, because factual issues

---

11. See *National Strategy for the Physical Protection of Critical Infrastructure and Key Assets* (February 2003), available at www.whitehouse.gov (accessed March 13, 2006); and HSPD-7 (December 2003), available at www.whitehouse.gov (accessed March 14, 2006).

12. Authors' calculations based on 2002 BEA and Census data, available at www.bea.gov and www.census.gov.

drive CFIUS's national security analysis, transactions must be reviewed on a case-by-case basis. It would be both impossible and inappropriate for CFIUS agencies to provide full "bright-line" guidance, listing criteria that, if a transaction met them, surely would or would not trigger a CFIUS investigation, or require mitigation measures. At the same time, however, the security landscape has changed, and public guidance from CFIUS agencies has not clarified what new risks from foreign investment have arisen in the new post–September 11 environment, in even a general sense.

Thus in its regulations, or in any amendment to Exon-Florio, Congress and the CFIUS agencies should formally clarify that protecting critical infrastructure is a factor in assessing national security risk. In addition, the DHS, coordinating with other agencies, should provide greater guidance, through speeches, testimony, and other means, on the particular subsectors in the US economy that would raise national security concerns if foreign investors were to acquire companies in them. Not only would such guidance help foreign investors seeking to acquire US firms operating in the "critical infrastructure" sectors, but it might help DHS identify exactly in what ways foreign ownership of such firms might actually threaten US national security. As chapter 2 notes, the linkages between foreign ownership of firms with operations that can be classified as "critical infrastructure" and national security is anything but clear, and exactly what threats to infrastructure are created by foreign ownership have not been identified. Clarifying for foreign investors what sorts of transactions raise security concerns might thus help DHS and other relevant agencies think through whether, and under what circumstances, foreign ownership creates a security risk.

Establishing Security Standards for Employment of Nonnationals in Sensitive Positions

CFIUS faces the difficult issue of assessing whether foreign ownership of a US company might result in sensitive information, pertinent to national security, falling into hostile hands. One way this could happen, of course, is by such information passing to hostile parties from employees who are not US nationals but brought into the US operation by the foreign owner. The Department of Justice (DOJ), FBI, and DHS have sought to mitigate the national security risks of foreign ownership of companies in sensitive sectors by requiring in security agreements that either the US government or the acquirers conduct security screening on personnel operating in sensitive positions. This approach borrows from long-standing practices used for foreign-owned companies with classified contracts with the DOD or other US government agencies. In the telecommunications sector, which, as we have noted in chapter 2, is the only sector for which security agreements are published, recent network security agreements (NSAs) have background checks of personnel involved in network operations and handling of data requests from the DOJ and FBI, either by the US government or by an independent third party, using a screening mechanism approved by the DHS and DOJ.

Screening of personnel involved in sensitive aspects of a company's business is arguably a low-cost, effective way to identify potential security vulnerabilities in a company. However, in many cases, key officials in foreign-owned companies operating in the United States are neither US citizens nor are they based in the United States. Deutsche Telecom, which runs T-Mobile, the fourth-largest wireless carrier in the United States, most likely has non-US citizens running key parts of the US network. Verizon, AT&T, and other large US-owned telecommunications companies almost surely do the same thing. In addition, Deutsche Telecom almost surely has officials based in Germany that regularly make decisions affecting its US subsidiary. For both non-US citizens working in the United States and non-US citizens working abroad, traditional screening practices employed by the US government or third-party screening companies might not be available.

In these circumstances, security agencies have two choices: They could require that company officials involved in sensitive activities be US citizens, or that the company screen non-Americans under screening processes and laws in those individuals' home countries. For certain activities, including handling classified information or processing a wiretap request from the FBI, it is entirely reasonable for the US government to require that the responsible officials be US citizens. However, for other positions, including technical positions key to running a telecommunications network, or operating a chemical plant in the United States, limiting these positions to US citizens could deny a firm the best global talent, without necessarily enhancing security. Moreover, American citizens are regularly employed in similar positions around the world by both subsidiaries of US companies and non-US companies. Precluding non-US citizens from these positions in foreign-owned operations in the United States could lead to foreign companies precluding American citizens from similar opportunities overseas.

US security agencies could potentially address any security concerns by having foreign nationals employed in sensitive positions screened by their own governments, or by independent screening agencies operating under the laws of a particular individual's home country. In doing so, US security agencies would need to accept the validity and integrity of a foreign country's screening process. But there are a number of countries for which this should not prove problematic. A number of British telecommunications, defense, chemical, and energy firms, some of them in the nuclear energy sector, operate in both the United Kingdom and the United States and even handle sensitive contracts for both the US and UK governments. British firms handling classified work for the UK government need to satisfy the British security screening process known as ListX, an approach similar to DOD's regulations for foreign ownership of companies doing business with the Pentagon. If a British citizen is cleared to handle classified work in the United Kingdom, which is one of the United States' closest allies on security and political issues, surely that individual should, at a minimum, be deemed sufficiently trustworthy to run a telecommunications network or chemical plant in the United States.

The issue would arise, of course, as to exactly which countries' standards could be mutually recognized. Nevertheless, if security agencies are increasingly going to screen employees to mitigate perceived national security risks, because a global company needs to access talent from around the world, security agencies would benefit from putting in place mutual recognition arrangements on security screenings, at least with the United States' closest allies.

Enhancing Disclosure of Information to Congress

In the wake of the Dubai controversy, virtually every one of the bills introduced to reform the CFIUS process includes measures to enhance disclosure of information to Congress.[13] These initiatives respond to the widespread view that CFIUS agencies have failed to adequately consult or share information with Congress on particular transactions. Critics make three complaints: First, CFIUS has failed to provide reports to Congress on investigations, as required by the amendment; second, CFIUS has failed to provide a quadrennial report, as required by the amendment; third, CFIUS should generally provide more information to Congress, since Congress is exempted from the amendment's confidentiality requirements.

In the first area of concern, Congressman Don Manzullo (R-IL) has argued that the Treasury Department takes too narrow a reading of the reporting requirement in the Exon-Florio Amendment, which reads as follows:

> Report to the Congress. The President shall immediately transmit to the Secretary of the Senate and the Clerk of the House of Representatives a written report of the President's determination of whether or not to take action under subsection (d), including a detailed explanation of the findings made under subsection (e) and the factors considered under subsection (f). Such report shall be consistent with the requirements of subsection (c) of this Act.[14]

Subsection (d) of Exon-Florio, which provides the president with authority to block a transaction, reads:

---

13. *Committee on Foreign Investment in the United States Reform Act*. See also *United States Security Improvement Act of 2006*, HR 4813, 109th Congress, 2nd sess., February 2006 (introduced by Congressman M. Foley).

14. Exon-Florio Amendment, § 2170(g).

[t]he President may take such action for such time as the President considers appropriate to suspend or prohibit any acquisition, merger, or takeover, of a person engaged in interstate commerce in the United States proposed or pending on or after the date of enactment of this section by or with foreign persons so that such control will not threaten to impair the national security. The President shall announce the decision to take action pursuant to this subsection not later than 15 days after the investigation described in subsection (a) is completed. The President may direct the Attorney General to seek appropriate relief, including divestment relief, in the district courts of the United States in order to implement and enforce this section.[15]

Manzullo criticized CFIUS agencies in general, and the Department of the Treasury in particular, after CFIUS refused to share documents and national security analyses related to a recent case that required an investigation, but was resolved without needing a presidential decision. Manzullo believed that section (g) of Exon-Florio required a detailed report to Congress any time a transaction proceeded to the investigation stage. CFIUS agencies demurred, arguing that a report to Congress under section (g) is required only where the president personally decides on a transaction.

CFIUS agencies have also been criticized for failing to provide a quadrennial report to Congress, as the Exon-Florio Amendment requires. According to the amendment, the president (as opposed to CFIUS agencies) must issue a report to Congress every four years that "(a) evaluates whether there is credible evidence of a coordinated strategy by 1 or more countries or companies to acquire United States companies involved in research, development, or production of critical technologies for which the United States is a leading producer; and (b) evaluates whether there are industrial espionage activities directed or directly assisted by foreign governments against private United States companies aimed at obtaining commercial secrets related to critical technologies."[16]

In a June 24, 2005, letter to Senators Thad Cochran and Robert Byrd, the chairman and ranking member of the Senate Appropriations Committee, C. Richard D'Amato and Roger W. Robinson, the chair and vice chair of the US-China Economic and Security Review Commission, wrote,

[I]t has come to our attention that the reporting requirement included in the Defense Production Act amendments of 1992—i.e., for the President to report to the Congress every four years "whether foreign governments or companies have a coordinated strategy to acquire US critical technology companies"—has not been met since the initial report was delivered in 1993 (see attachment). This omission clearly violates the law, and we strongly recommend that the report, which has not been produced in the last 12 years, be requested and executed as soon as possible. Having the content of this report will significantly help Congress properly evaluate the appropriateness of CFIUS decisions on whether foreign acquisitions

---

15. Exon-Florio Amendment, § 2170(d).

16. Exon-Florio Amendment, § 2170(k).

of US firms, particularly by Chinese government-controlled companies, should be approved or disapproved given the national security dimensions involved.[17]

Third, critics have contended that CFIUS agencies have withheld information from Congress, even though Congress is exempted from the confidentiality requirements of the amendment. Specifically, the amendment provides

> Confidentiality of information. Any information or documentary material filed with the President or the President's designee pursuant to this section shall be exempt from disclosure under section 552 of title 5, United States Code, and no such information or documentary material may be made public, except as may be relevant to any administrative or judicial action or proceeding. *Nothing in this subsection shall be construed to prevent disclosure to either House of Congress or to any duly authorized committee or subcommittee of the Congress.*[18] (emphasis added)

The calls for greater disclosure to Congress must be balanced by a recognition that, from an investment policy and national security perspective, strict confidentiality within the CFIUS process is warranted for a variety of reasons. Just as in antitrust reviews by the DOJ or the Federal Trade Commission, parties filing with CFIUS turn over a significant amount of confidential business information. The filing companies might be severely damaged not only if this information became public, but also if competitors obtained it. Perhaps more important, because the essence of any review includes the president's and CFIUS's judgments on national security issues, it is imperative that the proceedings remain confidential. Not only would CFIUS's national security judgments potentially embarrass the parties to a transaction, as well as the acquirer's host country, but US national security interests could be compromised if information related to a CFIUS review were made public.

Given the conflicting requirements that Congress be adequately informed of operations under Exon-Florio and the need for confidentiality in the CFIUS process, in our view, CFIUS agencies should develop a protocol with the relevant congressional committees (Banking and Financial Services, Homeland Security, and Armed Services) to establish better ground rules for the type of information CFIUS might share with Congress. As the amendment requires, the president should produce a quadrennial report, and inform Congress any time he personally makes a decision on a particular transaction. Beyond these statutory requirements, CFIUS should provide, on an annual basis, more aggregate data to Congress on the cases they process than is now provided. Such aggregate data could include

---

17. C. Richard D'Amato and Roger W. Robinson, Letter to Senators Thad Cochran and Robert C. Byrd, June 24, 2005, available at www.uscc.gov (accessed March 14, 2006).

18. Exon-Florio Amendment, § 2170(c).

- the number of transactions CFIUS reviews;

- the number of 30-day reviews, investigations, withdrawals, and decisions by the president;

- trends in the number of filings, investigation withdrawals, and presidential decisions;

- the sectors in which filings have been made, and the countries from which investments have emanated; and

- data disclosing whether companies that have withdrawn CFIUS notices later refiled such notices or, alternatively, abandoned the transaction.

CFIUS should also provide frequent, high-level classified briefings to key congressional committees on the types of national security issues that have arisen in transactions before the committee. Regular briefings would increase the confidence that key congressional committees show to CFIUS and help preserve the integrity of both the CFIUS process and the Exon-Florio Amendment.[19]

At the same time, Congress should not demand, nor should CFIUS provide, any confidential business data that parties to a particular transaction give to CFIUS. In many respects, Congress is better equipped to handle and preserve the confidentiality of national security briefings and information than confidential business data. Members of Congress can be expected to act vigorously as advocates for constituents, including business interests in their districts or state. A senator or congressperson, or their staff, may find the pressures to share business proprietary information irresistible if a constituent demands such information. By contrast, one would expect a member of Congress to face less pressure and be more discreet with national security information. CFIUS should feel comfortable informing Congress about their national security analysis of particular cases, but should resist pressure to share specific business information. Agencies do not provide confidential business information to Congress in any other regulatory review processes, such as those before the DOJ, Department of Transportation (DOT), or the Federal Communications Commission (FCC). Moreover, for statistical purposes, both domestically owned and foreign-owned businesses are required to supply certain information, often of a sensitive nature, to a number of federal agencies, such as the Bureau of the Census and the Bureau of Economic Analysis. But this information is also subject to very strict confidentiality requirements. Information supplied by firms to federal antitrust agencies—the Federal Trade Commission or the Antitrust Division of the DOJ under Hart-Scott-Rodino

---

19. For a full discussion of transparency issues, see David Marchick, Testimony Before the House Financial Services Committee on Foreign Investment, Jobs and National Security: The CFIUS Process, March 1, 2006.

investigations—is often highly sensitive, but subject to strict confidentiality requirements. CFIUS filings also include highly sensitive, proprietary company information, including market-sensitive information that competitors would love to have. CFIUS should not be an exception to the rule that confidential business information submitted to the federal government be kept confidential.

Congress should also not create a public notice requirement for Exon-Florio reviews.[20] A national security review process should remain confidential precisely because it affects US national security. In virtually every CFIUS review, the executive branch conducts background checks on companies and individuals, undertakes an intelligence assessment, and discusses highly classified national security issues. US national security could be negatively affected if these matters were discussed, or even if the public were notified.

Finally, Congress should avoid transparency measures that could facilitate the politicization of individual CFIUS reviews. It is fairly easy for domestic competitors to dream up fallacious national security arguments against a foreign acquisition of a US company. But CFIUS is meant to consider real national security threats, and not dubious threats that benefit a domestic competitor over a foreign company. The CFIUS process is and should remain a serious, sober inquiry into the national security implications of a particular acquisition, insulated from politicization in the same way as filings under the Hart-Scott-Rodino antitrust review process.

Improving and Clarifying the "Control" Standard

One of the most complicated factual determinations CFIUS frequently needs to make is whether a foreign acquirer will "control" a US entity. As mentioned above, the Exon-Florio Amendment requires a determination of whether there is foreign control; whether a foreign person might act to threaten US national security; and whether current laws, other than the International Emergency Economic Powers Act (IEEPA) or Exon-Florio, adequately mitigate the risk. But the Exon-Florio control test, which in practice has been interpreted to presume control any time a foreign interest owns more than 10 percent of a US company, is extraordinarily broad, lacking the texture associated with many other control tests under US law. CFIUS agencies should clarify the critical elements of the control test, and consider raising the 10 percent threshold above which control is presumed.

---

20. Congressman Manzullo has called for CFIUS to provide a notice and comment period in the *Federal Register,* hold a public hearing, and inform the relevant congressional committees any time an application is filed. See Statement of Congressman Donald Manzullo, Hearing before the House Financial Services Committee on Foreign Investment, Jobs and National Security: The CFIUS Process, March 1, 2006.

The Exon-Florio regulations define control to mean "the power, direct or indirect, whether or not exercised, and whether or not exercised or exercisable through the ownership of a majority or a dominant minority of the total outstanding voting securities of an issuer, or by proxy voting, contractual arrangements or other means, to determine, direct or decide matters affecting an entity."[21] Control is implied by the power to direct decisions about the disposition of any or all of the company's principal assets, dissolution, closing or relocating production or research and development facilities, terminating contracts, or amending the articles of incorporation regarding any of the above matters.[22]

CFIUS decisions about control are straightforward for complete acquisitions and majority investments, but involve a high degree of judgment and ambiguity for minority investments. The regulations do not define "a dominant minority," but exempt from review transactions undertaken "solely for the purpose of investment" if the foreign person will hold 10 percent or less of the outstanding voting securities. Foreign debt does not imply control without evidence that the foreign lender has acquired it, such as an imminent or actual default.[23] Although the 10 percent ownership threshold has been a presumption of control in practice, the regulations reject a bright-line percentage shareholder test as "inappropriate" and likely to "make it relatively easy to structure transactions to circumvent the statute." In addition, the regulations do not distinguish between direct control, such as ownership of shares in a US company by foreign citizens, governments, or other entities, and indirect control, such as foreign ownership of a corporation that controls a US company.[24]

Commentators have characterized the CFIUS review process as "loose, ambiguous, highly discretionary, and not subject to judicial review, with no formal procedures, due process protections, opportunities to respond to opposing evidence, or standards for assessing the credibility of evidence, and except when a formal presidential determination is made, no written decisions" (Marans et al. 2004, 595). The control test, as articulated in CFIUS regulations, is an example of this ambiguity. CFIUS agencies should revise the control test, taking account of standards for control that

---

21. Regulations Pertaining to Mergers, Acquisitions, and Takeovers by Foreign Persons, *Code of Federal Regulations,* title 31, sec. 800.204 (2003).

22. Regulations Pertaining to Mergers, Acquisitions, and Takeovers, sec. 800.204(a)(1–5).

23. Regulations Pertaining to Mergers, Acquisitions, and Takeovers, sec. 800.303(a)(2): "The Committee will accept notices concerning transactions that involve loans or financing by foreign persons where, because of imminent or actual default or other condition, there is a significant possibility that the foreign person may obtain control of the US entity."

24. Regulations Pertaining to Mergers, Acquisitions, and Takeovers, sec. 800.213, defines "foreign person" as a foreign national or any entity "over which control is exercised or exercisable by a foreign interest."

other US government agencies use, as well as the greater specificity that other laws and regulations provide for determining control.

For another formulation of a US government control test, CFIUS agencies need look no further than the agency that regulates different aspects of a significant number of the transactions reviewed under Exon-Florio: the FCC. Under FCC regulations and case law, control can be de jure or de facto. Ownership of more than 50 percent of an entity's voting shares constitutes de jure control.[25] Whether minority ownership constitutes de facto control depends on a fact-specific determination made on a "case-by-case basis" that "var[ies] with the circumstances presented by each case."[26] Relevant factors are the minority shareholder's "power to dominate the management of corporate affairs,"[27] including the power to appoint more than 50 percent of a license holder's board of directors; authority to appoint, promote, demote, and fire senior executives; a role in major management decisions; authority to pay financial obligations, including expenses; ability to receive monies and profits from facility operations; and unfettered use of all facilities and equipment.[28]

In one leading case, the FCC held that a party contributing 45 percent of a licensee's total equity, and holding 25 percent of its nonvoting stock, did not exercise de facto control.[29] Although the minority shareholder held an option to convert its nonvoting shares to voting shares, and to purchase an additional 25 percent of voting shares, thereby acquiring effective veto power over corporate affairs, the FCC emphasized the presence of a de jure controlling entity that had a majority of board votes, the members of which had significant experience in the industry.[30] By contrast, CFIUS agencies would certainly find control by a minority shareholder under the same conditions.

Similarly, the Department of Transportation uses an "actual control" test to determine whether a foreign person controls a US carrier. Actual control may be triggered by "myriad potential avenues" of influence,[31] and has

25. See, e.g., Extension of Lines, New Lines, and Discontinuance, Reduction, Outage and Impairment of Service by Common Carriers; and Grants of Recognized Private Operating Agency Status, *Code of Federal Regulations,* title 47, sec. 63.24 (2004): "A change from less than 50 percent ownership to 50 percent or more ownership shall always be considered a transfer of control."

26. Extension of Lines, sec. 63.24(c).

27. In re BBC License Subsidiary, Federal Communications Commission Record 10: 7926 (April 27, 1995).

28. Extension of Lines, sec. 63.24(c).

29. In re BBC License Subsidiary, 7926, 7931–33.

30. In re BBC License Subsidiary, 7926, 7931–33.

31. Acquisition of Northwest Airlines by Wings Holdings, Department of Transportation Order 89-9-51, Docket 46371 (September 29, 1989).

been found when there is a "substantial ability to influence the carrier's activities," encompassing "actual and potential control . . . both positive and negative" and control originating in debt, equity, and personal relationships. Factors relevant to control include supermajority voting provisions or other minority-enhancing voting rights; minority veto power; buyout clauses; board representation; foreign nonvoting equity ownership; dependence on foreign contracts; foreign debt accompanied by creditor control provisions; and substantial business relationships. The Department of Transportation has ruled that foreign companies owning up to 25 percent of a US carrier's voting stock and 49 percent of a US carrier's equity do not have "actual control" over a US airline.[32] It is hard to imagine that CFIUS would ever determine that a foreign company did not have control over a US company under the same conditions. At the time of this writing, the DOT had issued proposed regulations to loosen the control standard.[33]

To be fair, the CFIUS control test is not the most restrictive control test that the US government uses. Under the regulations in the DOD's National Industrial Security Program Operating Manual (NISPOM), facility security clearances may not be granted to contractors "under foreign ownership, control, or influence (FOCI)" (US DOD 1995, § 2.102(d)). The manual defines FOCI as

> whenever a foreign interest has the power, direct or indirect, whether or not exercised, and whether or not exercisable through the ownership of the US company's securities, by contractual arrangements or other means, to direct or decide matters affecting the management or operations of that company in a manner which may result in unauthorized access to classified information or may affect adversely the performance of classified contracts. (US DOD 1995, § 2.301(a))

The language in the DOD regulations covering foreign ownership of companies that do business with the Pentagon (the NISPOM FOCI) is strikingly similar to the CFIUS regulatory definition of control (US DOD 1995). The main substantive difference stems from the distinct objectives of Exon-Florio and NISPOM. For CFIUS, the control test focuses on the US entity itself and the foreign acquirer's power to "determine, direct or decide matters affecting an entity." NISPOM focuses on the more narrowly tailored exercise of power "in a manner which may result in unauthorized access to classified information or may affect adversely the performance of classified contracts." To the extent that such textual nuances are material, they suggest that the CFIUS control test covers more transactions than NISPOM, as there are some aspects of control relevant to "matters affecting an entity" that would not necessarily involve either disclosing classified information or the potential to affect adversely the performance of sensitive or classified contracts.

---

32. Acquisition of Northwest Airlines by Wings Holdings.

33. See US DOT (2005), Office of the Secretary, DOT, Actual Control of US Air Carriers, DOT Docket No. OST-03-15759-15 (November 2, 2005) (Notice of Proposed Rulemaking).

At the same time, NISPOM sets forth a number of factors to determine FOCI, none of which is necessarily sufficient, and all of which must be considered in the aggregate. These include direct or indirect ownership of 5 percent of voting stock, or 25 percent of nonvoting stock; the presence of non-US citizens in management positions; foreign power to elect directors; foreign contracts; foreign debt if the borrower's overall debt-to-credit ratio is 40 to 60 or greater; 5 percent or more of total revenues originating in a single foreign person, or 30 percent from foreign sources overall; or ownership by the US company of 10 percent or more of any foreign interest (US DOD 1995, § 2.302(b)). Notably, the final clause—in which foreign control is inferred from a US company's ownership of foreign interests, rather than vice versa—turns the traditional test for foreign control on its head. Thus, in many respects, including the consideration of a 5 percent threshold of voting stock, foreign contracts, and sales to foreign persons, the NISPOM control test is broader and captures more transactions than the CFIUS control test does. At the same time, the factors that NISPOM considers are spelled out in greater detail than the CFIUS factors.

Other US government control tests also define control more clearly than the CFIUS regulations. The Change in Bank Control Act (CBCA), administered by the Office of the Comptroller of the Currency (OCC, an agency of the Treasury Department), defines control as "the power, directly or indirectly, to direct the management or policies of an insured depository institution or to vote 25 per cent or more of any class of voting securities of an insured depository institution."[34] The OCC presumes that acquiring 10 percent or more of any class of voting securities constitutes the power to direct a bank's management or policies, if the securities are subject to the registration requirements of section 12 of the Securities Exchange Act of 1934,[35] or if, immediately after the proposed acquisition, the acquirer is the largest single shareholder in that class.[36] The OCC also aggregates holdings between individuals, corporations, or other entities acting "in concert."[37] Here, the statute and accompanying regulations not only cre-

---

34. *Change in Bank Control Act* (CBCA), Public Law 95-630, *US Statutes at Large* 92: 3683, codified at *US Code* 12 (2000), § 1817(j)(8)(B), and *Code of Federal Regulations*, title 12, sec. 5.50(d)(3) (2005), define control as "the power, directly or indirectly, to direct the management or policies of a national bank or to vote 25 percent or more of any class of voting securities of a national bank."

35. *Securities Exchange Act of 1934*, Public Law 73-291, *US Statutes at Large* 48: 881, codified at *US Code* 15 (2000), § 78l.

36. Rules, Policies, and Procedures for Corporate Activities, *Code of Federal Regulations*, title 12, sec. 5.50(f)(2)(ii) (2005).

37. CBCA, § 1817(j)(1); and *Code of Federal Regulations*, title 12, sec. 5.50(d)(2) (2005) define "acting in concert" to be "knowing participation in a joint activity or parallel action towards a common goal of acquiring control whether or not pursuant to an express agreement" or "a combination or pooling of voting or other interests in the securities of an issuer for a common purpose pursuant to any . . . agreement . . . written or otherwise."

ate a bright-line test—an approach CFIUS rejected—but they also lay out standards for control in great detail and with some precision.

The need for greater clarity in the Exon-Florio regulations is bolstered by the fact that, in virtually all of these other contexts, the parties have either the right to a hearing or appeal, or the right to participate in a public adjudicative proceeding (for the DOT and FCC) or hearing (in the case of bank regulation before the Office of Thrift Supervision, Federal Reserve, and Federal Deposit Insurance Corporation). Under Exon-Florio, while parties retain the right to judicial review of various procedural elements of the amendment, there is no right of judicial review of the president's national security decisions. Nor are CFIUS agencies obligated to explain their decisions to the parties; because of the confidential nature of the process, they are not even obliged to inform the parties that CFIUS has determined control regarding either a foreign entity or a foreign government.

Because CFIUS bases its determinations on national security concerns, there is strong justification for the confidential nature of its deliberations. But because the proceedings are confidential, there is an even stronger argument that CFIUS should provide more detailed guidance to foreign investors on what constitutes control. In the past, CFIUS has been concerned that a bright-line test would encourage "gaming" of the rules, but appropriately articulated criteria could guide investors without the risk of manipulation. Foreign investors seek certainty, and should be able to assess the regulatory risk associated with an investment before making an investment decision. For their part, CFIUS agencies have no interest in reviewing complicated or contentious cases, in which an unclear control test potentially forces the agencies, or the president, to bar or condition an investment. Ultimately, CFIUS agencies care most about having the discretion to make control determinations, but maintaining this discretion and providing greater clarity to investors are not mutually exclusive.

CFIUS agencies should also reconsider whether the 10 percent ownership threshold is too low, even when the purpose of acquiring voting stock is not solely for investment. As discussed above, the essence of the Exon-Florio control test is whether the acquirer has the power to "determine, direct or decide matters affecting an entity."[38] An investor could own 20 percent of a company's voting securities, and a seat or two on its board of directors, without having the power to determine, direct, or decide company matters. And, in the case of a default to a syndicate of banks, the Exon-Florio regulations would not find control even when a foreign bank owns up to 49 percent of a US company through its share of a syndicated loan, so long as the foreign bank, or banks, need "the majority consent of the US participants in the syndicate to take action."[39] Simi-

---

38. *Code of Federal Regulations*, title 31, sec. 800.204(a).

39. Rules, Policies, and Procedures for Corporate Activities, *Code of Federal Regulations*, title 12, sec. 800.303(a)(3)(b)(1).

larly, other government agencies allow much larger ownership stakes without finding control.

Developing International Standards
for National Security Review Processes

Last summer, French politicians expressed concerns over rumors that PepsiCo was seeking to acquire Danone, the French yogurt and water company; French prime minister Dominique de Villepin identified "[t]he Danone Group [as] one of the jewels of French industry" and promised "to defend the interests of France"[40] against the threatening acquisition.[41] Subsequently, and notwithstanding existing mechanisms for reviewing certain foreign investments affecting security interests, the French government announced that it would establish a list of "strategic industries" to be shielded from foreign investment.

Leaving aside the almost humorous merits of any claims about the strategic significance of yogurt—which, as it turned out, did not make the French government's list of strategic industries to be shielded from foreign ownership—the French reaction to the potential PepsiCo acquisition was not unusual or, for that matter, unexpected. Almost every country limits foreign ownership in certain sectors but often these limitations are narrowly defined to focus on particularly sensitive domestic industries. Over the last year, however, a number of countries have begun to reevaluate their laws governing permissible foreign direct investment (FDI), considering or adopting proposals to either impose tighter national security-based restrictions on FDI, or define such restrictions in broader economic and strategic terms, or both. In addition to France's initiative, Russia has moved to identify sectors in which foreign investment would be limited.

In a May 2005 address to the Duma, Russian President Vladimir Putin called for a new law to protect "strategic industries." At the time of this writing, legislation to protect these industries was being drafted, and at least 39 industries were on the initial list. In addition, the Russian Ministry of Natural Resources recently presented a proposal identifying specific natural resource deposits that would be subject to a new law on natural resources, which would effectively restrict the percentage of foreign ownership of those deposits. Not surprisingly, those in the Russian government supporting greater restrictions on foreign investment in

---

40. *LCI News,* July 20, 2005, available at www.lci.fr (accessed March 14, 2006).

41. This section is drawn from Marchick, Plotkin, and Fagan (2006), which is based in large part on a presentation the authors gave to senior Russian government officials in Moscow in October 2005, and an earlier meeting with Russian officials in Washington. At the latter meeting, Chris Caine, vice president for government programs for IBM, articulated a number of ideas included in this section.

"subsoil" resources have justified their position as preserving "national security."[42]

In Canada, the minister of industry recently proposed amendments to the Investment Canada Act, which currently requires review of investments of a certain monetary value, or in certain specified sensitive sectors, to determine their "net benefit" to Canada. The amendments would permit the review of any foreign investment, regardless of size or sector, that could compromise "national security" (Blakes Bulletin on Competition and Trade 2005).

In September 2005, Germany's cabinet expanded the country's foreign investment review mechanism to capture a broader set of foreign investments. This comes only a year after Germany implemented a new law allowing the government to veto foreign ownership of more than 25 percent of German defense companies.[43]

Although they are distinct, the proposals in France, Russia, Canada, and the United States, as well as the expansion of the previous law in Germany, share some common ground. To varying degrees, the five proposals fundamentally signify the potential appeal of protectionist sentiments. The Canadian and US legislative proposals were spurred in part by Chinese companies' failed bids for leading domestic natural resource companies; the changes in Germany came as a result of increased investments in Germany by US private equity funds.[44] Perhaps most important, in France, Russia, and Canada, there also has been a common thread in the debate over the proposals—namely, that because the United States already has a law (Exon-Florio) restricting foreign investment on national security grounds, so too should they.[45] The US experience under Exon-Florio has become a central issue for policy debate at home and abroad.

42. Bureau of National Affairs, "Russia Plans to Limit Foreign Investment in Move Seen as Threat to Trade Climate," March 10, 2006.

43. Martin Aguera, "Germany Tightens Rules on Foreign Ownership," Defense News and Army Times Publishing Co., September 19, 2005, 20.

44. In Canada, the proposed amendments were partly reacting to China Minmetals Corporation's bid for Noranda, Inc., a leading Canadian mining company. Supporters of expanding Exon-Florio in the United States to include economic security received a boost from the public and congressional reaction to the failed bid of China National Offshore Oil Corporation for Unocal.

45. See, e.g., "Participation of Foreign Capital in Strategic Industries of Russia to Be Limited," *Russian Business Monitor* (Russia), May 18, 2005. Russian officials clearly pointed the official Russian press to US and European restrictions: "The government has decided to use the experience of the US and France where there are stringent limitations for purchase of assets by foreign investors. Like Russia both countries are presidential republics. In the US if a foreign company is going to buy more than 5% of shares in a company that fulfills orders of the Department of Defense, the permit for such a deal is issued by the president. A similar system is in effect in France with the only difference that there the threshold for foreigners is either 5% of shares or three seats on the board of directors. Germany is preparing a similar bill."

In a recent speech, Russian Economy Minister German Gref said that proposed Russian legislation blocking foreign investment would be "more liberal" than similar legislation in the United States.[46] A spokesman for the Russian Ministry of Industry and Energy stated that the draft law had been based on concepts similar laws in the United States, Spain, France, and Finland, among others.

In India, the government's proposed restrictions on US investors seem to be directly linked to security commitments imposed by CFIUS on a company from that country. The Indian government, spurred on in part by a domestic company that had a difficult time clearing CFIUS, announced its intention to impose extremely broad security restrictions on foreign investments in telecommunications. These restrictions were announced in the context of a proposal to raise the ceiling on permitted foreign investment in the telecommunications sector, from 49 percent foreign ownership to 74 percent. It appears that the Indian government was responding to a request by the Indian company Videsh Sanchar Nigam Limited (VSNL), which signed a network security agreement (NSA) related to one of its investments in the United States. VSNL requested that the government impose similar security restrictions on US and other foreign investors. In a letter publicly filed with Indian regulatory officials, VSNL wrote,

> [we] propose that TRAI [the Indian regulatory authority] consider whether, in the interests of a level competitive playing field as well as regulatory symmetry, a similar security agreement process should exist in India for U.S. and other foreign carriers who desire a license to provide domestic or international services. (VSNL 2005, appendix D)

VSNL further wrote,

> While we certainly do not recommend that the Indian Government force foreign carriers to wait as long as VSNL has been made to wait for its license to enter the U.S. telecommunications market, we believe that the existence of these agreements in India and other countries will have a beneficial result by moderating the willingness of the U.S. government to impose burdensome conditions and requirements in their own security agreements, which of course hinder the ability of VSNL and other foreign carriers to compete fairly against U.S. carriers who are not subject to such requirements. (VSNL 2005, appendix D)

A number of other major countries, including the United Kingdom, Japan, and Germany, already have laws allowing them to restrict foreign investment on national security grounds.[47] To minimize the chilling effect on foreign investment of what seems to be a proliferation of new or ex-

---

46. Bureau of National Affairs, "Russia Plans to Limit Foreign Investment in Move Seen as Threat to Trade Climate," March 10, 2006.

47. Germany requires screening foreign acquisitions of 25 percent or more of German armament companies under a law that took effect in July 2004. See US Department of State (2005) and US GAO (1996).

panded foreign investment review measures, we believe it would be useful for members of the Organization for Economic Cooperation and Development (OECD),[48] joined by China, India, and Russia,[49] to develop principles that govern laws for national security–related screening processes for foreign investment. Such principles need not be legally binding, but should have the political support of each participating country. China, India, and Russia are not members of the OECD, though they receive large amounts of foreign investment. As such, they should be invited to participate in these deliberations on an equal basis.

In the mid- to late 1990s, the OECD's 29 members attempted to negotiate the Multilateral Agreement on Investment (MAI), a treaty that would have expanded investor protection among them. The MAI negotiations broke down in 1999 over a number of issues, including protection of culturally sensitive sectors, the environment, investments in public services, and protecting national security (Graham 2001, chapters 1 and 2). Although we support most of the goals that MAI negotiators pursued, we call for something much more modest: an agreed set of principles governing national security reviews, focused primarily on procedural and due process safeguards among leading FDI recipients. The United States, as the largest recipient of FDI, and with the most formal national security–based investment review process, should lead the effort to develop these principles, but each country should also appropriately define its own national security interests. Common ground could be developed on the procedures governing a national security review process, and such procedures could provide greater confidence for foreign investors, expanding foreign investment throughout the world. A number of the issues discussed earlier in this chapter could form the basis for an agreed set of principles, which could, among others, include

- a voluntary, not mandatory, national security–based investment review process;[50]

---

48. As of this writing, the members of the OECD were Australia, Austria, Belgium, Canada, Czech Republic, Denmark, Finland, France, Germany, Greece, Hungary, Iceland, Ireland, Italy, Japan, Korea, Luxembourg, Mexico, Netherlands, New Zealand, Norway, Poland, Portugal, Slovak Republic, Spain, Sweden, Switzerland, Turkey, United Kingdom, and the United States.

49. India has blocked a number of foreign investments on security grounds, including a recent proposed investment by Huawei, the Chinese telecommunications equipment maker. India's defense ministry has been quoted as saying that "there are general security concerns regarding activities of Chinese companies. Safeguards are practically difficult to implement in highly technical areas." In addition, the Indian intelligence agency, the Research and Analysis Wing (RAW), has been highly critical of Huawei, stating: "This company has been responsible for sweeping and debugging operations in the Chinese embassy. In view of China's focus on cyber warfare there is a risk of exposing our strategic telecom network to the Chinese." See Nicole Willig, "India Blocks Foreign Telecom Gear," October 11, 2005, available at www.lightreading.com (accessed March 14, 2006).

50. See pages 166 to 169 for a full discussion of this issue.

- a review process that provides predictability to transaction parties by ensuring that reviews will be conducted within a reasonable and definite time frame; focuses on national security, not economic security; and is led by an economic agency, with consultation from security agencies;

- a review mechanism that ensures confidentiality of proprietary business information;

- the decision to not use national security as a pretext for blocking transactions to protect domestic industry; and

- investment review decisions not made by legislative bodies.

Rejecting Proposed Amendments

Congress and the executive branch can protect national security while maintaining and promoting inward foreign direct investment. To achieve these twin goals, however, a number of ideas currently in play in Congress and elsewhere should be rejected. These include mandatory filings, moving the CFIUS chair out of the Treasury Department, and including economic security tests in the Exon-Florio process.

Mandatory Filings

One of the centerpieces of the Exon-Florio Amendment is that filing, or providing notice, with the Department of the Treasury is voluntary. This policy has frequently come under fire from various members of Congress, CFIUS observers,[51] and even the DOD, which drafted legislation in 2001 requiring CFIUS to review all foreign acquisitions above $100 million.[52] This proposal, which was included in a draft military authorization bill circulated within the US government for review, was later withdrawn after protests from the Treasury and Commerce Departments and foreign governments.[53] The administration's decision not to pursue this initiative was the right decision, because mandatory filing is both unnecessary and inconsistent with the philosophy underlying Exon-Florio and broader US international economic priorities.

---

51. See testimony of Patrick A. Mulloy before the Senate Banking, Housing and Urban Affairs Committee Hearing on the Implementation of the Exon-Florio Amendment and the Committee on Foreign Investment in the United States, 109th Congress, 1st sess., October 20, 2005.

52. Peter Spiegel, "Defense Hawks Gain Upper Hand After Long Crusade," *Financial Times,* April 6, 2002.

53. Peter Spiegel, "Pentagon Retracts Plans for Review of Mergers," *Financial Times,* April 18, 2002.

Mandatory filing proposals assume that foreign acquisitions of US firms that raise national security concerns will evade CFIUS review if providing notice is voluntary. However, parties to an acquisition of a US firm by a foreign investor have a strong incentive to file with CFIUS if there is any potential security issue, because the Exon-Florio Amendment allows CFIUS agencies to review and potentially unwind any transaction at any time, even after a particular acquisition closes. By contrast, if CFIUS reviews a transaction and the president does not bar it, CFIUS may not revisit or reopen its review.

To facilitate both review of transactions of interest and deterrence of companies avoiding provision of notice to CFIUS, the Department of the Treasury has set up an interagency process, through which any agency can request that CFIUS review a transaction for which the parties have not provided notice. CFIUS agencies regularly scour business pages for transactions they would like to review. If the Department of the Treasury or other CFIUS agencies collectively decide that they would like to review a transaction, a Treasury official typically contacts the company and requests that it provide notice. The Exon-Florio Amendment also allows any CFIUS agency to submit notice of a proposed or completed acquisition to the Department of the Treasury, thereby starting the national security review process.[54]

CFIUS agencies have debated the propriety of asking parties to a transaction to file when those parties have not done so, but in the post–September 11 environment, this internal debate has shifted toward asking for a filing. Almost always, if one agency wants to review a transaction, the other agencies will follow. In a sense, internal CFIUS practice has returned to a concept embodied, but never adopted, in the original Exon-Florio bill: requiring the secretary of commerce to investigate any transaction pursuant to the request of the head of any department or agency.[55]

However, requiring that all foreign acquisitions be filed with CFIUS would be unwieldy, and could hamper CFIUS's ability to protect national security. In recent years, there have been hundreds of foreign acquisitions of US companies every year, but a relatively small number of these have had potential security implications of any sort. CFIUS has received formal filings for between 50 and 80 transactions each year.[56] But even to preliminarily investigate this relatively small number of formal notifications, the Treasury and interagency staff that handle CFIUS matters have been stretched. The Office of International Investment at the Department of the Treasury, responsible for coordinating the interagency CFIUS process today, employs only four professional staff members. Most of the other

---

54. *Code of Federal Regulations,* title 800, sec. 402(a)(2).

55. *Trade and International Economic Policy Reform Act of 1987,* § 905(a).

56. See table 2.1 for the actual number of filings since 1988.

agencies assign one or two professional staff persons to act in coordinating roles, drawing on subject-matter experts as needed. Unless staffing levels were significantly increased, mandatory filings for all foreign acquisitions would completely overwhelm the CFIUS process. Even with the existing caseload, congressional funding for additional CFIUS staff is needed.

Thus the sheer volume of filings that would accompany a requirement that all foreign acquisitions be notified would make it much more difficult for CFIUS to identify cases that genuinely present national security issues. When a large, complex case moves to the investigation phase, or the security agencies are negotiating an NSA, the sheer volume of work of one difficult case can overwhelm the CFIUS staff. Adding hundreds of new filings per year, most of which would in no way implicate national security, would draw the attention of CFIUS agencies away from cases that really do matter, undermining CFIUS's ability to spend the time and resources necessary to review, investigate, and develop mitigation measures to address national security risks.

We thus believe that the present voluntary system of notification has worked well because most foreign acquisitions create no national security issues whatsoever, regardless of how broadly the term "national security" is defined. Transactions that warrant review generally have been notified, and in instances where parties to a transaction were reluctant to do so, pressure has been brought to bear to achieve the desired notification. Mandatory notification would require that the staff in the CFIUS agencies assigned to Exon-Florio cases be substantially enlarged, with no enhancements to national security.

Finally, there are strong international economic policy reasons to retain voluntary, as opposed to mandatory, filings. A mandatory filing requirement would transform CFIUS, from an interagency body that reviews transactions that could involve national security, into a more generic foreign investment review board. The United States has long pressed other countries not to create, or to eliminate, their own investment review boards. In the US-Australia Free Trade Agreement, signed in 2004, one of the United States' top priorities, and one of the last issues to be closed, was eliminating the Australian Foreign Investment Review Board. While the United States could not persuade the Australians to eliminate the board, it was able to exempt from review all US investments in new businesses, and raise the threshold for review of US acquisitions of Australian entities in most sectors from 50 million to 800 million Australian dollars. Similarly, the United States worked for years to convince Canada to eliminate its investment review structure, negotiated preferential terms for investment reviews in Canada for American investments under the US-Canada Free Trade Agreement, and has negotiated bilateral investment treaties (BITs) with more than 40 countries, guaranteeing nondiscriminatory treatment of investments from the United States. As the United States seeks to eliminate investment restrictions abroad, requiring mandatory filings under Exon-Florio would be a step in the wrong direction, undermining the United States' moral authority to press for removal of restrictions on investment in other countries.

Moving the CFIUS Chair Out of Treasury

As previously discussed, Senator Inhofe introduced a bill in August 2005 that would have transferred the CFIUS chair to the DOD. In March 2006 Senator Susan Collins (R-ME) introduced a bill moving the CFIUS chair to the Department of Homeland Security (the Collins bill). The original amendment offered by Senator Exon in 1988 placed the responsibility for heading the interagency review process with the secretary of commerce. Congressman Manzullo and others in the House of Representatives have similarly advocated that Commerce assume CFIUS leadership. As discussed in chapter 2, after a heated debate over the original Exon bill, including a blunt and rare (in the sense that Washington agencies typically seek to expand, not limit, their authority) statement from then-Secretary of Commerce Malcolm Baldrige: "I do not want the authority."[57] Congress passed the amendment without designating a particular agency to chair the review process. The version of the bill that the Reagan administration finally endorsed did not assign this responsibility to the secretary of commerce but granted authority to the president or the president's designee. Shortly after the enactment of the Exon-Florio Amendment, President Reagan designated CFIUS as the body responsible to "receive notices and other information, to determine whether investigations should be undertaken and to make investigations" under Exon-Florio.[58] Reagan also appointed the Secretary of the Treasury, the most investment-friendly Cabinet agency, to chair CFIUS and implement Exon-Florio. Reagan's decision was right at the time, and remains right even in the current post–September 11 environment.

Though the Exon-Florio Amendment was silent on the chairmanship of CFIUS, designating Treasury as its chair was consistent with legislative intent. Even the most hawkish members of Congress who advocated the original Exon-Florio measure were clear that they did not seek to stop or slow foreign investment into the United States. By designating Treasury as the CFIUS chair, the Reagan administration signaled its intention to continue to "welcome foreign investment," as articulated in President Reagan's policy statement with regard to foreign investment. Indeed, the current description of the CFIUS process on the Department of the Trea-

---

57. Senate Committee on Commerce, Science and Transportation: Hearing on HR 3, Foreign Acquisitions of Domestic Companies, 100th Congress (1987).

58. Executive Order no. 12,661, *Federal Register* 54 (1989): 779, § 3-201(1)(f).

sury's Web site makes clear that US policy continues to favor foreign investment, and presumes that such investment should be restricted only when national security interests are at stake.[59]

The same checks and balances that characterize the US system of government can be found in the CFIUS process. In general, most transactions notified to CFIUS do not require significant scrutiny. For hard or complex cases, debate is frequently fierce between the economic and security agencies. The economic agencies typically include the departments of the Treasury, Commerce, and State, and the US Trade Representative. The security agencies typically include the DOD, DHS, DOJ, and FBI. In certain cases, State and Commerce have split views on a particular transaction, since both agencies have bureaus with an economic focus, the Economics and Business Bureau and the International Trade Administration respectively, and a security focus, the Political Military Bureau and Bureau of Industry and Security respectively.

These checks and balances would be upset by handing the CFIUS chair to a security agency. Whereas economic agencies try to move the process along, security agencies have been known to simply dig in and avoid engagement. While only the president—and not the Treasury—can overrule the security agencies, Treasury's leadership, with White House support, in pressing CFIUS agencies to engage is critical for the CFIUS process to function effectively. If the DOD or DHS were to chair CFIUS, security agencies would not only dominate the debate over national security issues (rightly so, given their expertise), but they would also control the process. More transactions would be blocked, and even more transactions would be unnecessarily delayed. At least as a signal, the presumption would potentially shift from foreign investment being a positive development unless US national security interests were threatened to the opposite: Unless the parties could prove that national security interests were not implicated by a transaction, the proposed foreign investment would be deemed unwelcome.

The question of whether the Department of Commerce should chair CFIUS is a closer call. After all, Commerce not only has a strong proinvestment and protrade philosophy (notwithstanding exceptions for textiles and steel, among others), but also strong security credentials on export control issues, identified in the Exon-Florio Amendment as a factor CFIUS should consider in its security analysis. At the same time, Commerce's international focus is primarily in promoting exports, and not, as in the case of Treasury, promoting inward investment. In tough cases,

---

59. "The Exon-Florio provision is implemented within the context of this open investment policy. The intent of Exon-Florio is not to discourage FDI generally, but to provide a mechanism to review and, if the President finds necessary, to restrict FDI that threatens the national security." Office of International Affairs, US Department of the Treasury, Exon-Florio Provision, available at www.treas.gov (accessed January 12, 2006).

when Commerce is split internally between the International Trade Administration and the Bureau of Industry and Security, the department's effectiveness in leading CFIUS would be undermined. Finally, as discussed in chapter 5, CFIUS has increasingly become politicized. While Treasury is not immune to political influence or interference, it tends to be less susceptible than Commerce. Treasury is better equipped to chair the process in a fair, impartial, and nonpoliticized manner.

There are many critics of Treasury's leadership of CFIUS. In their view, as recently expressed by Congressman Manzullo (we paraphrase), Treasury has never seen a foreign investment it did not like. A recent Government Accountability Office report (US GAO 2005) also criticized Treasury's handling of a number of CFIUS cases, suggesting that Treasury sought to impose too narrow a definition of national security on other agencies.[60] Patrick Mulloy, a member of the US-China Economic and Security Review Commission, recently argued that Treasury's proinvestment "culture" inhibits its leadership of CFIUS.[61] Further, critics argue, Treasury lacks the security expertise required to evaluate and assess national security risks; though it still has some enforcement responsibilities that were not shifted to the DHS, Treasury's role is limited to that of a cheerleader for foreign investment, on one hand, and a processor of paper (the CFIUS notice, follow-up questions, etc.) on the other.

However, in our view, the inherent tension between the economic and security agencies is healthy and, in most cases, will help produce better, more rigorously debated decisions. Critics of Treasury are correct that the Treasury bureau responsible for CFIUS issues—the International Affairs Bureau—lacks real security expertise. However, the answer to this is not to remove Treasury as the chair of CFIUS, but to strengthen Treasury's leadership. The International Affairs Bureau, which serves the staff coordination role at Treasury, can and should bolster its security credentials by bringing security specialists onto its staff, or possibly by borrowing security experts from elsewhere in Treasury, such as the Terrorism and Financial Crimes division, or from other agencies, such as the CIA, NSA, DHS, or DOJ. In doing so, Treasury will solidify its already strong economic leadership credentials with a better ability to engage on the national security issues raised by the DOJ, DOD, DHS, and FBI. This approach would strengthen the CFIUS process and enhance CFIUS's ability to protect national security without chilling the foreign investment that the United States needs.

---

60. Other GAO reports have also been critical of various CFIUS policies and practices. See US GAO (1995, 2002).

61. Hearings on the Implementation of the Exon-Florio Amendment and the Committee on Foreign Investment in the United States before the Senate Committee on Banking, Housing and Urban Affairs, 100th Congress (October 20, 2005).

Introducing an Economic Security Test

The Exon-Florio Amendment is perhaps most frequently criticized for not allowing CFIUS and the president to consider economic as opposed to national security issues. As discussed in chapter 2, the original bill introduced by Senator Exon would have allowed an administration to block acquisitions that threatened the "essential commerce" of the United States.[62] Since the original Exon bill, a number of members of Congress have sought, unsuccessfully, to broaden the scope of review under Exon-Florio to include "economic security,"[63] acquisition of a "domestic steel company,"[64] and "the industrial and technological base of the United States."[65] Senator Inhofe recently rekindled this debate with his proposed amendment to Exon-Florio.

The same arguments used to thwart past efforts to broaden the scope of Exon-Florio are applicable today. First, adopting an "economic security" or "economic effects" test would undermine the United States' long-standing policy of welcoming foreign investment. More specifically, considering the economic security effects of an investment would create a broad-based investment review regime in the United States for virtually any significant foreign investment. The United States has long argued against such investment regimes, including the review mechanisms in Canada and Australia. Creating an investment review mechanism in the United States would encourage other countries to do the same, to the detriment of US companies. Second, an economic security test would be extremely difficult for CFIUS to implement, because it would be virtually impossible to define economic security. While national security is not defined in the statute, CFIUS includes three agencies—the DOD, DHS, and DOJ—charged with protecting US national security. By contrast, efforts to protect economic security would likely fall prey to domestic companies using it to shield themselves from international competition. Third, expanding the scope of a CFIUS inquiry to include economic security would increase the likelihood and frequency of Congress politicizing the CFIUS process. It would be much easier for a US company seeking either to avoid being acquired, or to protect itself from additional competition, to argue that US economic security demands that a foreign acquisition be blocked. A domestic company could point to the possible negative employment ef-

---

62. See statement of Senator Exon, *Foreign Investment, National Security and Essential Commerce Act of 1987*, HR 3, 100th Congress (1987).

63. *Foreign Investment and Economic Security Act of 1991*, HR 2386, 102nd Congress (1991).

64. *Steel and National Security Act*, HR 2394, 107th Congress (2001).

65. *To Amend the Defense Production Act of 1950 to Clarify and Strengthen Provisions Pertaining to National Security Takeovers*, HR 5225, 101st Congress, 2nd sess. (1990).

fects of an acquisition, arguing that protecting particular jobs in a particular community is important for the United States' economic security. Finally, expanding the review criteria would likely violate a number of the United States' international agreements, including BITs, treaties of friendship, commerce, and navigation (FCNs), and various free trade agreements, including those with major investment partners such as Canada, Australia, Mexico, and Singapore. Since the United States began BIT negotiations in the early 1980s, it has ratified more than 40 BITs with developing countries. While the terms of these BITs vary from agreement to agreement, a core provision in them is a national treatment commitment, under which the United States has agreed to accord investors from the other party "treatment no less favorable than it accords, in like circumstances, to its own investors."[66] All BITs include a "national security" or "essential security" provision that exempts a party from, among other things, BIT national treatment obligations. However, the national or essential security provisions in BITs have traditionally only covered investments that truly compromise national, as opposed to economic, security interests.[67] Jose Alvarez, a leading authority on Exon-Florio and international investment treaties, argues that the essential security exception in BITs must be read narrowly to apply to acts "legally justified under international law, such as self-defense under the U.N. Charter or legitimate acts of reprisal," or, alternatively, to "vital or fundamental security issues."[68] Indeed, Alvarez argues that the national security standard "assaults" the national treatment and most favored nation (MFN) guarantees in US treaties (Alvarez 1989, 120). While we have qualms about whether a foreign country would actually challenge the United States' right to prohibit investments for national security reasons, we do believe that if Exon-Florio were expanded to cover economic security, the United States would be at substantial risk of violating its treaty obligations. For these reasons, we believe it would be harmful to US economic and national security interests to expand Exon-Florio's criteria to include economic security.

---

66. See, e.g., Article 3 of the US Model Bilateral Investment Treaty, available at www.state. gov (accessed March 14, 2006). The model BIT states, "Each Party shall accord to investors of the other Party treatment no less variable than it accords, in like circumstances, to its own investors with respect to the establishment, acquisition, expansion, management, conduct, operation, and sale or other disposition of investments in its territory."

67. See e.g., Article 18 of the US Model Bilateral Investment Treaty, which states, "Nothing in this Treaty shall be construed ... to preclude a Party from applying measures that it considers necessary for the fulfillment of its obligations with respect to the maintenance or restoration of international peace or security, or the protection of its own essential security interests."

68. Alvarez (1989, footnote 626). Alvarez discusses at length the potential incompatibility of Exon-Florio with the United States' various international obligations.

Conclusion

The Dubai controversy has created an extraordinary amount of pressure to reform CFIUS. Critics charge that the process is secretive, politically tone-deaf, and unreasonably biased toward economic policy interests at the expense of national security. One irony of the congressional brouhaha over the transaction is that it has ignored the important changes in CFIUS that have taken place in recent years. As discussed in chapter 2, since September 11, 2001, CFIUS has applied greater scrutiny to foreign investments, imposed even tougher requirements as a condition for approval, and enhanced enforcement of security agreements negotiated through the Exon-Florio process. CFIUS has also intensely scrutinized any transaction involving investments from greater China and has done so in a difficult, politicized environment, as discussed in chapters 4 and 5.

CFIUS can be improved within the current statutory framework, which is sufficiently flexible to allow the needed improvement without new legislation to force what could be steps in the wrong direction. CFIUS faces the challenge of simultaneously protecting US national security, which has to be the United States' first priority, while maintaining an open investment climate. As discussed in several sections of this book, the vast majority of foreign acquisitions do not threaten US national security interests in any respect. It is hard to see a national security issue in a German parent firm controlling a Daimler-Chrysler auto assembly plant, or a Japanese firm controlling a Hollywood film studio, or a Dutch company owning Ben & Jerry's, the favorite ice cream maker of one of the coauthors' children. For the narrow set of transactions that genuinely threaten US national security, we believe that the Exon-Florio Amendment gives the president ample authority to block a transaction, or otherwise mitigate any concerns raised by a particular acquisition. Moreover, CFIUS agencies have demonstrated their willingness to use the full authority of the law when circumstances warrant it.

Why then is there current discomfort on Capitol Hill over Exon-Florio and the CFIUS process? As noted in earlier chapters and discussed in depth in chapter 4, one source of this discomfort has been the very recent, but thus far very limited, rise of China as a foreign investor. In the future, there might be additional efforts by Chinese firms to acquire US firms, and CFIUS is likely to give some of those transactions special scrutiny. But at the same time, the authority already granted to the president, and administered by CFIUS, adequately addresses the security-related concerns that such future acquisitions may create.

Clearly, not all members of Congress share our views on either the overall adequacy of the CFIUS process or its specific ability to block a transaction that poses a true security threat. If we were to be asked why this is, we probably would answer that it is because CFIUS has done an inadequate job of informing Congress of the work it actually does, and how, in practice, it has safeguarded legitimate security interests. CFIUS agencies must submit the reports called for in the statute; Treasury should hire additional staff to produce these reports and provide Congress with relevant information regarding the process. CFIUS should also keep records of informal consultations with foreign investors that frequently precede announcements of transactions or formal filings. Such consultations do occur and have resulted in some proposed acquisitions not proceeding because the parties became convinced, on the basis of consultations, that a formal review would lead to a block of the transaction, or to security-motivated conditions being placed on it that the parties could not accept. It would be entirely appropriate for CFIUS to report aggregate information to Congress regarding such consultations, such as numbers and the sectors involved, without disclosing specific information deemed business-sensitive or proprietary. Such reporting could include CFIUS estimates of how many transactions failed to materialize because of CFIUS concerns. There is no reason this could not be done without revealing confidential information.

In the current environment, some foreign investors might be forgiven for wondering if their money is still welcome in the United States. Of course, it is; the United States, as we have emphasized, has a strong interest and need to attract foreign investment. Indeed, because of its savings gap, the United States must either borrow or receive in foreign investment a total of over $800 billion each year. Moreover, as stressed in chapter 3, FDI in the United States creates considerable benefits that go beyond its role in helping to close the US saving-investment gap.

Unfortunately, the congressional reaction to the Dubai Ports deal and other controversial transactions has cast doubt on the United States' interest in encouraging foreign direct investment. Under these circumstances, it would seem to us entirely appropriate that President Bush, with the support of Congress, reissue a statement along the lines of that of President Ronald Reagan in 1982, in which Reagan indicated that foreign investment in the United States was welcome if it did not raise national security concerns. Such a statement might not only reassure foreign investors but also prove vital to US national security. Without continued and growing inflows of foreign investment, the US manufacturing base, employment, competitiveness, and innovation will all be at risk. Unless the United States remains open to foreign investment, it will alienate its allies. And unless the United States continues to welcome foreign investment, it could find itself more and more isolated in an increasingly interdependent world. There are those who would restrict this investment in the name of strengthening the economy and national security. If they have their way, the United States will lose what has been an important source of economic vitality, and the result will be exactly the contrary of what they set out to achieve. Maintaining an open environment for FDI is, in itself, deeply in the national security interest of the United States.

Appendix 6A
US Critical Infrastructure Sectors

The Department of Homeland Security (DHS) has designated 12 sectors and subsectors of the US economy as comprising "critical infrastructure." A bill introduced by Congressman Duncan Hunter (R-CA) into the US House of Representatives will greatly restrict or forbid foreign ownership in critical infrastructure sectors. Also, a bill introduced by Senator Richard Shelby (R-AL) would require an extended CFIUS review of foreign ownership in these sectors. As of the time of this writing, these bills have not passed.

Table 6A.1 lists the sectors DHS apparently had in mind when compiling its critical infrastructure list. We say "apparently had in mind" because, as noted in chapter 6, DHS has been somewhat less than precise in compiling the designation of these sectors. The US Bureau of the Census exhaustively categorizes economic activity in the United States into sectors and subsectors under the newly developed North American Industrial Classification System (NAICS). Officials of the United States, Canada, and Mexico jointly developed this system to consistently classify economic activity throughout the North American Free Trade Agreement (NAFTA) area. Rather incredibly, the DHS seems to have developed its list without reference to the NAICS.

Thus, we have attempted to match the (imprecise) DHS critical infrastructure categories with the (precise) NAICS categories. Some of the DHS categories seem to include more than one NAICS category, so the table has more than 12 sectors and subsectors. They nonetheless correspond, as best as we can determine, to the intent of DHS. Using data from the Bureau of the Census and the Bureau of Economic Analysis, the table indicates total US employment in each of these sectors and subsectors and employment by US affiliates of foreign investors.

Note that US affiliates of foreign investors that operate US seaports do not employ any US workers. This is because foreign-owned port operators in the United States undertake port operations as long-term service contracts, where these operators do not actually own the ports (even though some press articles at the time of this writing have reported otherwise). The activities of these operators thus are not classified under "water transport support activities," the broad category under which seaport operations are classified, but rather appear elsewhere in the NAICS.

Table 6A.1 **US employment in critical infrastructure sectors and employment by US affiliates of foreign investors in these sectors, 2002**

NAICS category	Sector	Total US employment		Employment in US affiliates of foreign investors	
		Thousands[a]	As percent of total US nonagricultural employment	Thousands[b]	As percent of US employment in sector[c]
311	Food manufacturing	1,443.6	1.10	114.4	7.9
324	Petroleum and coal	100.4	0.08	20.6	20.5
325	Chemicals	827.4	0.63	257.6	31.1
332992–332995	Arms, ammunition, and ordnance	27.6	0.02	0	0
334	Computers and electronics	1,300.4	1.00	167.5	12.9
515	Broadcasting except Internet	254.2	0.20	12.9	5.1
3364	Aerospace products and parts, including aircraft and missiles	391.2	0.30	31.9	8.2
516 and 5112	Internet/software publishing	312.1	0.24	4.6	1.5
518	Internet service provider/online information services	149.1	0.11	10.0	6.7
517	Telecommunications services	1,144.0	0.88	36.3	3.2
5415	Computer systems design and related, including computer scientists and programmers, except as classified under "computers and electronics"	1,059.0	0.81	41.4	3.9
481	Air transport, excluding support	548.3	0.42	1.0	0.2
482 and 4882	Rail transport and support	20.7[d]	0.02	10.7	51.7
483	Water transport, excluding support	64.3	0.05	5.2	8.1
484	Truck transport, excluding support	1,333.3	1.02	10.2	0.8

(table continues next page)

Table 6A.1   US employment in critical infrastructure sectors and employment by US affiliates of foreign investors in these sectors, 2002   *(continued)*

NAICS category	Sector	Total US employment		Employment in US affiliates of foreign investors	
		Thousands[a]	As percent of total US nonagricultural employment	Thousands[b]	As percent of US employment in sector[c]
485	Transit and ground transport, including urban transit systems	387.3	0.30	58.5	15.1
486	Pipelines	50.4	0.04	2.1	4.2
4881	Air transport support services, including air traffic control and airport operations	126.3	0.10	0	0
4883	Water transport support activities, including seaports	77.2	0.06	0	0
4885	Freight handling	164.4	0.13	n.a.	n.a.
5221	Depository institutions (banking)	2,081.7	1.60	124.1	6.0
523–525	Finance except banking	4,382.0	3.36	230.2	5.2
493	Warehousing, etc.	149.4	0.11	29.1	19.5
62	Health care and social assistance	14,900.1	11.43	76.6	0.5
2211	Electrical power generation and transmission	535.6	0.41	21.5	4.0
2212	Natural gas distribution	85.4	0.07	2.8	3.3
2213	Water and sewage	41.9	0.03	10.9	26.0
	Total employment in the sectors above	31,867.3	24.45	1,180.1	3.7
Memorandum:					
	Total US nonagricultural employment[e]	130,341			

n.a. = not available

a. Data obtained from US Bureau of the Census, 2002 Economic Census, www.census.gov.
b. Data obtained from Bureau of Economic Analysis, www.bea.gov.
c. Authors' calculations.
d. Includes only rail transport support services.
e. Data obtained from US Department of Labor, Bureau of Labor Statistics, http://data.bls.gov.

References

Adams, Gordon. 2002. Transatlantic Defense—Industrial Cooperation and American Policy. Paper prepared for the International Institute for Strategic Studies/The Center for European Policy Studies European Security Forum, Brussels (November 25).

Aho, C. Michael, and Marc Levinson. 1988. *After Reagan: Confronting the Changed World Economy*. New York: Council on Foreign Relations.

Alfaro, L., C. Areendam, S. Kalemil-Ozcan, and S. Selin. 2003. FDI and Economic Growth: The Role of Local Financial Markets. *Journal of International Economics* 61, no. 1: 512–33.

Alvarez, Jose E. 1989. Political Protectionism and United States International Investments Obligations in Conflict: The Hazards of Exon-Florio. *Virginia Journal of International Law* 30, no. 1: 1–187.

Baily, Martin Neil, Diana Farrell, Ezra Greenberg, Jan-Dirk Henrich, Naoko Jinjo, Maya Jolies, and Jaana Remes. 2005. *Increasing Global Competition and Labor Productivity: Lessons from the US Automotive Industry*. San Francisco: McKinsey Global Institute.

Balasubaramanyam, V. N., M. Salisu, and D. Sapsford. 1996. Foreign Direct Investment and Growth in EP and IS Countries. *Economic Journal* 106, no. 1: 92–105.

Barnet, Richard J., and Ronald E. Mueller. 1974. *Global Reach: The Power of the Multinational Corporations*. New York: Simon and Schuster.

Bäumler, Ernst. 1968. *A Century of Chemistry*. Dusseldorf: Econ-Verlag.

Bergsten, C. Fred, Thomas Horst, and Theodore H. Moran. 1978. *American Multinationals and American Interests*. Washington: The Brookings Institution.

Bhagwati, Jagdish. 2004. *In Defense of Globalization*. New York: Oxford University Press.

Blakes Bulletin on Competition and Trade. 2005. Canada Proposes New Regime for Review of Foreign Investment Transactions Based on National Security Concerns. Available at www.blakes.com (accessed March 15, 2006).

Blomström, Magnus, Robert Lipsey, and Mario Zejan. 1994. What Explains Developing Country Growth? In *Convergence and Productivity: Gross National Studies and Historical Evidence*, ed. William Baumol, Richard Nelson, and Edward Wolff. Oxford: Oxford University Press.

Blonigen, Bruce A., and Miao Grace Wang. 2005. Inappropriate Pooling of Wealthy and Poor Countries in Empirical FDI Studies. In *Does Foreign Direct Investment Promote Development?* ed. Theodore H. Moran, Edward M. Graham, and Magnus Blomström. Washington: Institute for International Economics.

Borensztein, E., J. de Gregorio, and J. W. Lee. 1998. How Does Foreign Investment Affect Growth? *Journal of International Economics* 45, no. 1: 115–72.

Buckley, Peter J., and Mark C. Casson. 1976. *The Future of the Multinational Enterprise*. London: Macmillan.

Carkovic, Maria, and Ross Levine. 2005. Does Foreign Direct Investment Accelerate Economic Growth? In *Does Foreign Direct Investment Promote Development?* ed. Theodore H. Moran, Edward M. Graham, and Magnus Blomström. Washington: Institute for International Economics.

Chen, Jian. 2001. Ownership Structure as Corporate Governance Mechanism: Evidence from Chinese Listed Companies. *Economics of Planning* 34, no. 1/2: 53–72.

Crichton, Michael. 1992. *Rising Sun*. New York: Alfred A. Knopf.

Dayal-Gulati, A., and A. M. Husain. 2000. *Centripetal Forces in China's Economic Development*. Working Paper WP/00/86. Washington: International Monetary Fund.

Doms, Mark E., and J. Bradford Jensen. 1998. Comparing Wages, Skills, and Productivity Between Domestic and Foreign-Owned Manufacturing Establishments in the United States. In *Geography and Ownership as Bases for Economic Accounting*, ed. Robert E. Baldwin, Robert E. Lipsey, and J. David Richardson. Chicago: National Bureau of Economic Research and University of Chicago Press.

Dunning, John H. 1958. *American Investment in British Manufacturing Industry*. London: George Allen and Unwin.

Edwards, Corwin D. 1944. *Economic and Political Aspects of International Cartels*. Monograph for the US Senate Subcommittee on War Moblization. Reprinted as *Economic and Political Aspects of International Cartels*, by Corwin G. Edwards (New York: Arno Press, 1976).

Fenton, Christopher R. 2002. U.S. Policy Towards Foreign Direct Investment Post-September 11: Exon-Florio in the Age of Transnational Security. *Columbia Journal of Transnational Law* 41, no. 1: 195–249.

Friedman, Thomas L. 2000. *The Lexus and the Olive Tree*. New York: Farrar, Straus and Giroux.

Friedman, Thomas L. 2005. *The World Is Flat*. New York: Farrar, Straus and Giroux.

Graham, Edward M. 1974. Oligopolistic Imitation and European Direct Investment in the United States. Unpublished doctoral dissertation, Graduate School of Business Administration, Harvard University.

Graham, Edward M. 2001. *Fighting the Wrong Enemy: Antiglobal Activists and Multinational Enterprises*. Washington: Institute for International Economics.

Graham, Edward M. 2004. Do Export Processing Zones Attract FDI and its Benefits: The Experience from China. *International Economics and Economic Policy* 1, no. 1: 87–103.

Graham, Edward M. 2005. No Reason to Block the Deal. *Far Eastern Economic Review* 168, no. 7: 24–27.

Graham, Edward M., and Paul R. Krugman. 1994. *Foreign Direct Investment in the United States*. Washington: Institute for International Economics.

Graham, Edward M., and Erika Wada. 2001. *Foreign Direct Investment in China: Effects on Growth and Economic Performance*. Working Paper 01-3. Washington: Institute for International Economics.

Green, Stephen. 2003a. Two-Thirds Privatisation: How China's Listed Companies Are—Finally—Privatising. Royal Institute of International Affairs, Asia Programme, Briefing Note. London. Available at www.chathamhouse.org (accessed March 12, 2006).

Green, Stephen. 2003b. Two Thirds Privatisation: Is It Working? Briefing Note. London: Royal Institute of International Affairs.

Green, Stephen. 2005. The Privatization Two-Step at China's Listed Firms. In *Exit the Dragon? Privatization and State Control in China*, ed. Stephen Green and Guy S. Liu. Malden, MA: Blackwell Publishing.

Green, Stephen, and Alissa Black. 2003. *A Market in Control: Non-Tradable Shares Deals in Companies Listed at the Shenzhen Stock Exchange*. Working Paper 11. London: Royal Institute of International Affairs.

Green, Stephen, and Guy S. Liu. 2005. China's Industrial Reform Strategy. In *Exit the Dragon? Privatization and State Control in China*, ed. Stephen Green and Guy S. Liu. Malden, MA: Blackwell Publishing.

Hardie, W. F. D., and J. D. Pratt. 1966. *A History of the Modern British Chemical Industry.* Oxford: Pergamon Press.

Hexner, Erwin. 1945. *International Cartels.* Chapel Hill, NC: University of North Carolina Press.

Hildebrandt International. 2005. *Report on Opportunities in the Legal Services Market in China.* Chicago: Hildebrandt International.

Hong, Eunsuk, and Laixiang Sun. 2004. *Go Overseas Via Direct Investment: Internationalization Strategy of Chinese Corporations in a Comparative Prism.* Discussion Paper 40. London: Center for Financial and Management Studies, University of London.

Huang, Ray. 1997. *China: A Macrohistory.* New York: M. E. Sharpe.

Hymer, Stephen H. 1960. The International Operations of National Firms. Massachusetts Institute of Technology, Economics Department PhD thesis. Reprinted in 1976 as *The International Operations of National Firms* by Stephen H. Hymer (Cambridge, MA: The MIT Press, 1976).

International Labor Organization (ILO). 2001. Translation of Premier Zhu Rongji's Outline of the Tenth Five-Year Plan for National Economic and Social Development at the Fourth Session of the Ninth National People's Congress on March 5, 2001. Available at www.logos-net.net (accessed March 13, 2006).

Jackson, John H. 1977. *Legal Problems of International Economic Relations.* St. Paul, MN: West Publishing.

Jia, Wei. 1994. *Chinese Foreign Investment Laws and Policies.* Westport, CT: Quorum Books.

Karim, Syed Anwar. 1995. *Foreign Acquisitions of U.S. Companies.* Industrial College of the Armed Forces Executive Research Project. Washington: National Defense University.

Kumar, Nagesh, and Jaya Prakash Pradhan. 2005. Foreign Direct Investment, Externalities, and Economic Growth in Developing Countries: Some Empirical Evidence. In *Multinationals and Foreign Investment in Economic Development,* ed. Edward M. Graham. New York: Palgrave.

La Porta, Rafael, Florencio Lopez-de-Silanes, and Andrei Shleifer. 1999. Corporate Ownership Around the World. *Journal of Finance* 54, no. 2: 471–517.

Lardy, Nicholas R. 1994. *China in the World Economy.* Washington: Institute for International Economics.

Lemoine, Françoise. 2000. *FDI and Opening Up the Chinese Economy.* Working Paper 00-11. Paris: Centre d'Etudes Prospectives et d'Information Internationale.

Lemoine, Françoise, and Deniz Ünal-Kesenci. 2004. Assembly Trade and Technology Transfer: The Case of China. *World Development* 32, no. 5: 829–50.

Levathes, Louise E. 1994. *When China Ruled the Seas.* New York: Simon and Schuster.

Liebeler, Susan W., and William H. Lash III. 1993. Exon-Florio: Harbinger of Economic Nationalism? *Regulation* 16, no. 1: 44–51.

Lipsey, Robert E., and Fredrik Sjöholm. 2005. The Impact of FDI on Developing Countries: Why Such Different Answers? In *Does Foreign Direct Investment Promote Development?* ed. Theodore H. Moran, Edward M. Graham, and Magnus Blomström. Washington: Institute for International Economics.

Liu, Guy S., and Pei Sun. 2004. *Ultimate Control, Stock Pyramids, and Intermediate Shareholding Classes in Chinese Public Corporations.* Peking University Working Paper 7–8.

Liu, Guy S., and Pei Sun. 2005. Ownership and Control of Chinese Public Corporations: A State-Dominated Corporate Governance System. In *Corporate Governance: Accountability, Enterprise and International Comparisons,* ed. Kevin Keasey, Steve Thompson, and Michael Wright. Chichester: John Wiley & Sons.

Long, Guoqiang. 2005. China's Policies on FDI: Review and Evaluation. In *Does Foreign Direct Investment Promote Development?* ed. Theodore Moran, Edward M. Graham, and Magnus Blomström. Washington: Institute for International Economics and Center for Global Development.

Marans, J. Eugene, John H. Shenefield, Joseph E. Pattison, and John T. Byam, eds. 2004. *Manual of Foreign Investment in the United States.* 3rd ed. St. Paul, MN: West Group.

Marchick, David M., Mark E. Plotkin, and David N. Fagan. 2005. National Security Regulation of Foreign Investments and Acquisitions in the United States. *China Law and Practice* 19, no. 5: 23–26.

Marchick, David M., Mark E. Plotkin, and David N. Fagan. 2006. Foreign Investment Laws and National Security: Lessons from Exon-Florio. Essay prepared for the Critical Infrastructure Protection Program monograph on Exon-Florio. Arlington, VA: George Mason University School of Law.

Melitz, Marc. J. 2005. Comment. In *Does Foreign Direct Investment Promote Development?* ed. Theodore H. Moran, Edward M. Graham, and Magnus Blomström. Washington: Institute for International Economics.

Menard, David A. 2002. The Flexibility of the Exon-Florio Amendment and the Expansion of Telecommunications into the Global Economy. *Public Contract Law Journal* 31, no. 2, 313–37.

Morton, W. Scott. 1980. *China: Its History and Culture.* New York: McGraw-Hill.

National Commission on Terrorist Attacks upon the United States. 2004. *The 9/11 Commission Report.* New York: W. W. Norton.

Reagan, Ronald. 1983. Statement on International Investment Policy (September 9). Simi Valley, CA: Ronald Reagan Presidential Library. Available at www.reagan.utexas.edu (accessed March 13, 2006).

Rosen, Daniel H. 1999. *Behind the Open Door: Foreign Enterprises in the Chinese Marketplace.* Washington: Institute for International Economics.

Servan-Schreiber, Jean-Jacques. 1967. *Le Défi Américain.* New York: Atheneum.

Shearer, W. Robert. 1993. The Exon-Florio Amendment: Protectionist Legislation Susceptible to Abuse. *Houston Law Review* 30, no. 4: 1729–73.

Sidak, J. Gregory. 1997. *Foreign Investment in American Telecommunication.* Chicago: University of Chicago Press.

Stiglitz, Joseph E. 2002. *Globalization and Its Discontents.* New York: W. W. Norton & Company.

Sun, Qian, Wilson H. S. Tong, and Jing Tong. 2002. How Does Government Ownership Affect Firm Performance? Evidence from China's Privatization Experience. *Journal of Business Finance & Accounting* 29, no. 12: 1–27.

Tenev, Stoyan, and Chunlin Zhang. 2002. *Corporate Governance and Enterprise Reform in China: Building Institutions of Modern Markets.* Working Paper. Washington: World Bank, International Finance Corporation.

Thurow, Lester C. 1992. *Head to Head: The Coming Economic Battle among Japan, Europe and America.* New York: William Morrow & Co.

Tian, Lihui. 2001. *Government Shareholding and the Value of China's Modern Firms.* William Davidson Institute Working Paper 395. Ann Arbor, MI: University of Michigan Business School.

Tolchin, Martin, and Susan Tolchin. 1988. *Buying into America: How Foreign Money Is Changing the Face of Our Nation.* New York: Times Books.

Tolchin, Martin, and Susan Tolchin. 1992. *Selling Our Security: The Erosion of America's Assets.* New York: Alfred A. Knopf.

United Nations Conference on Trade and Development (UNCTAD). 2005. *World Investment Report 2005: Transnational Corporations and the Internationalization of R&D.* Geneva: UNCTAD.

US Central Intelligence Agency (CIA). 2003. Acquisition of Technology Relating to Weapons of Mass Destruction and Advanced Conventional Munitions. Unclassified Report to Congress from the Director of Central Intelligence, April 2003. Available at www.fas.org (accessed February 27, 2006).

US Central Intelligence Agency (CIA) and Federal Bureau of Investigation (FBI). 1999. *Report to Congress on Chinese Espionage Activities Against the United States,* December 12. Available at www.fas.org (accessed March 15, 2006).

US Department of Defense (DOD). 1995. National Industrial Security Program Operating Manual (NISPOM). Available at www.dss.mil/isec/nispom.htm (accessed March 10, 2006).

US Department of Defense (DOD). 2003. *Business Combinations Desk Book*. Deputy Under Secretary of Defense (Industrial Policy) and Deputy General Counsel (Acquisition & Logistics). Washington: Office of the Deputy Under Secretary of Defense.

US Department of Defense (DOD). 2005. *Annual Report to Congress: The Military Power of the People's Republic of China*. Washington: Office of the Secretary of Defense.

US Department of Homeland Security (DHS). 2003. The National Strategy for the Physical Protection of Critical Infrastructure and Key Assets. Available at www.whitehouse.gov (accessed March 15, 2006).

US Department of State. 2003. *Adherence To and Compliance With Arms Control and Nonproliferation Agreements and Commitments*. Washington: Department of State.

US Department of State. 2005. 2005 Investment Climate Statement—Germany. Available at www.state.gov (accessed March 14, 2006).

US Department of Transportation (DOT), Office of the Secretary. 2005. *Actual Control of US Air Carriers*. DOT Docket No. OST-03-15759-15 (November 2).

US General Accounting Office (GAO). 1995. *Implementation of Exon-Florio and Related Amendments*. GAO/NSIAD-96-12, December. Washington: Government Printing Office.

US General Accounting Office (GAO). 1996. *Foreign Laws and Policies Addressing National Security Concerns*. GAO/NSIAD-96-61, April. Washington: Government Printing Office.

US General Accounting Office (GAO). 2002. *Mitigating National Security Concerns under Exon-Florio Could Be Improved*. GAO-02-736, September. Washington: Government Printing Office.

US Government Accountability Office (GAO). 2005. *Defense Trade: Enhancements to the Implementation of Exon-Florio Could Strengthen the Law's Effectiveness*. GAO-05-686, September. Washington: Government Printing Office.

US House of Representatives Select Committee on US National Security and Military/Commercial Concerns with the People's Republic of China (Cox Committee). 1999. US National Security and Military/Commercial Concerns with the People's Republic of China (Cox Report). Available at www.house.gov (accessed March 15, 2006).

US Senate, Committee on Commerce, Science and Transportation. 1987. *Foreign Acquisitions of Domestic Companies: Hearing on H.R. 3 Before the Senate Committee on Commerce, Science and Transportation*, 100th Congress, 1st sess.

Vaupel, J. W., and J. P. Curhan. 1969. *The Making of Multinational Enterprise*. Cambridge, MA: Harvard University Press.

Vernon, Raymond. 1971. *Sovereignty at Bay*. New York: Basic Books.

Videsh Sanchar Nigam Limited (VSNL). 2005. Re: Response to Consultation Paper on "Measures to Promote Competition in International Private Leased Circuits (IPLC) in India." Available at www.trai.gov.in (accessed March 15, 2006).

Wei, Shang Jin. 1996. Foreign Direct Investment in China: Sources and Consequences. In *Financial Deregulation and Integration in East Asia*, ed. Takahashi Ito and Anne Krueger. Chicago: University of Chicago Press.

Wilkins, Mira. 1970. *The Emergence of Multinational Enterprise*. Cambridge, MA: Harvard University Press.

Wilkins, Mira. 1974. *The Maturing of Multinational Business: American Business Abroad from 1914 to 1970*. Cambridge, MA: Harvard University Press.

Wilkins, Mira. 1989. *The History of Foreign Investment in the United States to 1914*. Cambridge, MA: Harvard University Press.

Wilkins, Mira. 2004. *The History of Foreign Investment in the United States 1914–1945*. Cambridge, MA: Harvard University Press.

Wolf, Martin. 2004. *Why Globalization Works*. New Haven: Yale University Press.

Xu, Xiaonian, and Yan Wang. 1997. *Ownership Structure, Corporate Governance, and Firms' Performance: The Case of Chinese Stock Companies.* World Bank Policy Research Working Paper 1794. Washington: The World Bank.

Xu, Xiaonian, and Yan Wang. 1999. Ownership Structure and Corporate Governance in Chinese Stock Companies. *China Economic Review* 10, no. 1: 75–98.

Zhang, Z., and Kang Chen. 1997. China: A Rapidly Emerging Light-Manufacturing Base in Guangdong Province. In *Multinationals and East Asian Integration,* ed. Wendy Dobson and Chia Sui Yue. Ottawa: International Development Research Centre.

Zilg, Gerard Colby. 1974. *DuPont: Behind the Nylon Curtain.* Englewood Cliffs, NJ: Prentice-Hall.

Index

Manzullo, Don, 49, 152–53, 169, 170
Mao Zedong, 98–99
Maytag-Haier transaction, 119
Merchant Marine Act of 1920, Section 27 (Jones Act), 12
mergers and acquisitions (M&As), 25–26, 100
Micronesian Telecommunications Corporation (MTC). *See* Pacific Telecom and Micronesian Telecommunications Corporation (MTC)
Mineral Lands Leasing Act, 13–14
Mitsubishi Trading Company, 17
Model Bilateral Investment Treaty, US, 173*n*
Multilateral Agreement on Investment, 165
multinational businesses
　localization, 53–55
　ownership, 56

National Aniline and Chemical Company, 7
National Aniline and Film, 7. *See also* General Aniline and Film (GAF)
National Defense Authorization Act, Byrd Amendment, 37
National Emergencies Act of 1976, 20–21
National Industrial Security Program Operating Manual (NISPOM), 70–72
National Strategy for the Physical Protection of Critical Infrastructure and Key Assets (DHS), 149–50
Navy, US, 9–10, 11–12, 13–15
network security agreements (NSAs), 64–67, 120, 127–28, 150–51, 164
　costs of, 68
　security concerns, 67–69
NewComm. *See* Telefonica and NewComm
Nextel, 68
NISPOM. *See* National Industrial Security Program Operating Manual (NISPOM)
nitrogen fixation, 17
nonmanufacturing sectors, wages and salaries, 82*t*
Norinco, 110
North American Industrial Classification System (NAICS), 176
Northrop Grumman, 70
Norton Company. *See* British Tire and Rubber (BTR) and Norton Company

oil, 13–15, 20. *See also* China National Offshore Oil Corporation (CNOOC) and Unocal
　China and, 120, 129–30

Omnibus Trade and Competitiveness Act of 1988, 29
Organization for Economic Cooperation and Development (OECD), 165, 165*n*
Organization of Petroleum Exporting Countries (OPEC), 20

Pacific Telecom and Micronesian Telecommunications Corporation (MTC), 66–67
Peninsular and Oriental Steam Navigation Company (P&O) and Dubai Ports World, 2, 29–30, 37, 52, 95–96, 123, 136–41, 146–47, 174
　characteristics of, 138–39
　Committee on Foreign Investment in the United States (CFIUS) and, 137–39
　House Appropriations Committee and, 140, 145
　letter of assurances, 138
　timing, 137–39
PepsiCo and Danone Group, 162
personnel security standards
　Committee on Foreign Investment in the United States (CFIUS) and, 150–52
　screening options, 151–52
PetroKazakhstan, 101
politicization costs, 141
Pombo, Richard, 129, 132–33
portfolio investment, 3
Portman, Rob, 131–32
Ports, Customs, and Free Zones Corporation, 137. *See also* Peninsular and Oriental Steam Navigation Company (P&O) and Dubai Ports World
Putin, Vladimir, 162

Radio Act of 1912, 10
Radio Act of 1927, 10–11
radio broadcasting sector, 9–10
Radio Corporation of America (RCA), 10
Rand Corporation, 114
Raytheon Systems, 70
Reagan, Ronald, 20, 33, 58, 169, 175
reciprocity, 14, 14*n*, 130
Report to Congress on Chinese Espionage Activities Against the United States (CIA), 113
research and development (R&D)
　sector expenditures, US, 85–86

Other Publications from the Institute for International Economics

WORKING PAPERS

POLICY BRIEFS

* = out of print

POLICY ANALYSES IN
INTERNATIONAL ECONOMICS Series

International Debt: Systemic Risk and Policy
Response*   William R. Cline
1984   ISBN 0-88132-015-3
Trade Protection in the United States: 31 Case
Studies* Gary Clyde Hufbauer, Diane E. Berliner,
and Kimberly Ann Elliott
1986   ISBN 0-88132-040-4
Toward Renewed Economic Growth in Latin
America* Bela Balassa, Gerardo M. Bueno, Pedro-
Pablo Kuczynski, and Mario Henrique Simonsen
1986   ISBN 0-88132-045-5
Capital Flight and Third World Debt*
Donald R. Lessard and John Williamson, editors
1987   ISBN 0-88132-053-6
The Canada-United States Free Trade Agreement:
The Global Impact*
Jeffrey J. Schott and Murray G. Smith, editors
1988   ISBN 0-88132-073-0
World Agricultural Trade: Building a Consensus*
William M. Miner and Dale E. Hathaway, editors
1988   ISBN 0-88132-071-3
Japan in the World Economy*
Bela Balassa and Marcus Noland
1988   ISBN 0-88132-041-2
America in the World Economy: A Strategy for
the 1990s*   C. Fred Bergsten
1988   ISBN 0-88132-089-7
Managing the Dollar: From the Plaza to the
Louvre*   Yoichi Funabashi
1988, 2d. ed. 1989   ISBN 0-88132-097-8
United States External Adjustment and the World
Economy*   William R. Cline
May 1989   ISBN 0-88132-048-X
Free Trade Areas and U.S. Trade Policy*
Jeffrey J. Schott, editor
May 1989   ISBN 0-88132-094-3
Dollar Politics: Exchange Rate Policymaking in
the United States*
I. M. Destler and C. Randall Henning
September 1989   ISBN 0-88132-079-X
Latin American Adjustment: How Much Has
Happened?*   John Williamson, editor
April 1990   ISBN 0-88132-125-7
The Future of World Trade in Textiles and
Apparel*   William R. Cline
1987, 2d ed. June 1999   ISBN 0-88132-110-9
Completing the Uruguay Round: A Results-
Oriented Approach to the GATT Trade
Negotiations*   Jeffrey J. Schott, editor
September 1990   ISBN 0-88132-130-3
Economic Sanctions Reconsidered (2 volumes)
Economic Sanctions Reconsidered:
Supplemental Case Histories
Gary Clyde Hufbauer, Jeffrey J. Schott, and
Kimberly Ann Elliott
1985, 2d ed. Dec. 1990   ISBN cloth 0-88132-115-X
                          ISBN paper 0-88132-105-2

Economic Sanctions Reconsidered: History and
Current Policy   Gary Clyde Hufbauer,
Jeffrey J. Schott, and Kimberly Ann Elliott
December 1990   ISBN cloth 0-88132-140-0
                     ISBN paper 0-88132-136-2
Pacific Basin Developing Countries: Prospects for
Economic Sanctions Reconsidered: History
and Current Policy   Gary Clyde Hufbauer,
Jeffrey J. Schott, and Kimberly Ann Elliott
December 1990   ISBN cloth 0-88132-140-0
                     ISBN paper 0-88132-136-2
Pacific Basin Developing Countries: Prospects
for the Future*   Marcus Noland
January 1991   ISBN cloth 0-88132-141-9
                     ISBN paper 0-88132-081-1
Currency Convertibility in Eastern Europe*
John Williamson, editor
October 1991   ISBN 0-88132-128-1
International Adjustment and Financing: The
Lessons of 1985-1991* C. Fred Bergsten, editor
January 1992   ISBN 0-88132-112-5
North American Free Trade: Issues and
Recommendations*
Gary Clyde Hufbauer and Jeffrey J. Schott
April 1992   ISBN 0-88132-120-6
Narrowing the U.S. Current Account Deficit*
Alan J. Lenz/June 1992   ISBN 0-88132-103-6
The Economics of Global Warming
William R. Cline/June 1992   ISBN 0-88132-132-X
US Taxation of International Income: Blueprint
for Reform*   Gary Clyde Hufbauer,
assisted by Joanna M. van Rooij
October 1992   ISBN 0-88132-134-6
Who's Bashing Whom? Trade Conflict in High-
Technology Industries Laura D'Andrea Tyson
November 1992   ISBN 0-88132-106-0
Korea in the World Economy* Il SaKong
January 1993   ISBN 0-88132-183-4
Pacific Dynamism and the International
Economic System*
C. Fred Bergsten and Marcus Noland, editors
May 1993   ISBN 0-88132-196-6
Economic Consequences of Soviet Disintegration*
John Williamson, editor
May 1993   ISBN 0-88132-190-7
Reconcilable Differences? United States-Japan
Economic Conflict*
C. Fred Bergsten and Marcus Noland
June 1993   ISBN 0-88132-129-X
Does Foreign Exchange Intervention Work?
Kathryn M. Dominguez and Jeffrey A. Frankel
September 1993   ISBN 0-88132-104-4
Sizing Up U.S. Export Disincentives*
J. David Richardson
September 1993   ISBN 0-88132-107-9

NAFTA: An Assessment
Gary Clyde Hufbauer and Jeffrey J. Schott/rev. ed.
October 1993   ISBN 0-88132-199-0
Adjusting to Volatile Energy Prices
Philip K. Verleger, Jr.
November 1993   ISBN 0-88132-069-2
The Political Economy of Policy Reform
John Williamson, editor
January 1994   ISBN 0-88132-195-8
Measuring the Costs of Protection
in the United States
Gary Clyde Hufbauer and Kimberly Ann Elliott
January 1994   ISBN 0-88132-108-7
The Dynamics of Korean Economic Development*
Cho Soon/March 1994   ISBN 0-88132-162-1
Reviving the European Union*
C. Randall Henning, Eduard Hochreiter, and
Gary Clyde Hufbauer, editors
April 1994   ISBN 0-88132-208-3
China in the World Economy   Nicholas R. Lardy
April 1994   ISBN 0-88132-200-8
Greening the GATT: Trade, Environment, and
the Future   Daniel C. Esty
July 1994   ISBN 0-88132-205-9
Western Hemisphere Economic Integration*
Gary Clyde Hufbauer and Jeffrey J. Schott
July 1994   ISBN 0-88132-159-1
Currencies and Politics in the United States,
Germany, and Japan   C. Randall Henning
September 1994   ISBN 0-88132-127-3
Estimating Equilibrium Exchange Rates
John Williamson, editor
September 1994   ISBN 0-88132-076-5
Managing the World Economy: Fifty Years after
Bretton Woods   Peter B. Kenen, editor
September 1994   ISBN 0-88132-212-1
Reciprocity and Retaliation in U.S. Trade Policy
Thomas O. Bayard and Kimberly Ann Elliott
September 1994   ISBN 0-88132-084-6
The Uruguay Round: An Assessment*
Jeffrey J. Schott, assisted by Johanna W. Buurman
November 1994   ISBN 0-88132-206-7
Measuring the Costs of Protection in Japan*
Yoko Sazanami, Shujiro Urata, and Hiroki Kawai
January 1995   ISBN 0-88132-211-3
Foreign Direct Investment in the United States,
3d ed., Edward M. Graham and Paul R. Krugman
January 1995   ISBN 0-88132-204-0
The Political Economy of Korea-United States
Cooperation*
C. Fred Bergsten and Il SaKong, editors
February 1995   ISBN 0-88132-213-X
International Debt Reexamined*   William R. Cline
February 1995   ISBN 0-88132-083-8
American Trade Politics, 3d ed., I. M. Destler
April 1995   ISBN 0-88132-215-6

Asia Pacific Fusion: Japan's Role in APEC*
Yoichi Funabashi
October 1995   ISBN 0-88132-224-5
Korea-United States Cooperation in the New
World Order*
C. Fred Bergsten and Il SaKong, editors
February 1996   ISBN 0-88132-226-1
Why Exports Really Matter!* ISBN 0-88132-221-0
Why Exports Matter More!*   ISBN 0-88132-229-6
J. David Richardson and Karin Rindal
July 1995; February 1996
Global Corporations and National Governments
Edward M. Graham
May 1996   ISBN 0-88132-111-7
Global Economic Leadership and the Group of
Seven   C. Fred Bergsten and C. Randall Henning
May 1996   ISBN 0-88132-218-0
The Trading System after the Uruguay Round*
John Whalley and Colleen Hamilton
July 1996   ISBN 0-88132-131-1
Private Capital Flows to Emerging Markets after
the Mexican Crisis*   Guillermo A. Calvo,
Morris Goldstein, and Eduard Hochreiter
September 1996   ISBN 0-88132-232-6
The Crawling Band as an Exchange Rate Regime:
Lessons from Chile, Colombia, and Israel
John Williamson
September 1996   ISBN 0-88132-231-8
Flying High: Liberalizing Civil Aviation in the
Asia Pacific*
Gary Clyde Hufbauer and Christopher Findlay
November 1996   ISBN 0-88132-227-X
Measuring the Costs of Visible Protection
in Korea*   Namdoo Kim
November 1996   ISBN 0-88132-236-9
The World Trading System: Challenges Ahead
Jeffrey J. Schott
December 1996   ISBN 0-88132-235-0
Has Globalization Gone Too Far?   Dani Rodrik
March 1997   ISBN paper 0-88132-241-5
Korea-United States Economic Relationship*
C. Fred Bergsten and Il SaKong, editors
March 1997   ISBN 0-88132-240-7
Summitry in the Americas: A Progress Report
Richard E. Feinberg
April 1997   ISBN 0-88132-242-3
Corruption and the Global Economy
Kimberly Ann Elliott
June 1997   ISBN 0-88132-233-4
Regional Trading Blocs in the World Economic
System   Jeffrey A. Frankel
October 1997   ISBN 0-88132-202-4
Sustaining the Asia Pacific Miracle:
Environmental Protection and Economic
Integration   Andre Dua and Daniel C. Esty
October 1997   ISBN 0-88132-250-4

Trade and Income Distribution   William R. Cline
November 1997   ISBN 0-88132-216-4
Global Competition Policy
Edward M. Graham and J. David Richardson
December 1997   ISBN 0-88132-166-4
**Unfinished Business: Telecommunications
after the Uruguay Round**
Gary Clyde Hufbauer and Erika Wada
December 1997   ISBN 0-88132-257-1
Financial Services Liberalization in the WTO
Wendy Dobson and Pierre Jacquet
June 1998   ISBN 0-88132-254-7
Restoring Japan's Economic Growth
Adam S. Posen
September 1998   ISBN 0-88132-262-8
Measuring the Costs of Protection in China
Zhang Shuguang, Zhang Yansheng, and Wan
Zhongxin
November 1998   ISBN 0-88132-247-4
**Foreign Direct Investment and Development:
The New Policy Agenda for Developing
Countries and Economies in Transition**
Theodore H. Moran
December 1998   ISBN 0-88132-258-X
**Behind the Open Door: Foreign Enterprises
in the Chinese Marketplace**
Daniel H. Rosen
January 1999   ISBN 0-88132-263-6
**Toward A New International Financial
Architecture: A Practical Post-Asia Agenda**
Barry Eichengreen
February 1999   ISBN 0-88132-270-9
Is the U.S. Trade Deficit Sustainable?
Catherine L. Mann
September 1999   ISBN 0-88132-265-2
**Safeguarding Prosperity in a Global Financial
System: The Future International Financial
Architecture**, Independent Task Force Report
Sponsored by the Council on Foreign Relations
Morris Goldstein, Project Director
October 1999   ISBN 0-88132-287-3
**Avoiding the Apocalypse: The Future of the
Two Koreas**   Marcus Noland
June 2000   ISBN 0-88132-278-4
**Assessing Financial Vulnerability: An Early
Warning System for Emerging Markets**
Morris Goldstein, Graciela Kaminsky, and
Carmen Reinhart
June 2000   ISBN 0-88132-237-7
Global Electronic Commerce: A Policy Primer
Catherine L. Mann, Sue E. Eckert, and Sarah
Cleeland Knight
July 2000   ISBN 0-88132-274-1
The WTO after Seattle   Jeffrey J. Schott, editor
July 2000   ISBN 0-88132-290-3

**Intellectual Property Rights in the Global
Economy**   Keith E. Maskus
August 2000   ISBN 0-88132-282-2
**The Political Economy of the Asian Financial
Crisis**   Stephan Haggard
August 2000   ISBN 0-88132-283-0
**Transforming Foreign Aid: United States
Assistance in the 21st Century**   Carol Lancaster
August 2000   ISBN 0-88132-291-1
**Fighting the Wrong Enemy: Antiglobal Activists
and Multinational Enterprises**   Edward M. Graham
September 2000   ISBN 0-88132-272-5
**Globalization and the Perceptions of American
Workers**
Kenneth F. Scheve and Matthew J. Slaughter
March 2001   ISBN 0-88132-295-4
World Capital Markets: Challenge to the G-10
Wendy Dobson and Gary Clyde Hufbauer,
assisted by Hyun Koo Cho
May 2001   ISBN 0-88132-301-2
Prospects for Free Trade in the Americas
Jeffrey J. Schott/*August 2001*   ISBN 0-88132-275-X
**Toward a North American Community:
Lessons from the Old World for the New**
Robert A. Pastor/*August 2001*   ISBN 0-88132-328-4
**Measuring the Costs of Protection in Europe:
European Commercial Policy in the 2000s**
Patrick A. Messerlin
September 2001   ISBN 0-88132-273-3
Job Loss from Imports: Measuring the Costs
Lori G. Kletzer
September 2001   ISBN 0-88132-296-2
**No More Bashing: Building a New Japan–United
States Economic Relationship**   C. Fred Bergsten,
Takatoshi Ito, and Marcus Noland
October 2001   ISBN 0-88132-286-5
Why Global Commitment Really Matters!
Howard Lewis III and J. David Richardson
October 2001   ISBN 0-88132-298-9
Leadership Selection in the Major Multilaterals
Miles Kahler
November 2001   ISBN 0-88132-335-7
**The International Financial Architecture:
What's New? What's Missing?**   Peter Kenen
November 2001   ISBN 0-88132-297-0
**Delivering on Debt Relief: From IMF Gold
to a New Aid Architecture**
John Williamson and Nancy Birdsall,
with Brian Deese
April 2002   ISBN 0-88132-331-4
**Imagine There's No Country: Poverty,
Inequality, and Growth in the Era
of Globalization**   Surjit S. Bhalla
September 2002   ISBN 0-88132-348-9

Reforming Korea's Industrial Conglomerates
Edward M. Graham
January 2003   ISBN 0-88132-337-3
Industrial Policy in an Era of Globalization:
Lessons from Asia
Marcus Noland and Howard Pack
March 2003   ISBN 0-88132-350-0
Reintegrating India with the World Economy
T. N. Srinivasan and Suresh D. Tendulkar
March 2003   ISBN 0-88132-280-6
After the Washington Consensus:
Restarting Growth and Reform
in Latin America   Pedro-Pablo Kuczynski
and John Williamson, editors
March 2003   ISBN 0-88132-347-0
The Decline of US Labor Unions and
the Role of Trade   Robert E. Baldwin
June 2003   ISBN 0-88132-341-1
Can Labor Standards Improve
under Globalization?
Kimberly Ann Elliott and Richard B. Freeman
June 2003   ISBN 0-88132-332-2
Crimes and Punishments? Retaliation
under the WTO   Robert Z. Lawrence
October 2003   ISBN 0-88132-359-4
Inflation Targeting in the World Economy
Edwin M. Truman
October 2003   ISBN 0-88132-345-4
Foreign Direct Investment and Tax
Competition   John H. Mutti
November 2003   ISBN 0-88132-352-7
Has Globalization Gone Far Enough?
The Costs of Fragmented Markets
Scott Bradford and Robert Z. Lawrence
February 2004   ISBN 0-88132-349-7
Food Regulation and Trade:
Toward a Safe and Open Global System
Tim Josling, Donna Roberts, and David Orden
March 2004   ISBN 0-88132-346-2
Controlling Currency Mismatches in
Emerging Markets
Morris Goldstein and Philip Turner
April 2004   ISBN 0-88132-360-8
Free Trade Agreements: US Strategies
and Priorities   Jeffrey J. Schott, editor
April 2004   ISBN 0-88132-361-6
Trade Policy and Global Poverty
William R. Cline
June 2004   ISBN 0-88132-365-9
Bailouts or Bail-ins? Responding
to Financial Crises in Emerging Economies
Nouriel Roubini and Brad Setser
August 2004   ISBN 0-88132-371-3
Transforming the European Economy
Martin Neil Baily and Jacob Kirkegaard
September 2004   ISBN 0-88132-343-8

Chasing Dirty Money: The Fight Against
Money Laundering
Peter Reuter and Edwin M. Truman
November 2004   ISBN 0-88132-370-5
The United States and the World Economy:
Foreign Economic Policy for the Next Decade
C. Fred Bergsten
January 2005   ISBN 0-88132-380-2
Does Foreign Direct Investment Promote
Development ?   Theodore Moran, Edward
M. Graham, and Magnus Blomström, editors
April 2005   ISBN 0-88132-381-0
American Trade Politics, 4th ed.
I. M. Destler
June 2005   ISBN 0-88132-382-9
Why Does Immigration Divide America?
Public Finance and Political Opposition
to Open Borders
Gordon Hanson
August 2005   ISBN 0-88132-400-0
Reforming the US Corporate Tax
Gary Clyde Hufbauer and Paul L. E. Grieco
September 2005   ISBN 0-88132-384-5
The United States as a Debtor Nation
William R. Cline
September 2005   ISBN 0-88132-399-3
NAFTA Revisited: Achievements
and Challenges
Gary Clyde Hufbauer and Jeffrey J. Schott,
assisted by Paul L. E. Grieco and Yee Wong
October 2005   ISBN 0-88132-334-9
US National Security and Foreign Direct
Investment
Edward M. Graham and David M. Marchick
May 2006   ISBN 0-88132-391-8
          ISBN 978-0-88132-391-7

SPECIAL REPORTS

1   **Promoting World Recovery: A Statement**
     on Global Economic Strategy*
     by 26 Economists from Fourteen Countries
     December 1982   ISBN 0-88132-013-7
2   **Prospects for Adjustment in Argentina,**
     Brazil, and Mexico: Responding to the
     Debt Crisis*   John Williamson, editor
     June 1983   ISBN 0-88132-016-1
3   **Inflation and Indexation: Argentina, Brazil,**
     and Israel*   John Williamson, editor
     March 1985   ISBN 0-88132-037-4
4   **Global Economic Imbalances***
     C. Fred Bergsten, editor
     March 1986   ISBN 0-88132-042-0
5   **African Debt and Financing***
     Carol Lancaster and John Williamson, eds.
     May 1986   ISBN 0-88132-044-7

**Banking System Fragility
in Emerging Economies**
Morris Goldstein and Philip Turner

**Second among Equals: The Middle-Class
Kingdoms of India and China**
Surjit Bhalla

DISTRIBUTORS OUTSIDE THE UNITED STATES

Australia, New Zealand,
and Papua New Guinea
D. A. Information Services
648 Whitehorse Road
Mitcham, Victoria 3132, Australia
Tel: 61-3-9210-7777
Fax: 61-3-9210-7788
Email: service@dadirect.com.au
www.dadirect.com.au

India, Bangladesh, Nepal, and Sri Lanka
Viva Books Private Limited
Mr. Vinod Vasishtha
4737/23 Ansari Road
Daryaganj, New Delhi 110002
India
Tel: 91-11-4224-2200
Fax: 91-11-4224-2240
Email: viva@vivagroupindia.net
www.vivagroupindia.com

Mexico, Central America, South America,
and Puerto Rico
US PubRep, Inc.
311 Dean Drive
Rockville, MD 20851
Tel: 301-838-9276
Fax: 301-838-9278
Email: c.falk@ieee.org
www.uspubrep.com

Southeast Asia (*Brunei, Burma, Cambodia,*
Indonesia, Malaysia, the Philippines,
Singapore, Taiwan, Thailand, and Vietnam)
APAC Publishers Services PTE Ltd.
70 Bendemeer Road #05-03
Hiap Huat House
Singapore 333940
Tel: 65-6844-7333
Fax: 65-6747-8916
Email: service@apacmedia.com.sg

Canada
Renouf Bookstore
5369 Canotek Road, Unit 1
Ottawa, Ontario KlJ 9J3, Canada
Tel: 613-745-2665
Fax: 613-745-7660
www.renoufbooks.com

Japan
United Publishers Services Ltd.
1-32-5, Higashi-shinagawa
Shinagawa-ku, Tokyo 140-0002
Japan
Tel: 81-3-5479-7251
Fax: 81-3-5479-7307
Email: purchasing@ups.co.jp
For trade accounts only. Individuals will find
IIE books in leading Tokyo bookstores.

Middle East
MERIC
2 Bahgat Ali Street, El Masry Towers
Tower D, Apt. 24
Zamalek, Cairo
Egypt
Tel. 20-2-7633824
Fax: 20-2-7369355
Email: mahmoud_fouda@mericonline.com
www.mericonline.com

United Kingdom, Europe
(*including Russia and Turkey*)**, Africa,**
and Israel
The Eurospan Group
c/o Turpin Distribution
Pegasus Drive
Stratton Business Park
Biggleswade, Bedfordshire
SG18 8TQ
United Kingdom
Tel: 44 (0) 1767-604972
Fax: 44 (0) 1767-601640
Email: eurospan@turpin-distribution.com
www.eurospangroup.com/bookstore

Visit our Web site at:
www.iie.com
E-mail orders to:
IIE mail@PressWarehouse.com